OCCASIONAL PAPER 148

Nigeria
Experience with Structural Adjustment

Gary Moser, Scott Rogers, and Reinold van Til
with Robin Kibuka and Inutu Lukonga

INTERNATIONAL MONETARY FUND
Washington DC
March 1997

HC
1055
.M68
1997

© 1997 International Monetary Fund

Library of Congress Cataloging-in-Publication Data

Moser, Gary G. (Gary Gene), 1958–
  Nigeria: experience with structural adjustment / Gary Moser, Scott Rogers, and Reinold van Til with Robin Kibuka and Inutu Lukonga.
    p. cm. — (Occasional paper, ISSN 0251–6365; no. 148)
    Includes bibliographical references (p.)
    ISBN 1-55775-630-9
  1. Structural adjustment (Economic policy)—Nigeria. 2. Finance Public—Nigeria. 3. Nigeria—Economic conditions—1970 – I. Rogers, Scott, 1955– . II. Til, Reinold H. van. III. Title. IV. Series: Occasional paper (International Monetary Fund) ; no.148.
HC1055.M68   1997
338.9669—dc21   97-1966
                                                                              CIP

Price: US$15.00
(US$12.00 to full-time faculty members and
students at universities and colleges)

Please send orders to:
International Monetary Fund, Publication Services
700 19th Street, N.W., Washington, D.C. 20431, U.S.A.
Tel.: (202) 623-7430   Telefax: (202) 623-7201
Internet: publications@imf.org

recycled paper

Contents

		Page
Preface		vii
Map		viii
I	**Introduction**	1
II	**Economic and Political Setting**	3
III	**Austerity and Controls in the First Half of the 1980s**	7
IV	**Structural Reform and Macroeconomic Policy, 1986–90**	11
	Price Liberalization and Subsidy Policy	11
	Reform of the Exchange Rate	13
	Trade and Tariff Reform	15
	External Debt Policy	16
	Paris Club Agreements	16
	London Club Agreements	16
	Fiscal Adjustment and Reform	17
	State and Local Government Finances	18
	Monetary Policy and Financial Sector Reform	19
	Credit Controls	20
	Interest Rate Policy	21
	Financial Intermediation	22
	Public Enterprise Reform	25
V	**Adjustment and Growth, 1986–90**	27
	Sectoral Growth	27
	Savings and Investment	30
	Inflation	31
	External Sector	36
	Employment and Wages	37
VI	**Post-Adjustment Decline, 1991–94**	39
	Fiscal Deterioration	39
	Monetary Expansion and Interest Rates	39
	Foreign Exchange Market	42
	Domestic Petroleum Prices	43
	Privatization	43

CONTENTS

VII	Concluding Observations	45

Appendices

I	Determinants of Inflation in Nigeria	46
II	Money Demand in Nigeria, 1970–94	55
III	Nigeria's Non-Oil Exports: Determinants of Supply and Demand, 1970–90	63
IV	Oil Smuggling, Fiscal Policy, and Macroeconomic Imbalances	74
V	Statistical Appendix	79

Boxes

Section

II	1. Nigeria's Resource Endowment	5
	2. Nigeria's Regional Importance	6
IV	3. Experience with Fund-Supported Programs	12
	4. Fiscal Federalism	19
	5. Measuring the Stance of Fiscal Policy in an Oil Economy	20
	6. Oil Revenue in Nigeria	22
IV	7. Main Determinants of Inflation	32
	8. Macroeconomic Policies and Growth: A Quantitative Analysis, 1980–94	34
	9. Inefficient Public Investment	37
VI	10. Monetary Policy Targets and Outcomes	42

Tables

Section

II	1. Social Indicators	4
	2. Selected Economic and Financial Indicators, 1970–80	5
III	3. Selected Economic and Financial Indicators, 1980–85	9
IV	4. Structural Reforms and Policy Implementation	13
	5. Summary of Federal Government Fiscal Operations	18
	6. Structure of Federal Government Expenditures	23
	7. Monetary Targets and Outcomes	24
	8. Credit Guidelines for Commercial Banks	25
V	9. Selected Economic and Financial Indicators, 1986–90	29
	10. Farm Profitability Under the Structural Adjustment Program	30
	11. Savings and Investment	33
VI	12. Selected Economic and Financial Indicators, 1990–94	41

Appendix

I	13. Consumer Price Index Market Basket	47
	14. Matrix of Factors Influencing Inflation	48
	15. Selected Price, Money, and Exchange Rate Indicators	49
	16. Inflation Database	53
II	17. Long-Run Real Money Demand	57
	18. Short-Run Real Money Demand	58
	19. Database	61

Section			
III	20.	Comparative Growth Rates of Selected Commodities	65
	21.	Equilibrium Model, Export Supply Elasticities for Selected Export Crops	69
	22.	Disequilibrium Model, Export Supply Elasticities for Selected Export Crops	70
	23.	Average Time Lags	71
IV	24.	Retail Prices of Premium Gasoline in Nigeria and Neighboring Countries	76
	25.	Composition of Retail Prices of Premium Gasoline in Selected CFAF Countries, 1991	77
V	26.	Selected Economic and Financial Indicators	80
	27.	Federal Government Fiscal Operations	82
	28.	Summary of Budgetary Operations of State and Local Governments and Special Funds	84
	29.	Consolidated General Government Fiscal Operations	85
	30.	Monetary Survey	86
	31.	Balance of Payments	87
	32.	Stock of Public and Publicly Guaranteed Debt	88
	33.	Domestic Petroleum Prices	89
	34.	Gross Domestic Product by Sector of Origin at Current Prices	90
	35.	Gross Domestic Product by Sector of Origin at Constant 1984 Prices	91
	36.	Gross National Expenditure	92
	37.	Index of Agricultural Production	93
	38.	Index of Manufacturing Production	94
	39.	Non-Oil Exports, 1970-80	95
	40.	Non-Oil Exports, 1981–90	96
	41.	Structure of Exports, 1970-80	97
	42.	Structure of Exports, 1981-90	98
	43.	Structure of Non-Oil Exports, 1970-80	99
	44.	Structure of Non-Oil Exports, 1981-90	100
	45.	Agricultural Exports—Selected Indicators, 1970-80	101
	46.	Agricultural Exports—Selected Indicators, 1981-90	102
	47.	Export Volumes, Export Prices, Consumer Price Index, GDP at Factor Cost, and Index of Manufacturing	103
	48.	Selected Financial Institutions	104

Figures

Section

III	1.	Selected Economic Indicators	8
IV	2.	Domestic Gasoline Prices,	14
	3.	Exchange Rate Developments	14
	4.	Selected Interest Rates	26
	5.	Financial Intermediation	26
V	6.	Developments in the Real Sector	28
	7.	Manufacturing and Agricultural Output	30
	8.	Capacity Utilization Rates	31
	9.	Federal Government Savings and Investment	31
	10.	Inflation, Money, and Exchange Rate Developments	31
	11.	External Sector Developments	36
	12.	Quarterly National Unemployment Rates	37
VI	13.	Selected Economic Indicators	40

CONTENTS

Appendix

I	14.	Consumer Prices	47
	15.	Inflation, Money, and Exchange Rate Developments	48
	16.	Acual and Fitted Inflation	51
	17.	Structural Stability of Price Equation	52
	18.	Dynamic Response of Inflation	52
II	19.	Actual and Fitted Money Demand	59
	20.	Dynamic Response of Broad Money	59
	21.	Dynamic Response of Narrow Money	60
III	22.	Structure of Non-Oil Exports	64
	23.	Developments in Non-Oil Exports	64
IV	24.	Retail Gasoline Prices	75

The following symbols have been used throughout this paper:

. . . to indicate that data are not available;

— to indicate that the figure is zero or less than half the final digit shown, or that the item does not exist;

– between years or months (e.g., 1991–92 or January–June) to indicate the years or months covered, including the beginning and ending years or months;

/ between years (e.g., 1991/92) to indicate a crop or fiscal (financial) year.

"Billion" means a thousand million.

Minor discrepancies between constituent figures and totals are due to rounding.

The term "country," as used in this paper, does not in all cases refer to a territorial entity that is a state as understood by international law and practice; the term also covers some territorial entities that are not states, but for which statistical data are maintained and provided internationally on a separate and independent basis.

Preface

This paper originated as part of the country work on Nigeria during the 1993–95 period. Some of the material was prepared as background for the 1994 Article IV consultation. The authors would like to thank Jean Claude Nachega for research assistance, Janet Bungay for editorial assistance, and Vera Da Luz for secretarial assistance. The authors are also grateful to David Driscoll of the External Relations Department, who edited the paper for publication and coordinated production. The views expressed here are the sole responsibility of the authors, and do not necessarily reflect the opinions of the Government of Nigeria or the Executive Directors of the IMF. The study was completed in May 1996.

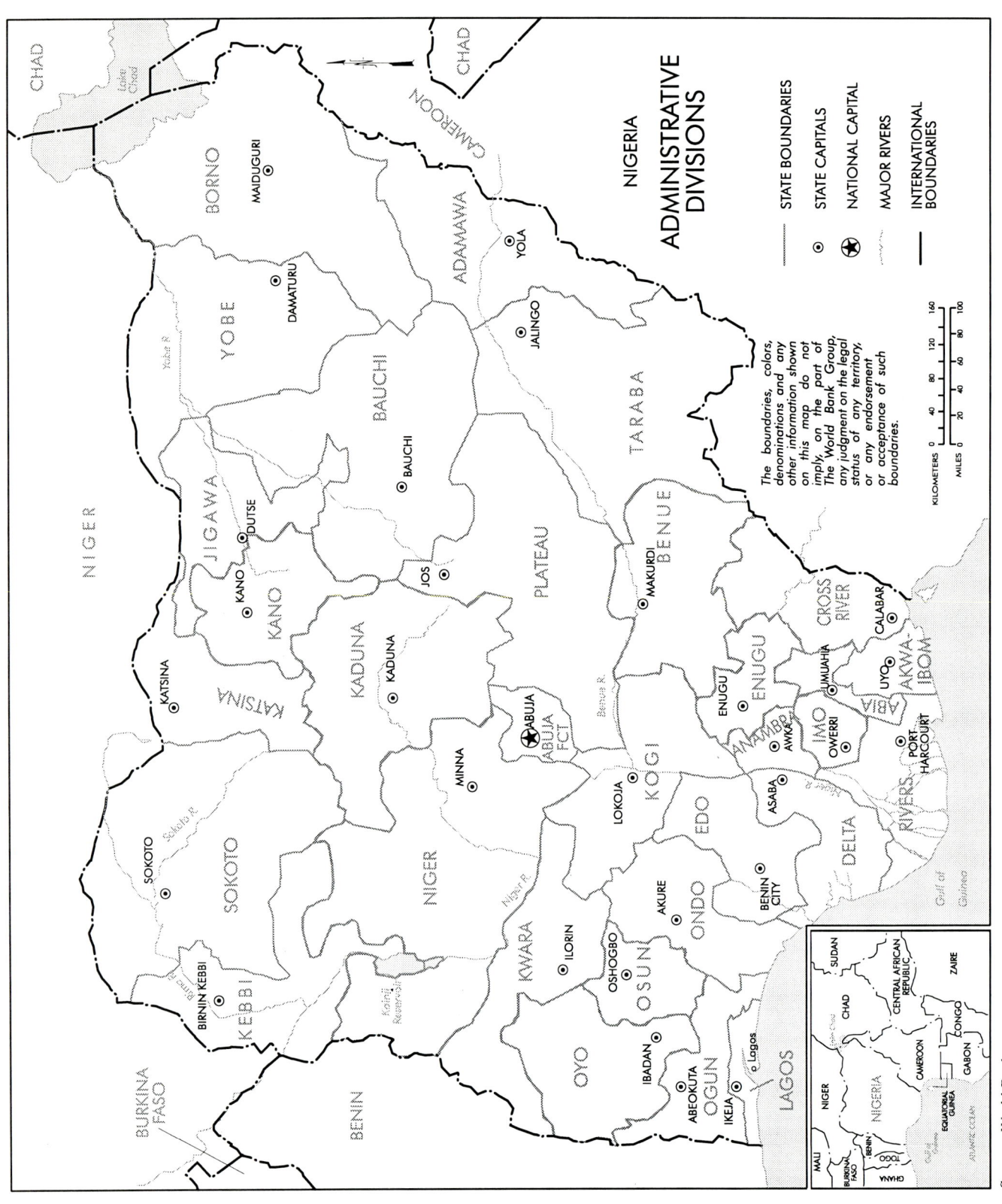

Source: World Bank.

I Introduction

Over the past two decades, Nigeria has not reaped fully the benefits of its national wealth. Apart from a promising but brief interlude in which structural adjustment was pursued vigorously, the country's development has stagnated and its economic and social conditions have deteriorated. During the 1980s and early 1990s, the population grew by more than 3 percent per annum, outstripping real GDP growth, and real per capita GDP declined by a cumulative 15 percent. Taking into account the deterioration in the terms of trade during this period, real per capita national income has dropped by some 45 percent.

Nigeria's economic and financial performance has suffered from erratic macroeconomic policies, weak management of its natural resources, and major inefficiencies of its public investments, which have given rise to waste and opportunity for substantial patronage rents. These policies were also inspired by the wish to create a state-sponsored industrial complex, which was not exposed to the discipline of the market, operated behind high protective walls, and was heavily subsidized.

Oil has dominated the economy and has led to the neglect of the agricultural sector, thus compromising employment creation, export diversification, and the development of the rural economy. Oil wealth also largely explains why Nigeria has been able for so long to sustain fundamentally unsustainable macroeconomic policies, characterized most of the time by excessively expansionary financial policies, a substantially overvalued currency, and a lopsided structure of public finance, on both the revenue and the expenditure sides.

One of the most intriguing aspects of the country's economic policy debate has been a strong resistance to structural adjustment, which has been held responsible for most of the economic ills of the country, including the debasement of the naira, the high rate of inflation, the crippling of domestic industry, high interest rates, high unemployment, and the spread of poverty. These strong sentiments culminated in the official abandonment of structural adjustment in 1994, when the Government announced a reversal of what it believed to be the misguided policies of deregulation and structural reform. Thus, the Government reimposed interest rate controls, eliminated the free market for foreign exchange, and reaffirmed its belief in the stability of the official exchange rate, irrespective of the underlying economic fundamentals. It was convinced that inflation was caused primarily by the depreciation of the naira and that economic activity was stifled by high import costs and high interest rates. The outcome of this recent policy experiment, however, demonstrated that a stable macroeconomic environment cannot be engineered by fixing a few key variables. It also proved that the main determinant of inflation is not the exchange rate. It became abundantly clear that the artificially cheap pricing of foreign exchange did not help domestic industries, as scarcities became even more pronounced.

This paper provides an overview of economic and financial developments during 1980–94, with particular emphasis on the period of structural adjustment pursued during 1986–90. The main conclusion of the paper is that the facts do not support the negative image that structural adjustment has had in Nigeria. Despite its shortcomings, including that it lasted too short a time, the vigorous implementation of market reforms and tight financial policies resulted in substantial economic growth and employment expansion. The subsequent reversals and weakening of policies, most notably since the end of 1990, have brought about prolonged stagflation.

Cognizant of the failure of the policy shift in 1994, the Government moved to a partial deregulation of the economy again in 1995, which entailed the introduction of a dual exchange rate system, the liberalization of exchange controls, and the restoration of the role of the foreign exchange bureaus. A package of stabilization measures was introduced, which centered on a substantial tightening of fiscal policy. Thus, gains were made in reducing demand pressures, which resulted in some moderation of inflation and a stabilization of the foreign exchange rate.

The paper is organized in the following manner. Section II gives the background to the reform efforts, focusing on the transformation of the Nigerian economy during the 1960s and early 1970s from a largely

I INTRODUCTION

agricultural economy to an oil-dominated one. Section III presents an overview of Nigeria's ill-fated efforts to stabilize the economy during 1981–85 in the face of a substantial decline in the terms of trade. Section IV reviews the objectives and measures under the country's structural adjustment program during 1986–90 and Section V discusses the impact of adjustment on growth. Section VI sketches the post-adjustment decline in recent years (1991–94), and the final chapter offers some concluding observations. The appendices contain more detailed empirical work on inflation, money demand, the longer-term evolution of non-oil exports, as well as the impact of oil smuggling on fiscal policy.

II Economic and Political Setting

Nigeria, with a population of about 95 million, is Africa's most populous country and the continent's third largest economy. Oil dominates the economy, accounting in 1993 for roughly 30 percent of GDP, 80 percent of federal government revenues, and 95 percent of foreign exchange earnings. With a per capita income of US$370 in 1993 and comparatively unfavorable social indicators (Table 1), Nigeria is one of the poorest oil producing countries. Since its independence in 1960, the country has undergone major political and economic changes. It has attempted to forge a unified nation out of diverse regional, ethnic, and religious groups through a federal structure of government, whose leadership has changed no fewer than eight times, mostly through military coups. Oil has been an economic blessing but also a source of political strife. It was discovered in a small area in the Niger Delta in 1956, and production began in 1958. The management of oil resources has been the responsibility of the Federal Government. The distribution of oil revenue among the three regions of the country (the north, east, and west) became a highly sensitive political issue during the mid-1960s, and to this day, the control and distribution of oil revenue has remained at the center of the country's political agenda.

During the 1970s, Nigeria evolved from a poor agricultural economy into a relatively rich, oil-dominated one (Box 1). In 1969 the oil sector accounted for less than 3 percent of GDP and a modest US$370 million in exports (42 percent of total exports); per capita income was only US$130; and more than half of GDP was generated in the agricultural sector. By 1980, the oil sector had come to account for nearly 30 percent of GDP, oil exports totaled US$25 billion (96 percent of total exports), and per capita income exceeded US$1,100. Following the discovery and exploration of oil, the economy experienced many symptoms of the "Dutch disease," with the real effective exchange rate appreciating steadily during the 1970s. The steady erosion of competitiveness of the non-oil tradable goods sector was reflected in the substantial decline of agricultural exports, which began in the mid-1960s, and continued through 1976, when oil production reached its peak. Notwithstanding the dramatic rise in oil revenue in the 1970s, the Government[1] failed to strengthen public finances. The excessive expansion of public expenditure, from an average of 13 percent of GDP during 1970–73 to 25 percent in 1974–80, moved the fiscal balance from a small surplus to a deficit, averaging 2½ percent of GDP a year (Table 2). The monetary financing of these deficits contributed to a rapid growth in broad money and a sharp acceleration in inflation. The real effective appreciation of the naira that followed the surge in oil prices toward the end of 1973 eroded Nigeria's competitiveness, and growth of real GDP slowed markedly. A buoyant oil sector sustained an average external current account surplus of 1½ percent of GDP during this period, while gross international reserves averaged the equivalent of about seven months of imports. By 1980, the country's external debt was only US$4.1 billion, or 5 percent of GDP, and the debt-service ratio was a modest 3.7 percent.

The economic policy orientation during the 1970s left the country ill prepared for the eventual collapse of oil prices in the first half of the 1980s. Public investment was concentrated in costly, and often inappropriate, infrastructure projects with questionable rates of return and sizable recurrent cost implications, while the agricultural sector was largely neglected. Nigeria's industrial policy was inward-looking, with a heavy emphasis on protection and government controls,[2] which bred an uncompetitive manufacturing

---

[1]The terms "Government," "fiscal deficit," and "public expenditure" refer to the Federal Government, unless stated otherwise.

[2]High protective tariffs, import bans, an import licensing scheme, and export bans on food crops characterized the external trade regime. The proliferation of government controls was reflected in the establishment of price controls (*Price Control Decree of 1971*), marketing boards (*Commodity Board Decree of 1977*), state trading corporations (in 1977, the Nigerian National Supply Company, the Nigerian National Freight Company, and the National Fertilizer Board), and the effective nationalization of all land (*Land Use Decree of 1978*, which brought all land under the control of state governments). In addition, through the *Nigerian Enterprise Decree (1972)*, the Government promoted indigenous participation in industrial investment and discouraged foreign investment.

II ECONOMIC AND POLITICAL SETTING

Table 1. Social Indicators

	Unit of Measure	1970–75 Nigeria	1980–85 Nigeria	1988–93 Nigeria	1988–93 Sub-Saharan Africa	1988–93 All low-income countries
Population						
Total population	Millions	62.8	83.1	105.3	559.0	3,091.8
Growth rate	Annual, in percent	2.6	2.9	3.1	2.9	1.9
Urban	Annual, in percent	5.6	5.5	5.3	5.0	3.9
Density	Population/sq. km	68.0	89.9	110.5	22.4	77.6
Health						
Infant mortality	Thousands/live births	111	99	83	93	63
Under 5 years	Thousands/live births	...	...	191.0	172.3	101.4
Immunization						
Measles	In percent of age group	...	9.0	34.0	49.9	87.3
DPT	In percent of age group	...	9.0	29.0	51.9	89.9
Population per hospital bed	Persons	1,844	1,169	599	1,269	1,016
Access to safe water						
Urban	Percent of population	...	60	52	...	78.7
Rural	Percent of population	...	30	20	...	62.0
Total life expectancy	Years	43	46	51	52	63
Total fertility rate	Birth/woman	6.5	6.5	6.4	6.2	3.6
Education						
Gross enrollment						
Primary schools	Percent of school-age population	57	82	76	67	108
Secondary schools	Percent of school-age population	8	29	20	18	41
Pupil-teacher ratio						
Primary schools	Pupil/teacher	34	44	39	40	39
Illiteracy rate	Percent of population (age 15 and over)	...	57	49	50	41
Newspaper circulation	Per thousand population	10	17	18	12	...
Other						
GNP per capita	U.S. dollars	510	950	300	520	380
Irrigated land	Percent of land	1.2	1.2	1.2	0.8	18.0
Forests and woodland	Thousand sq. km	...	0.2	0.2	5.3	7.2
Food production per capita	Index (1987=100)	127	104	129	101	113
Fertilizer consumption	Kg/ha	0.8	4.1	7.8	4.6	59.9
Energy consumption per capita	Kg of oil equivalent	71	148	141	257	364

Source: World Bank, *Social Indicators of Development* (1995).

sector. Nonetheless, because of its size, Nigeria's economy has remained dominant in the region (see Box 2 on Nigeria's regional importance).

Nigeria has been ruled by the military for 25 of its 35 years as an independent nation. The last elected civilian government was overthrown by the military in December 1983, and a largely civilian interim national government was ousted by the military on November 17, 1993. The origin of political instability in Nigeria has been the inability to forge a national entity that transcends ethnic, regional, religious, and economic interests. These diverging interests led to scores of political coups and counter coups. The principal ethnic groups in Nigeria are the Hausa in the north, the Yoruba in the west, and the Ibo in the east, and the principal religious groups are the Muslims in the north and the Christians in the south.[3] The federal structure of Nigeria has changed dramatically during the past decades; the country's original three regions have since been divided into 30 states, including 9 new states created in 1991, the Federal Capital Territory of Abuja, and more than 589 local governments.

---

[3]The distinctions between north, south, east, and west are made to simplify what is actually a more fluid geographic distribution of religious and ethnic affiliations.

Box 1. Nigeria's Resource Endowment

Nigeria spans an area of 913,000 square kilometers bordering the Gulf of Guinea. The topography ranges from mangrove swampland along the coast to tropical rain forest and savannah to the north. The Sahara Desert encroaches upon the extreme northern part of the country. Some 10 percent of the land is covered with forest, and Nigeria's wood resources include large stands of mahogany, walnut, and obeche. However, rapid deforestation has reduced Nigeria's forests by 50 percent in the last 15 years, and the potential for their future exploitation is extremely limited. The country's fishery resources are fairly small and are concentrated in the coastal area.

The importance of oil in the Nigerian economy notwithstanding, agriculture is the dominant economic activity in terms of employment and linkages with the rest of the economy. Roughly 90 percent of Nigeria's land is arable and about 40 percent of this is cultivated. The United Nation's Food and Agricultural Organization rates Nigeria's farmland from low to medium in productivity, but notes that most of the country's cultivable land would have medium to good productivity, if properly managed. Despite the existence of two major rivers, the Niger and the Benue, agriculture is predominantly rainfed. Yams, cassava, sorghum, and millet constitute the main food crops. The principal export crops are cocoa and rubber, which together account for nearly 60 percent of non-oil merchandise exports.

The country's proven oil reserves, all located in the southeast coastal area, amount to an estimated 18 billion barrels, sufficient to last for 25 years at the current rate of production. Annual production of 2 million barrels per day (mbd) compares favorably to 1.2 mbd in Algeria and 2.7 mbd in Mexico. Proven natural gas reserves are estimated at 3.4 trillion cubic meters, with an energy content slightly higher than the country's oil reserves. These reserves are comparable to those of Algeria, and will last for 110 years at current production levels. Nearly 80 percent of the natural gas produced is presently being flared, and most of the remaining 20 percent is used for electricity generation. It is expected that the export of gas will be substantial after the year 2000. Nigeria's rivers also constitute a substantial energy resource, providing the country with nearly half of its electricity.

Limited information is available on the size and quality of Nigeria's labor force other than what can be inferred from broad social indicators. The adult illiteracy rate is 49 percent. About 76 percent of children of primary school age attend school; the participation rate falls to 20 percent for children of secondary school age. Average life expectancy at birth is 51 years.

Table 2. Selected Economic and Financial Indicators, 1970–80

	1970–73	1974–80
	(Average annual percentage change)	
Nominal GDP	30.1	24.1
Real GDP (at constant factor cost)	9.0	2.3
Oil GDP (at constant factor cost)	19.4	–0.2
Non-oil GDP (at constant factor cost)	3.6	2.8
Consumer prices (annual average)	9.5	18.0
Consumer prices (end of period)	10.3	18.1
Broad money	24.8	35.3
	(In percent of GDP)	
Federal Government expenditure	13.3	24.9
Overall fiscal balance	0.3	–2.7
External current account balance	–2.8	1.4
External debt service due (in percent of exports)	2.7	1.8
External debt	4.4	3.5
	(In units indicated)	
Oil production (in millions of barrels a day)	1.6	2.1
Oil export price (average; in U.S. dollars per barrel)	2.6	18.3
Real effective official exchange rate (1988=100)	197	268
Terms of trade (1988=100)	67	197

From early 1986 through late 1989, the Babangida regime laid the political foundation for the transition to elected government through the establishment of the National Electoral Commission (1987), the election of a Constituent Assembly (1988), the approval of a new constitution (1989), and the establishment of a two-party system (1989), comprising the Social Democratic Party (SDP) and the National Republican Convention (NRC). Following an attempted coup in 1990, the Government moved more aggressively to implement the rest of the political reform agenda. Legislative elections at the state level were held in December 1991 and at the federal level in July 1992. In the latter, the SDP won the majority in both the Senate and the House of Representatives.

The presidential elections, however, proved problematic and created a serious political crisis. The results of a series of presidential primaries were an-

II ECONOMIC AND POLITICAL SETTING

> ### Box 2. Nigeria's Regional Importance
>
> Nigeria's economy is the second largest in sub-Saharan Africa and by far the largest in West Africa. While trade with African countries accounts for less than 3 percent, officially, it is significant for some countries in the region, particularly those in West Africa belonging to the CFA franc zone. Nigeria accounted for nearly 6 percent of Niger's officially recorded exports and 10 percent of Côte d'Ivoire's imports in 1990; actual trade flows are probably much higher. It is estimated that Nigeria's exports to Cameroon exceed officially recorded trade by a factor of 10; official exports to Cameroon were estimated at US$4 million in 1990. Nigeria is also a major employer of migrant workers from the region, most notably from Benin.
>
> Neighboring countries have been particularly affected by Nigeria's domestic petroleum pricing and exchange rate policies. The smuggling of subsidized petroleum products from Nigeria has contributed to the evasion of domestic gasoline taxes by citizens of neighboring countries, thereby affecting these countries' fiscal positions, and has influenced the structure of prices and production throughout the region. The extremely low retail price of petroleum products in Nigeria, coupled with the real effective depreciation of its currency, contributed to a decline in the competitiveness of industries in neighboring countries, particularly in textiles and other light industries, which compete with Nigerian producers in local markets. (See Appendix IV for a discussion of the relationship between Nigeria's fiscal policy, domestic petroleum product pricing policy, and the smuggling of fuel to other countries in the region.) In response to the growing cost of the subsidy, and increased smuggling, the Nigerian Government raised gasoline prices by 364 percent in 1993, and by a further 238 percent in 1994, effectively eliminating the subsidy.
>
> Nigeria's real effective exchange rate depreciated by some 88 percent between 1985 and 1992, which gave a boost to producers of tradable goods. However, this improvement in competitiveness imposed a cost on neighboring producers. While the currencies of other countries in the region have generally depreciated in real effective terms since 1985, all of them have substantially appreciated in real bilateral terms against the naira. This has led to a surge of Nigerian exports within the region, particularly to Cameroon, where recorded imports from Nigeria have increased by more than 400 percent since 1985 in nominal terms, while exports to Nigeria have fallen. This trend reversed itself temporarily in 1994 when the naira appreciated by 83 percent in real effective terms, as the Government eliminated the free market for foreign exchange, while the CFA franc depreciated by 14 percent in real effective terms in Cameroon in FY1994.

nulled in September 1992 because of alleged irregularities, and the candidates were declared ineligible to participate in the presidential elections. Subsequently, President Babangida postponed the transition to an elected government and in January 1993 announced the formation of an interim government which consisted of an all-civilian Transitional Council, headed by Chief Shonekan, to handle the day-to-day affairs of government under the National Defense and Security Council chaired by President Babangida.[4] Presidential elections were set for June 13, 1993, and a new government was scheduled to assume office on August 27, 1993. In the event, the elections were annulled after Chief Abiola, a businessman and leader of the SDP, had emerged as the apparent winner. The annulment led to domestic unrest and international protest. Against this background, President Babangida, the military leadership, and the leadership of the SDP and the NRC agreed to another transitional government. On August 26, 1993, amid widespread labor unrest and civil strikes, President Babangida resigned as Head of State and Commander-in-Chief of the Armed Forces, and Chief Shonekan was sworn in as Head of the Interim National Government for the period through March 31, 1994, when an elected government was scheduled to assume office. On November 17, 1993, the Interim National Government was ousted by the military under General Sani Abacha. All democratic institutions were dissolved, and all elected officials were removed from office.

---

[4]The Transitional Council was sworn in on January 4, 1993, together with the members of the House of Representatives and of the Senate.

III Austerity and Controls in the First Half of the 1980s

The collapse of world oil prices and the sharp decline in petroleum output, the latter resulting from a lowering of Nigeria's OPEC quota in the early 1980s, brought to the forefront the precarious nature of the country's economic and financial position. Rising and ill-directed government spending during the 1970s, neglect of the agricultural sector, and inward-looking industrial policies left Nigeria vulnerable to profound changes in the external environment in the following decade. Thus, the dramatic fall in oil export revenues entailed a sharp deterioration in the country's public finances and balance of payments. The overall fiscal deficit rose from ½ percent of GDP in 1980 to 9½ percent in 1981, and the external current account balance shifted from a surplus of 4½ percent to a deficit of 7½ percent in the same period. The severe weakening of the external position was reflected in a dwindling of international reserves. Stepped-up foreign borrowing by federal and state governments and public enterprises increased external debt to the equivalent of 23 percent of GDP by 1985, from only 5 percent in 1980 (Figure 1 and Table 3). The growing scarcity of foreign exchange affected output in the import-intensive manufacturing sector, with capacity utilization falling from 73 percent in 1981 to 38 percent in 1985. The steady appreciation of the real effective exchange rate also depressed agricultural output, which remained at levels below those achieved in the early 1970s. As a result, annual GDP growth decelerated sharply and turned negative in 1981.

The sharp worsening of economic conditions prompted the Shagari Government to introduce in April 1982 significant budget cuts and measures to improve the external position. The latter consisted of a severe tightening of import controls, the imposition of exchange restrictions on current international transactions, substantial increases in customs tariffs, the introduction of an advance import deposit scheme, and ceilings on total central bank foreign exchange disbursements. Henceforth, the foreign exchange budget would be used as an exchange control instrument rather than, as before, as a monitoring device. The tightening of fiscal policies consisted of a freeze on capital expenditure, the curtailment of lower priority public investment projects, an increase in petroleum product prices and utility tariffs, and a freeze on wages and salaries in the public sector. In addition, foreign borrowing of the state and local governments was severely restricted, ceilings on bank credit to the private sector were progressively lowered, and administered bank lending rates were raised.

These measures resulted in some easing of inflationary pressures, but real GDP contracted in 1982–83, owing to the sharp decline in oil production, the scarcity of imported inputs, and a worsening drought. Although the external current account position improved somewhat in 1983, reflecting the severe compression of imports, the Government's financial position deteriorated as fiscal oil revenue dropped further and transfers to state and local governments and loans to parastatals expanded. The monetization of the Government's fiscal deficit resulted in a strong growth of broad money and, coupled with the impact of a severe drought, the rate of inflation accelerated to 39 percent in 1983, from 7 percent in 1982.

The worsening economic and financial conditions and alleged widespread corruption led to a military coup at the end of 1983. The new regime under General Buhari sought to reinforce the 1982 austerity measures by further tightening financial policies and introducing more administrative controls. Additional exchange and trade restrictions were announced in mid-1984, including stricter import controls, higher import tariffs, a more centralized system of foreign exchange allocation, and severe penalties for smuggling, hoarding, and corruption. The fiscal and monetary measures announced in May 1984 aimed at drastically reducing domestic demand pressures. The Government also implemented draconian expenditure cuts and substantial tax increases. It dismissed some 10,000 civil servants (almost 5 percent of the civil service) and continued the freeze on civil service salaries.

The expenditure cuts were particularly successful in the short run. They reduced the overall federal government fiscal deficit from 11 percent of GDP in 1983 to 3 percent in 1985. As a consequence, the Government's recourse to bank credit was virtually

III AUSTERITY AND CONTROLS IN THE FIRST HALF OF THE 1980s

Figure 1. Selected Economic Indicators

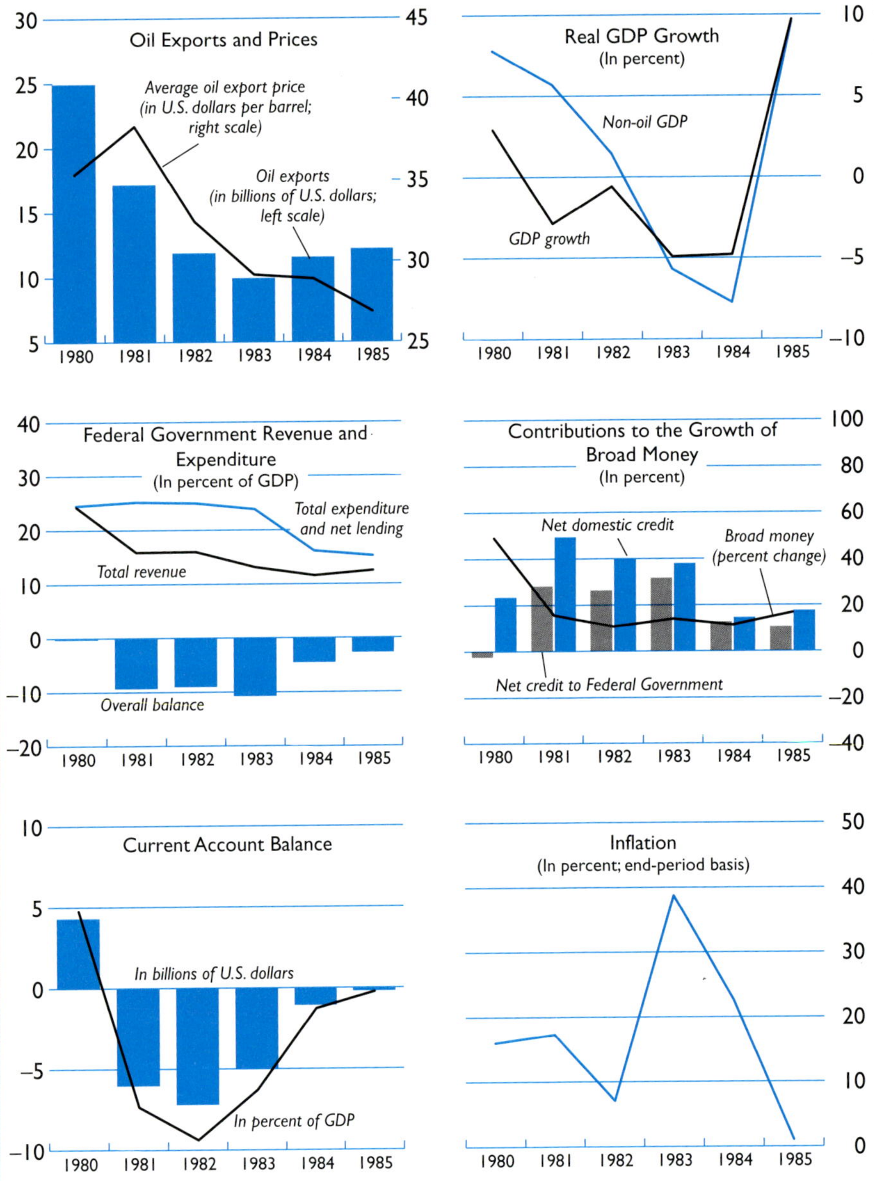

Sources: Government of Nigeria; and IMF staff estimates.

eliminated and inflationary pressures were significantly reduced. On the external front, the coverage of import licenses was extended considerably, and the authorities entered into barter arrangements to boost exports and secure essential imports in 1984. At the same time, the volume of oil exports rose and the external current account improved markedly in 1984 and 1985. Nonetheless, Nigeria accumulated external payments arrears throughout the period, and the heavy foreign borrowing resulted in an almost fivefold increase in the external debt during the first half of the 1980s.

The Government's austerity measures did meet with some success by 1985; inflation fell to 1 per-

Table 3. Selected Economic and Financial Indicators, 1980–85

	1980[1]	1981[1]	1982	1983	1984	1985
	(Annual percentage changes, unless otherwise indicated)					
National income and prices						
Real GDP (at 1984 market prices)	2.9	−2.9	−0.6	−4.9	−4.8	9.7
Oil GDP (at 1984 factor cost)	−11.6	−31.6	−11.4	−3.2	13.0	8.5
Non-oil GDP (at 1984 factor cost)	7.8	5.7	1.5	−5.7	−7.7	9.5
Consumer prices (end of period)	16.0	17.3	7.1	38.7	22.6	1.1
Nominal GDP (in billions of naira)	49.8	50.7	51.7	57.1	63.6	72.4
Oil production volume (in m/b per day)	2.060	1.440	1.280	1.240	1.390	1.500
Average oil export price (U.S. dollars per barrel, f.o.b.)	35.4	38.3	32.4	29.2	28.9	26.9
Population (millions)	61.4	63.5	65.7	67.9	70.2	72.6
External sector						
Exports f.o.b. (in billions of U.S. dollars)	26.0	17.7	12.2	10.4	11.9	12.6
Of which: oil (in billions of U.S. dollars)	(24.9)	(17.2)	(11.9)	(10.0)	(11.6)	(12.2)
Imports f.o.b. (in billions of U.S. dollars)	−14.7	−18.4	−14.9	−11.5	−8.9	−8.3
Oil export volume	−12.9	−36.0	−18.3	−6.7	17.3	13.6
Non-oil export volume	5.2	−33.9	−23.1	59.3	−38.6	10.3
Import volume	11.0	31.2	−15.4	−20.1	−19.8	−7.1
Nominal effective exchange rate	11.1	3.4	4.6	3.9	7.2	−8.3
Real effective exchange rate	6.5	10.8	2.7	18.1	37.7	−10.3
Average official exchange rate (naira/U.S. dollar)	0.55	0.62	0.67	0.72	0.77	0.89
Terms of trade	52.0	12.2	−12.1	−7.4	3.9	−7.3
Money and credit						
Net foreign assets	73.7	−54.5	−61.7	−61.8	172.9	78.8
Net domestic assets	33.5	72.5	26.1	18.9	7.9	−34.1
Net credit to the Federal Government	−6.5	116.8	58.1	48.9	15.0	12.1
Credit to the rest of the economy	61.9	46.5	24.1	9.8	3.1	12.2
Broad money	48.9	15.6	10.6	14.0	11.3	16.7
Velocity (GDP/average broad money)	...	3.7	3.4	3.3	3.3	3.3
Savings deposit rate (end of period)	6.0	6.0	8.5	7.5	9.5	9.5
	(In percent of GDP)					
Investment and savings						
Gross national savings	23.2	18.1	17.9	13.1	10.4	15.2
Gross domestic investment	18.5	25.5	27.3	19.4	11.7	15.5
Federal Government budget						
Revenue	24.2	15.9	16.0	13.1	11.5	12.4
Expenditure and net lending	24.5	25.2	25.0	23.8	16.1	15.2
Current expenditure	10.5	9.7	8.2	11.9	10.1	8.3
Capital expenditure	14.0	15.5	16.8	11.9	6.1	7.0
Federal Government budget deficit	−0.3	−9.3	−9.0	−10.8	−4.6	−2.8
External sector						
Current account balance	4.7	−7.4	−9.4	−6.3	−1.3	−0.3
Overall balance of payments	5.0	−7.5	−6.9	−7.3	−0.5	−0.1
External debt	4.5	7.4	16.1	22.4	21.0	23.3
	(In billions of U.S. dollars, unless otherwise indicated)					
Current account balance	4.3	−6.0	−7.2	−5.0	−1.1	−0.2
Overall balance of payments	4.5	−6.2	−5.3	−5.8	−0.4	−0.1
External public and publicly guaranteed debt	4.1	6.1	12.4	17.8	17.3	18.9
Gross international reserves (end of period)	10.4	4.5	2.0	1.2	1.5	1.7
(in months of imports of goods and nonfactor services)	5.9	2.3	1.3	1.1	1.7	1.9

Sources: Data provided by the Nigerian authorities; and IMF staff estimates.
[1]Figures prior to 1982 are based on constant 1977/78 prices.

III AUSTERITY AND CONTROLS IN THE FIRST HALF OF THE 1980s

cent, the external current account moved into balance, and real GDP growth jumped to 9½ percent. The substantial growth in real GDP was due principally to an increase in oil production arising from the upward adjustment in OPEC quotas and to the recovery of the agricultural sector from a two-year drought. However, improvements in the fiscal and external positions in 1984 and 1985 proved transitory and failed to establish a basis for sustained economic growth. Short-run fiscal stabilization measures and quantitative trade controls dominated the adjustment efforts, while underlying economic and financial conditions continued to worsen. Between 1980 and 1985 government revenue fell from 24 percent of GDP to 12 percent, reflecting the sharp decline in oil prices as well as the diminished buoyancy of non-oil taxes. The adverse impact of the overvalued exchange rate on oil and customs revenue, coupled with the depressing effect of increasingly complex import controls on the customs tax base, exacerbated the difficulties.

Gross national savings fell substantially during 1980–85, from 23 percent of GDP in 1980 to 15 percent in 1985, reflecting in particular a sharp drop in government savings. As the Federal Government's savings-investment balance worsened significantly, the public investment program was financed by the other tiers of government, the drawdown of reserves, and the running up of arrears on external debt-service obligations. Private sector savings, on the other hand, increased from 4½ percent of GDP in 1980 to 8 percent in 1985, though the private sector savings-investment balance deteriorated as well over the period.

Despite the strong real appreciation of the naira during the first half of the 1980s, the Government resisted a fundamental reform of the exchange system. The adjustments of the official exchange rate against the U.S. dollar during this period only offset the appreciation of the U.S. dollar against other major currencies and failed to correct for the significant overvaluation of the naira. Given the relatively high rate of inflation in Nigeria, the real effective exchange rate appreciated by 85 percent between 1980 and 1984, and depreciated in 1985 by some 10 percent following the sharp deceleration in Nigeria's inflation rate. The sizable overall balance of payments deficits during 1981–85 resulted in a depletion of international reserves, which fell to the equivalent of only two months of imports by the end of 1985, from six months in 1980.

The authorities' policy to foster employment through the creation of public sector jobs continued to exert strong pressure on the budget during 1981–84. Following a 109 percent increase in 1977–81, public sector employment grew by a further 18 percent between 1981 and 1984. This policy promoted migration into cities, as government salaries compared very favorably with income opportunities in the rural areas. Urban migration and its attendant unemployment problems became even more pronounced in 1981 when the Government increased the minimum wage rate to the entry level salary of public sector employees. Urban unemployment increased substantially, from 2½ percent in 1980 to 10 percent in 1985, while rural unemployment rose from 3 percent to 5 percent over the same period.[5] Real per capita income fell significantly as well, from US$1,010 in 1981 to US$850 in 1985.

The emphasis on short-run stabilization measures reflected the Government's belief, at the time, that Nigeria's economic and financial problems were transient and would eventually disappear with a recovery in oil export prices. In the event, oil prices did not recover, and it became clear that the stabilization policies had failed to address the underlying economic problems, including the lopsided reliance on oil, the neglect of the agricultural sector, the inward-looking industrial strategy, the inefficiency of the public enterprise sector, and the misdirected capital investment projects of the Federal Government. In addition to the inefficient allocation of large oil receipts, intervention in key areas of the economy, including the fixing of the exchange rate, of interest rates, and of domestic and export prices and the marketing of non-oil exports, remained pervasive and impeded the supply response essential to a sustained recovery of the Nigerian economy. The extensive system of direct controls suppressed market signals and discouraged private sector activity. Crippling import shortages and growing social and political discontent set the stage for another military coup, under General Babangida, who assumed power in October 1985.

---

[5]Official unemployment statistics, while providing an indication of the trends in the labor market, substantially underestimate trends by excluding underemployment, which was estimated to be in the range of 40 percent in 1985.

IV Structural Reform and Macroeconomic Policy, 1986–90

It became clear to Nigeria's economic policymakers that short-run stabilization measures and increased regulation were not appropriate responses to deep-seated impediments to growth. After considerable popular debate, the Babangida Government adopted in June 1996 a comprehensive structural adjustment program (SAP) that signaled a radical departure from previous adjustment efforts. It emphasized reliance on market forces and deregulation. The SAP was originally intended to last for two years, but was extended when it was realized that implementing many of the reforms required more time. However, toward the end of 1990, the Government began to retreat from the basic reforms of the initial program, and much of the momentum of the reform effort had been lost by then. Nigeria's adjustment efforts were supported by three stand-by arrangements with the Fund, but the Government decided not to use the Fund's resources (Box 3). The World Bank also supported the adjustment program through a US$450 million trade policy and export diversification loan.

The objectives of the SAP were to (1) restructure and diversify the productive base of the economy so as to reduce dependency on the oil sector and imports; (2) achieve fiscal and balance of payments viability over the medium term; and (3) promote non-inflationary economic growth. The growth and inflation objectives for 1987–88 were a real GDP growth of 3–4 percent and a reduction of inflation to 20 percent per year on an average annual basis. It was thought that the anticipated devaluation of the naira would have a considerable impact on consumer prices.

The key policies designed to achieve these objectives were

- the tightening of financial policies through a reduction of the fiscal deficit to below 3 percent of GDP by 1988 and a limiting of the growth of broad money to 12 percent per year, the latter requiring limits on the expansion of net domestic bank credit on the order of 5–6 percent per year and net bank credit to the Government of 3 percent

- the adoption of a market-determined exchange rate
- the liberalization of the external trade and payments system
- the elimination of price controls and commodity boards
- the decontrol of interest rates
- the rationalization and restructuring of public expenditure
- the rationalization of the tariff structure and the overall lowering of tariffs
- the privatization or commercialization of most federal public enterprises (see Table 4).

Although significant progress was made in the liberalization of the economy, specifically through reform of the exchange and the trade system and the freeing of prices, macroeconomic policy implementation remained erratic and failed to bring inflation under control. Public criticism of economic policies increased, based on the notion that the disappointing results of the adjustment effort were a product of misguided policies under the SAP, rather than on the realization that incoherent implementation of SAP policies caused most the economic ills.

Price Liberalization and Subsidy Policy

The decontrol of prices at the start of the SAP was an important step in the liberalization of the economy. In 1986 the *Price Control Decree of 1971* and the *Commodity Board Decree of 1977* were repealed. The *Price Control Decree* had mandated the Productivity, Prices, and Incomes Board (PPIB) to announce annual price and wage guidelines for the private sector. The seven commodity boards[6] were

---

[6]The Cocoa Board (cocoa, coffee, and tea), the Groundnut Board (groundnuts, soya beans, benniseed, peanuts, and ginger), the Cotton Board, the Palm Produce Board (palm oil, palm kernel, and copra), the Rubber Board, the Grains Board (corn, millet, maize, wheat, rice, and beans), and the Tuber and Root Crops Board (yams and cassava).

IV STRUCTURAL REFORM AND MACROECONOMIC POLICY, 1986–90

> **Box 3. Experience with Fund-Supported Programs**
>
> Nigeria's adjustment efforts were supported by three stand-by arrangements (SBA) between 1986 and 1992, spanning a noncontinuous period of 42 months. The Fund committed a total of SDR 1.44 billion, but Nigeria decided, based on the results of a national referendum, not to make purchases under these arrangements. The arrangements with the Fund opened the door to official debt rescheduling, which was a high priority for the authorities. The first Fund program (January 1987–January 1988) quickly went off track; the second (February 1989–May 1990) was successfully implemented; and the third (January 1991–April 1992) also went off track soon after its approval.
>
> The three SBAs focused on fiscal adjustment and were designed against the background of volatile world oil prices. The last two SBAs incorporated some form of fiscal stabilization mechanism, which took account of deviations from programmed oil export prices. Over time, the stabilization mechanism did not prove very useful as it became a major source of funding of extrabudgetary projects. The first SBA incorporated a major exchange market reform and other liberalization measures, including a substantial increase in retail prices of petroleum products. It went off track early because of the diversion of oil revenue, which caused a budgetary shortfall and led to the accumulation of external payments arrears. The second SBA focused on fiscal adjustment, consolidation of earlier foreign exchange system reforms, adjustment of domestic petroleum product prices, and measures to strengthen the banking system. This program benefited from the recovery in oil prices, which, in combination with wide-ranging reforms at the outset of the SAP, led to a broad-based recovery of the economy. Fiscal adjustment was assisted by the establishment of a stabilization account to sterilize some of the windfall oil receipts, while monetary growth was controlled, in part, by the decision to transfer federal government accounts from commercial banks to the Central Bank in the summer of 1989. The vast improvement in the oil sector helped the country to achieve its macroeconomic objectives. The third SBA came in the aftermath of the 1990 oil price boom and in the midst of heightened efforts to regain the momentum of the transition to civilian rule. The emphasis of the program was on fiscal adjustment, but it went off track in the first quarter of 1991, mainly because of uncontrolled growth in federal government expenditures.
>
> In terms of design, the reform efforts undertaken under the different programs incorporated some structural fiscal reforms, particularly in the areas of budgetary practices, public expenditure programming and management, oversight of state and local government budgets, and prioritization of investment projects under the rolling plan. However, these formal changes in official procedures had little effect on actual budgetary practices. Overall, fiscal adjustment was limited to short-lived stabilization measures without addressing the structural fiscal problems that were the root cause of Nigeria's internal and external imbalances. The lack of a durable fiscal adjustment, the inability to develop efficient allocative and distributional budgetary functions, and the backsliding in the implementation of key policies undermined domestic and international confidence in Nigeria's adjustment efforts.

responsible for setting producer prices for the country's major agricultural crops. Their elimination, in conjunction with the devaluation of the naira, was instrumental in improving the profitability of non-oil export production, which increased substantially during the subsequent years.

Prices of goods and services provided by public enterprises remained largely under the control of the Government. This was especially true for the Nigerian National Petroleum Corporation (NNPC), the National Fertilizer Company of Nigeria (NAFCON), the Nigerian Electric Power Authority (NEPA), and other public utilities. Electricity tariffs remained unchanged between 1979 and 1989 at an average rate of ₦0.07 per kilowatt hour, equivalent to US$0.01.[7] They were raised to an average of ₦0.32 per kilowatt hour in mid-1989. The new tariff, equivalent to US$0.029 per kilowatt hour at the parallel exchange rate, was still less than half the rate prevailing in the United States in that year and substantially below the rate needed to improve services and eliminate the operating deficit of the parastatal.

The Government's efforts in the early part of the SAP to reduce further the subsidy on fertilizer and free up prices and marketing in the sector were overtaken by strong domestic pressure to stall the reforms, which led to higher subsidies during 1988–90. While the retail sales price of fertilizer was increased once during the SAP period (in 1986), the estimated subsidy element increased from about 30 percent in 1986 to more than 80 percent in 1989, largely as a result of the impact of the devaluation. The rising cost of the subsidy commanded some 70 percent of the agriculture ministry's capital budget in 1989, as compared with about 15 percent in 1983. With state and local governments sharing the cost of the subsidy equally with the Federal Government, the rising costs quickly overwhelmed their resources, with fertilizer-related costs accounting for an estimated 50

---
[7] At the average official exchange rate for 1989; the tariff was only 0.5 U.S. cents at the parallel exchange rate.

Table 4. Structural Reforms and Policy Implementation

	1986	1987	1988	1989	1990	1991	1992	1993	1994
Structural/Policy Reforms									
Foreign exchange market[1]	√	√		√	√		√	×	×
Import liberalization[2]	√	√	×	×	×	×			
Export promotion[3]	√	×	√×	×					
Debt conversion				√			√		
Prices	√							√	√
Privatization/commercialization				√					
Interest rates[4]	√	√			×		×	√	×
Credit guidelines	√	√					√		
Financial sector						√	√	√	
Budget (tax/expenditure)									
Policy Implementation									
Inflation	—	+	+	+	−	+	+	+	—
Fiscal deficit/GDP	+	+	+	−	−	+	+	+	−
Petroleum subsidy		*	*	*	*	*	*	*	*
Fertilizer subsidy	*	*	*	*	*	*	*	*	*
Extrabudgetary expenditures	—	+	+	+	+	+	+	+	−
Growth in broad money	−	+	+	−	+	−	+	−	−
Real effective exchange rate (+ appreciate)	−	−	+	−	−	−	−	+	+
Official and parallel exchange rate spread	−	−	+	+	−	+	−	+	+
External current account	−	+	−	+	+	−	−	−	−

Key: √ indicates reform, × indicates reversal of reform; change relative to previous year where, − indicates a decline, + indicates an increase; * indicates variable was positive; — indicates figure is zero, or that the item does not exist.

[1] Prorate allocation of foreign exchange by CBN in 1993, fixed exchange rate in 1994.
[2] During 1988–91 higher tariffs or import bans were introduced.
[3] In 1987 export bans on grains were introduced and bans were extended to other commodities in 1988 and 1989. In 1989 the rediscount/refinancing facility for exports was introduced by the CBN.
[4] On November 10, 1989, the CBN introduced a maximum interest rate spread between saving and prime lending rates, the prime and the highest lending rates, and the interbank and prime lending rates. Ceilings were imposed on maximum lending rates at the beginning of 1991 and 1994.

percent of state and local government capital outlays in 1989. As important as the rising fiscal implications of the subsidy were the growing distribution problems, including unequal and delayed distribution, increased smuggling to neighboring countries, and a disproportionate share of the subsidy going to marketers.

The pricing of domestic petroleum products, especially gasoline, contained a large subsidy element. Domestic petroleum product prices are set by the Federal Government, as is the amount of national oil production allocated for domestic consumption. However, in January 1986 product prices were increased between 24 and 725 percent, with gasoline prices rising by nearly 200 percent.[8] The increase in the price of gasoline raised the domestic price well above import parity.[9] Prices for domestic petroleum products were subsequently raised in 1988 and 1990, and the implicit subsidy was temporarily reduced each time until it caught up with the depreciation of the naira. Thus, the ratio of the domestic price of gasoline to the world price fell from 186 percent immediately after the 1986 price increase to a low of 37 percent in 1990 (Figure 2).

Reform of the Exchange Rate

The precipitous decline in the terms of trade (52 percent) in 1986 convinced the authorities that exchange rate reform was unavoidable. The foreign ex-

---

[8] The price of household kerosene remained unchanged. With this exception, the lowest increase was for liquefied petroleum gas (24 percent).

[9] Measured at the official exchange rate, the domestic price of gasoline was 186 percent of the world wholesale price after the increase. Measured at the parallel exchange rate, the domestic price was still 10 percent below the world price.

IV STRUCTURAL REFORM AND MACROECONOMIC POLICY, 1986–90

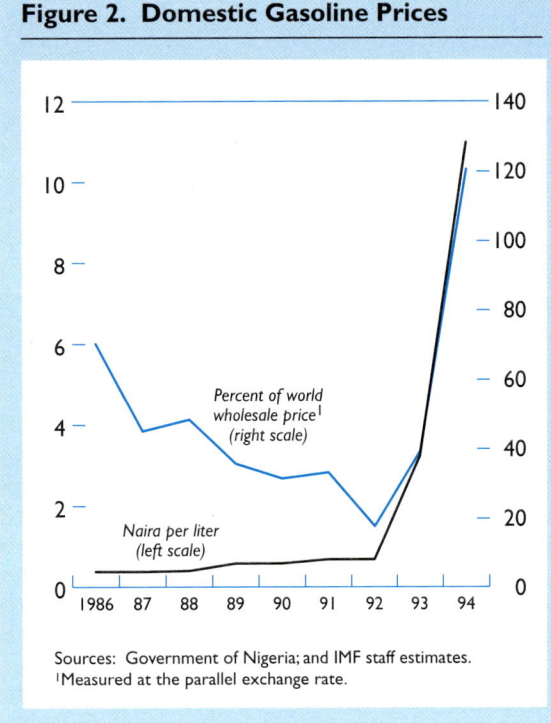

Figure 2. Domestic Gasoline Prices

Sources: Government of Nigeria; and IMF staff estimates.
[1]Measured at the parallel exchange rate.

Figure 3. Exchange Rate Developments
(Naira per U.S. dollar)

Sources: Data provided by the Nigerian authorities; and IMF staff estimates.

change market was liberalized in a number of steps, thereby allowing the economy to restore external competitiveness and to absorb severe terms of trade shocks.

On September 26, 1986, a dual exchange rate system was introduced, consisting of an administratively determined official rate and an auction rate. The official rate was applied to external debt-service payments, official foreign capital inflows, and other federal government transactions. The auction rate, determined in weekly foreign exchange auctions by the Central Bank of Nigeria (CBN), applied to all other transaction.[10] Foreign exchange obtained from the auction was traded in an interbank market, which was also funded from private non-oil export proceeds.[11] The official exchange rate was devalued by 22 percent, to ₦1.538 per U.S. dollar, and the first auction resulted in a 65 percent devaluation of the naira, to ₦4.20 per U.S. dollar (Figure 3).

The pricing of foreign exchange in the auctions was based on a marginal bid system. An important provision of the auction was the ceiling on the share of the total foreign exchange that could be purchased by individual dealer banks. The three largest dealer banks were each allowed to purchase no more than 5 percent of the total offering and the other banks no more than 3 percent. This provision intended to prevent the emergence of monopolistic or oligopolistic practices in the foreign exchange market, but also had the effect of depressing the price that emerged from the auction. To reinforce this policy, the Central Bank required all transactions in the interbank market to be carried out at the rate established in the previous auction, adjusted for a maximum buying and selling spread of 1 percent.

Official Supply of Foreign Exchange

	1987	1988	1989	1990
Official supply				
In billions of U.S. dollars	2.0	2.8	2.2	2.5
In percent of official foreign exchange earnings	...	54	33	...

In January 1987, however, the exchange rate in the interbank market was fully liberalized. Given the continued quantity restrictions on bids in the central bank auction and the segmentation of the two markets during the subsequent six months, a spread emerged between the interbank and auction rates that, however, never exceeded 5 percent.

---

[10]Only authorized dealer banks were allowed to participate in the auction, which was designated as the Secondary Foreign Exchange Market (SFEM).

[11]The foreign exchange surrender requirement to the Central Bank for non-oil export proceeds was lifted in 1986, but exporters were still required to surrender 75 percent of foreign exchange earnings to commercial banks at the prevailing interbank rate. In 1987, the surrender requirement was eliminated altogether.

In an effort to reduce speculative bids by authorized dealers, which had caused considerable volatility in the weekly auction rates, the marginal bid system was replaced with a Dutch auction system on April 2, 1987. Henceforth, auctions were held every fortnight. Furthermore, on July 2, 1987, following nine months of frequent devaluations of the official exchange rate, this rate was merged with the auction rate.[12] At the same time, the auction market for foreign exchange became more restrictive as dealer banks could now bid only on behalf of their customers. The interbank rate applied only to foreign exchange obtained outside the Central Bank. Consequently, despite the "unification" of the exchange rates, there were still two rates: the auction rate and the interbank rate, with the latter depreciating more rapidly over time. The differential between the two rates widened from 8 percent at the end of 1987 to 55 percent by the end of 1988.

The large spread between the two exchange rates prompted the authorities to unify the auction and the interbank rates into a "central" rate in January 1989. The new system incorporated an auction mechanism, but the Central Bank retained a large degree of discretion in setting the rate. Official foreign exchange was allocated among the participating banks on a daily basis in proportion to their capital base. During the next two years, the official exchange rate depreciated by 44 percent against the U.S. dollar. Small-scale purchasers of foreign exchange had limited access to the official market, and a broadening of the foreign exchange market was accomplished with the introduction of foreign exchange bureaus in September 1989. The bureaus were allowed to buy and sell currency and traveler's checks at freely negotiated rates. The funding of the foreign exchange bureaus was limited to private remittances, private capital inflows, and other invisible proceeds. While the bureaus operated on a relatively small scale, they provided an important source of additional foreign exchange for importers who could not fulfill their demands through the auction.

Trade and Tariff Reform

A major reform of the trade and tariff system was implemented concurrently with the introduction of the dual exchange rate system in September 1986. The import and export licensing schemes were abolished, the number of import bans was reduced from 74 to 16, and the number of export bans from 11 to zero.[13] The 30 percent import surcharge, which had been imposed in January 1986, was removed[14] and the 100 percent advance payment for import duty was reduced to 25 percent in 1987. Pending a comprehensive tariff reform, the *Customs and Excise Provisions Decree of 1986* was issued to provide immediate relief from the impact of the devaluation of the naira on the cost structure of selected tradable goods. As a result, the level and dispersion of tariffs were significantly reduced and the average nominal tariff rate was lowered from 33 percent to 23 percent. Reduced tariffs were applied to agricultural inputs, basic industrial raw materials, and selected agricultural commodities; but higher rates were introduced on capital goods, essential consumer goods, and agricultural machinery. Most tariffs were set in a range of 10–30 percent, but for agricultural and industrial imports that competed with major domestic producers high rates of 100 percent or more were maintained. The *Customs and Excise Tariff (Consolidation) Decree of 1988* superseded the 1986 decree and set out a tariff regime for the period through 1994. The decree reduced the (unweighted) average tariff rate for chemicals, base metals, machinery and equipment, and vehicles, but raised it for most textile products. More important, it significantly reduced the dispersion of tariffs within each SITC group, although the average unweighted tariff of 28 percent was higher than in 1986. Subsequently, in response to mounting pressures, there were numerous revisions to the 1988 decree, which aimed at increasing protection for domestic manufacturers. Duties were increased on 22 items in 1989 and 1990, mostly on finished goods, and reduced on 16 items, mostly on industrial inputs.

The progress in trade liberalization, made in the early years of the SAP, particularly with respect to the lifting of trade bans, suffered setbacks in the following years. Exports of unprocessed timber were banned in 1987 and exports of cassava, maize, yams, beans, and rice were banned in 1989. By 1990, the export bans applied to 63 percent of the volume of crop production. The immediate impact of these bans on trade was negligible, as these products accounted for a very small proportion of exports prior to the imposition of the bans. But their existence inhibited significantly the diversification of the country's export base. While the total number of import bans did not change, selected commodities were re-

---

[12]The two rates were unified at ₦3.73 per U.S. dollar (the prevailing auction rate) and the SFEM was renamed the FEM (foreign exchange market).

[13]The remaining import bans covered cigarettes, poultry, vegetables, rough wood, eggs, fruit, most textile fabrics, plastic wares, mineral water, jewelry and precious metals, rice, maize, wheat, selected alcoholic beverages, gaming machines, and vegetable oils.

[14]A 6.02 percent surcharge was reimposed in January 1987.

IV STRUCTURAL REFORM AND MACROECONOMIC POLICY, 1986–90

moved from the import prohibition list between 1987 and 1990, but others were added.

External Debt Policy

Prolific external borrowing during the first half of the 1980s increased Nigeria's official external debt from US$4.1 billion at the end of 1980 to US$24.6 billion by the end of 1986. The debt-service ratio rose from 6 percent to 72 percent during this period. The increased debt-service burden reflected, in part, the Federal Government's assumption of external debt-service obligations of state governments, but also the sharp contraction in export revenue, especially in 1986. Nigeria's external debt strategy aimed at regularizing relations with its external creditors, and reducing debt-service obligations to around 30 percent of official foreign exchange receipts. This was to be accomplished through a series of rescheduling agreements with Paris and London Club creditors, and, in 1988, through the introduction of a debt conversion scheme. The SAP paved the way for two rescheduling agreements with Paris Club creditors (October 1986 and March 1989) and three agreements with London Club creditors (November 1986, August 1987, and April 1989).

Paris Club Agreements

The 1986 Paris Club agreement covered current maturities on medium- and long-term debt falling due from October 1986 to the end of 1987 (US$2.8 billion), as well as arrears accumulated on short-term trade credits and medium- and long-term maturities (US$1.1 billion). Of the arrears, US$0.5 billion was to be paid between November 1987 and the end of 1989. The remaining rescheduled amounts were to be repaid over a 4½-year period commencing November 1992.

The agreement soon ran into trouble as the authorities were not able to honor their obligations. In an attempt to stabilize the newly established interbank exchange rate, the supply of official reserves to the market exceeded substantially the amounts programmed in the 1987 budget. Thus, the allocation of additional foreign exchange receipts to the FEM was achieved at the cost of accumulating arrears on Paris Club and other external debt. This problem continued well into 1988. As a result, US$230 million in external payment arrears were accumulated in 1987, and a further US$4.5 billion in the subsequent year. Following the approval by the Fund of a second stand-by arrangement with Nigeria, a new rescheduling agreement with Paris Club creditors was reached in March 1989.

In view of the previous rescheduling and the fact that arrears had accumulated on debt-service payments due on previously rescheduled debt, the terms of the new agreement were rather complex.[15] The total amount of debt relief (including arrears) involved for 1989 and the first four months of 1990 was about US$5.3 billion. Partially reflecting delays in bilateral negotiations and reconciliation efforts, Nigeria again began to accumulate arrears to Paris Club creditors in 1989 and continued to do so through 1990 pending the signing of the third stand-by arrangement with the Fund in January 1991, which facilitated the authorities' third rescheduling agreement with Paris Club creditors in that same year.

London Club Agreements

In 1984 Nigeria reached an agreement with the London Club commercial banks to reschedule arrears that had built up on trade credits during the 1982–83 period, and the final payments under this arrangement were made in October 1986. During 1986, faced with a large drop in export earnings, Nigeria accumulated an estimated US$2.8 billion in arrears on letters of credit extended by London Club banks (including late interest). In April 1986, an agreement was reached for a moratorium on payments on principal, pending a comprehensive rescheduling of all debt payments due to the banks. In November 1986, an agreement was concluded on the repayment of arrears on letters of credit over a four-year period starting December 1987. Due to delays in finalizing the agreement, however, the London Club creditors agreed to a modified repayment schedule in November 1987, involving US$520 million in new credits during 1988 and 1989, with repayment of interest and principal to occur over a three-year period commencing in January 1988. In the event, this agreement was never implemented owing to the delay in reaching an agreement with the Fund on a program and the London Club creditors' subsequent refusal to provide new money.

A breakthrough was finally achieved with the signing of a more comprehensive agreement in April 1989 on terms much more favorable to the authorities. The original US$2.6 billion in trade arrears were to be repaid in 144 equal monthly installments

---

[15]Creditors agreed to reschedule: (1) all principal and interest (excluding late interest) due from January 1, 1989, up to April 30, 1990 on medium- and long-term debt contracted before October 1, 1985 (the cutoff date used for the previous rescheduling); (2) all arrears (including late interest) outstanding as of end-1988 on medium- and long-term debt contracted before the cutoff date; (3) up to a maximum of 60 percent of the amounts that were due before December 31, 1988, and not paid, on previously rescheduled debt; and (4) all arrears outstanding at end-1988 on short-term credits, contracted before that date.

beginning in January 1992 at an interest rate of LIBOR plus ¹³⁄₁₆ In addition, the new agreement covered US$2.9 billion in arrears and current maturities, which were rescheduled over a 20-year period, also commencing in January 1992.

In 1991, Nigeria made substantial progress in reducing its commercial debt; following an agreement in principle with London Club creditors in March, which was finalized in December, a debt and debt-service reduction operation (DROP) was completed in January 1992. The DROP involved the purchase of US$3.4 billion of commercial debt at a 60 percent discount and the exchange of another US$2.0 billion at par for 30-year bonds carrying an interest rate of 5.5 percent per annum for the first three years and 6.25 percent per annum thereafter. Principal for the par bonds was collateralized by Treasury zero coupon bonds and 12 months of interest was collateralized by cash and certain permitted investments. As a result of the DROP, Nigeria's debt outstanding to the London Club banks was reduced from nearly US$6 billion at end-1991 to US$2.2 billion. The Nigerian authorities have since remained current on these obligations.

Fiscal Adjustment and Reform

Fiscal policy was erratic during the SAP period, as it had been during the first half of the 1980s. During the first two years (1987–88), the overall and primary fiscal balances deteriorated substantially, but increased world oil prices contributed to a marked improvement in the fiscal position during the 1989–90 period (see Table 5). Thus, in 1990 the overall deficit fell to below 3 percent of GDP, and the primary balance recorded a surplus of nearly 9 percent.

The deterioration in the fiscal position in 1987 was primarily due to the assumption of large external debt-service obligations of the state governments by the Federal Government (Box 4). Nondebt expenditure rose modestly in that year, and the primary fiscal balance turned to a surplus of 1 percent of GDP, from a deficit of ½ percent in 1986. In 1988, however, the Government adopted a "reflationary package" as part of its budget proposals to alleviate the adverse impact of the large increase in petroleum prices, the elimination of price controls, and the sizable devaluation of the naira. This caused nondebt expenditure to rise by more than 45 percent compared with the 1987 outcome, while government revenue rose by only about half that amount. In only two years, government nondebt expenditure increased by 90 percent, while under the influence of the devaluation and higher oil export volumes government revenue increased by 60 percent.

The improvement in the fiscal position during the 1989–90 period was attributable to a substantial moderation in the rate of growth of nondebt expenditure and a surge in oil revenue, owing to the rise in world oil prices. Nonetheless, the degree of fiscal adjustment was insufficient to redress inflationary and exchange rate pressures. In circumstances where the bulk of government revenue is coming from abroad, the usual indicators of the stance of fiscal policy, such as the overall or primary fiscal balance, may fail to provide a proper measure of the monetary impact of the Government's budget. In those circumstances, the evolution of nominal nondebt expenditure is a more useful indicator of the underlying fiscal stance (see Box 5). Thus, an increase in nominal government expenditure in excess of real output growth would result in inflation or in a crowding out of real private absorption, or a combination of both. This seems to have been the case in Nigeria, where nominal nondebt government expenditure increased by 213 percent during the SAP period, and by 44 percent in 1990 alone, compared with a growth of real GDP of 27 percent over the entire period.

Tax policy during the SAP was aimed primarily at attenuating the impact of higher import prices arising from the depreciation of the naira. Little was done to enhance non-oil tax revenue, which increased only to 5½ percent of GDP in 1990, from 4½ percent in 1986, largely on account of rising customs revenues. Tax reform at the federal level consisted of rate reductions in corporate and personal income taxes. The corporate income tax rate was reduced from 45 percent to 40 percent in 1987, and the top marginal rate in personal income taxes was lowered from 70 percent to 55 percent.[16] In 1988, the number of excisable items was reduced from 412 to 118, including the exemption of all imported intermediate inputs. There were other minor changes in the tax system, such as tax relief for dividend income, income of small-scale manufacturers, and capital investment. During 1986–90, no new taxes were introduced.

Government expenditure policy suffered from weak budgetary procedures and lack of transparency, as reflected in the underbudgeting of various expenditure categories, including domestic interest payments, and the emergence of sizable extrabudgetary spending. The structure of government spending changed significantly during the

---

[16]Since the personal income tax is levied at the state level, this measure had virtually no impact on federal government revenue. The Federal Government collects income taxes only from residents of the Federal Capital Territory (Abuja), and the armed forces.

IV STRUCTURAL REFORM AND MACROECONOMIC POLICY, 1986–90

Table 5. Summary of Federal Government Fiscal Operations

	1985	1986	1987	1988	1989	1990
	(In billions of naira)					
Federally collected revenue	15.1	15.9	23.3	29.5	55.4	93.7
Of which: oil revenue	(10.9)	(12.7)	(18.5)	(23.6)	(46.7)	(79.8)
Federally retained revenue	9.0	10.2	12.6	16.1	31.0	56.2
Total expenditure	11.0	14.0	25.4	35.8	46.6	63.8
Of which: non-debt	(8.1)	(10.5)	(11.7)	(20.2)	(22.3)	(32.9)
Overall balance	−2.1	−3.8	−12.8	−19.7	−15.6	−7.7
Primary balance	0.9	−0.4	1.0	−4.2	8.7	23.3
Financing	2.0	3.8	12.8	19.7	15.6	7.7
Foreign (net)	−0.4	−0.3	3.5	5.4	8.2	−0.3
Domestic	2.4	4.1	9.3	14.3	7.4	7.9
Of which: banking system	(1.6)	(−0.8)	(2.4)	(6.1)	(−9.3)	(2.8)
	(In percent of GDP)					
Federally collected revenue	20.9	21.7	21.4	20.3	24.6	35.9
Of which: oil revenue	(15.1)	(17.4)	(17.0)	(16.3)	(20.8)	(30.6)
Federally retained revenue	12.4	13.9	11.6	11.1	13.8	21.5
Total expenditure	15.2	19.1	23.3	24.7	20.7	24.5
Of which: non-debt	(11.2)	(14.4)	(10.7)	(13.9)	(9.9)	(12.6)
Overall balance	−2.8	−5.2	−11.7	−13.6	−7.0	−2.9
Primary balance	1.2	−0.5	0.9	−2.9	3.9	8.9
Financing	2.8	5.2	11.7	13.6	7.0	2.9
Foreign (net)	−0.5	−0.3	3.2	3.7	3.7	−0.1
Domestic	3.3	5.6	8.5	9.8	3.3	3.0
Of which: banking system	(2.2)	(−1.1)	(2.2)	(4.2)	(−4.1)	(1.1)

Sources: Data provided by the Nigerian authorities; and IMF staff estimates.

SAP period. With the assumption by the Federal Government in 1987 of the state government's external debt obligations, foreign interest obligations rose sharply, accounting for more than 30 percent of total expenditure during 1987–90. The lack of budget control was particularly evident in growing extrabudgetary spending, which reached by 1990 an estimated 17 percent of total spending, equivalent to 50 percent of budgeted nondebt expenditure. This development occurred despite the introduction of a warrant system in 1985, in which all expenditure was to be authorized by quarterly warrants issued by the Accountant General. In fact, the budgetary process became less and less transparent during the SAP period. Extrabudgetary outlays were financed from oil revenues kept outside the Federation Account; during 1989–90, this source of funding was augmented by spending from the stabilization account (Box 6). As these expenditures were not covered by the warrant system, their nature is largely unknown, but it is believed that much of it was spent on the construction of the federal capital of Abuja. As extrabudgetary expenditures grew, the official budgets lost much of their meaning (Table 6).

State and Local Government Finances

The state governments derive nearly 90 percent of their revenue from the Federation Account.[17] The remainder comes mostly from income and sales taxes. Local governments and the special funds rely almost entirely on transfers from the Federation Account.[18] The budgets of these tiers of government were broadly in balance during the SAP period. Total revenue from these sources increased from 9.8 percent of GDP in 1986 to 13.7 in 1990, while total expenditure increased from 10.3 percent of GDP to 13.1 percent during the same period.

---

[17]Data limitations preclude a comprehensive accounting of the fiscal operations of the state and local governments and the special funds. Data are available for allocations from the Federation Account, statutory claims on transfers to the Federation Stabilization Account, highly aggregated state budgetary data, and net bank credit to state and local governments. Little information is available on the financial operations of the special funds or revenue collected directly by local governments.

[18]Local governments collect some fees and municipal taxes, but these revenues are relatively small.

Monetary Policy and Financial Sector Reform

Box 4. Fiscal Federalism

The Government of Nigeria consists of the Federal Government, 30 state governments, and 589 local governments. The bulk of government revenue is collected at the federal level and shared among the three tiers of government, including oil proceeds, customs duties, excise taxes, and corporate income taxes. These revenues accrue to the Federation Account, from where they are distributed as follows: 48.5 percent to the Federal Government, 24 percent to state governments, 20 percent to local governments, and 7.5 percent to five special funds. These are the Ecology Fund, the Federal Capital Territory Fund, the Mineral Derivation Fund, the Mineral Producing Areas Fund, and the Statutory Stabilization Account. The Federation Account allocation to individual state and local governments is based on a distribution formula that takes into account equality (40 percent), population (30 percent), social development (10 percent), land mass (10 percent), and internal revenue mobilization efforts (10 percent). In addition to the Federation Account allocations, the revenue generated from the value-added tax, introduced in 1994, is shared between the Federal Government (20 percent, increased to 40 percent in 1995) and state governments (80 percent). Apart from the allocations from the Federation Account, state governments raise their own revenue from income taxes and fees. In the diagram below the main components of the resource flows are depicted, with illustrative figures for 1992 (in naira). Totals may not add due to rounding.

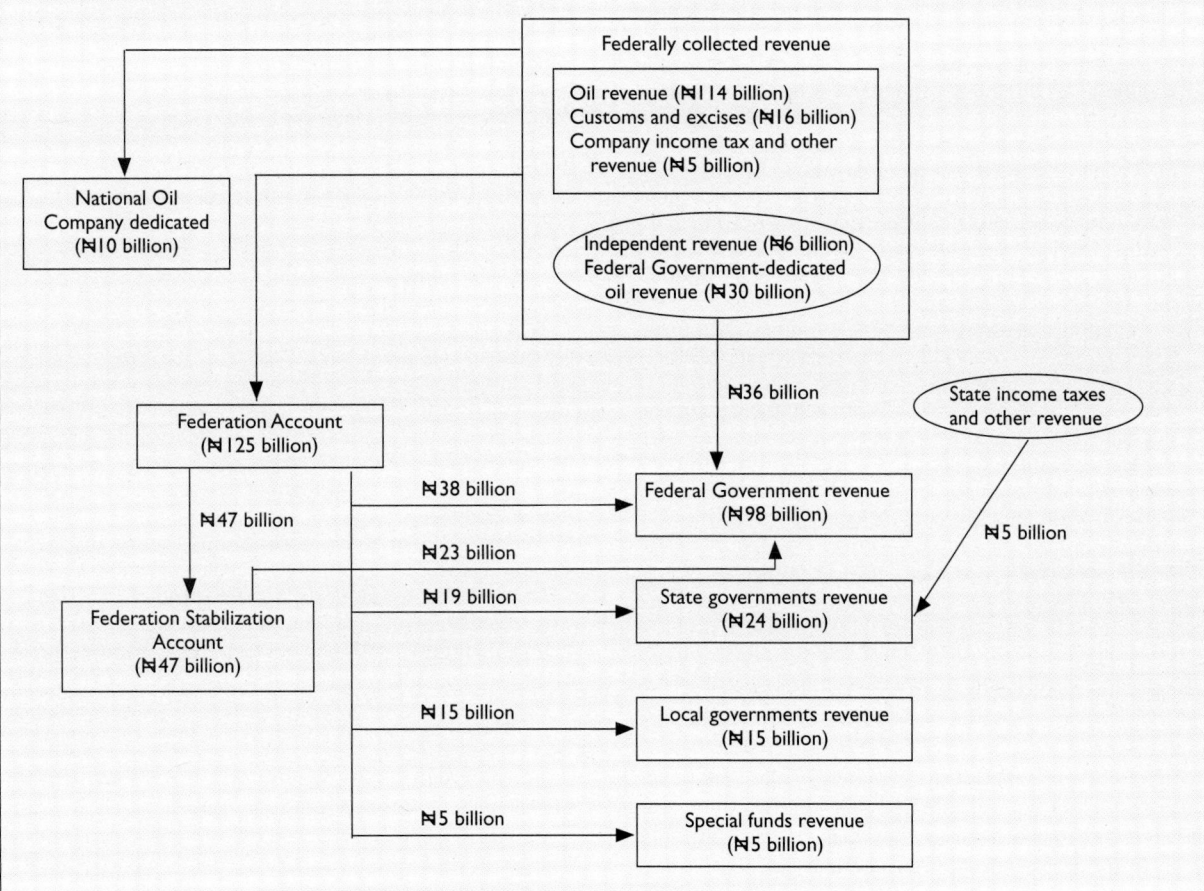

The consolidated fiscal position of federal, state, and local governments mirrored broadly the pattern of fiscal developments within the Federal Government, namely a sharp deterioration during the first two years of the SAP followed by a remarkable turnaround in 1989–90.

Monetary Policy and Financial Sector Reform

In the absence of a supportive fiscal policy, monetary policy had to play a dominant role in macroeconomic stabilization. However, at the same time its ef-

IV STRUCTURAL REFORM AND MACROECONOMIC POLICY, 1986–90

Box 5. Measuring the Stance of Fiscal Policy in an Oil Economy

A simple model can be used to analyze the inflationary impact of government expenditure when the bulk of fiscal revenue is generated from external trade:

$$Mv = Py, \quad (1)$$

$$M = NFACB + NFAOB + NDCG + NDCRE, \quad (2)$$

$$NFACB = NFACB_{t-1} + XOIL - FI + FGB + Z, \quad (3)$$

$$NDCG = NDCG_{t-1} - D - FBG - DNBBG, \quad (4)$$

$$D = t*XOIL + OGR - G - FI, \quad (5)$$

where: M = the stock of broad money; v = velocity; P = non-oil GDP deflator; y = real non-oil GDP; $NFACB$ = net foreign assets of the Central Bank (adjusted for valuation effects); $NFAOB$ = net foreign assets of the rest of the banking system (net of valuation effects); $NDCG$ = net bank credit to the Federal Government; $NDCRE$ = net bank credit to the rest of the economy (including other items net); $XOIL$ = value of oil exports; FI = foreign interest payments due; FGB = net external financing of the fiscal deficit; Z = the overall balance of payments, excluding $XOIL$, FI, and FGB; D = the overall fiscal balance; $DNBBG$ = domestic nonbank borrowing by the Government; t = government oil revenue as a share of oil export revenue; OGR = government non-oil revenue; and G = government expenditure excluding foreign interest due.

Equation (1) states the quantity theory of money. Since Nigeria is assumed to be a price taker with respect to exports, monetary shocks are assumed to affect only prices in the non-oil sector. Hence, the equation is defined in terms of non-oil GDP and the non-oil GDP deflator. Equation (2) defines the stock of broad money in terms of its counterparts in the balance sheet of the consolidated banking system. Equation (3) defines the relationship between the net foreign assets of the Central Bank and the overall balance of payments, which are here disaggregated into nominal oil exports, foreign interest obligations, and net external borrowing of the Government, and the remaining balance of payments, excluding changes in international reserves. Equation (4) states that the change in net bank credit to the Government is equal to the overall fiscal deficit minus net foreign financing and nonbank borrowing by the Federal Government, and equation (5) defines the government budget deficit.

Equations (1) through (5) can be combined to yield equation (6):

$$P = (v/y)*[NFACB_{t-1} + NDCG_{t-1} + NFAOB + NDCRE + (1-t)*XOIL + Z - DNBBG - OGR + G], \quad (6)$$

which defines the aggregate price level as a function of the income velocity of money, real non-oil GDP, and the stock of broad money, which has been decomposed into its constituent parts as defined by equations (2) through (5).

Equation (6) shows that an increase in government expenditure (G), excluding foreign interest payments, that is not offset by an increase in either domestic nonbank borrowing or in non-oil fiscal revenue, will be inflationary, unless there is an equivalent leakage through the balance of payments, or a corresponding contraction of net bank credit to the rest of the economy. The inflationary impact of additional oil revenue is equivalent, therefore, to an increase in domestic bank borrowing. Clearly, the future debt dynamics of the two cases differ, and, hence, so will the subsequent monetary impact.

This result captures the basic characteristic of the Government's fiscal policy during most of the 1986–90 period; during periods of low oil prices the deficit was large and the Government borrowed from the banking system; during periods of high oil prices the deficit was small and the Government monetized most of the higher oil revenues and reduced its borrowing from the banking system. In both cases, however, fiscal operations contributed to the expansion of broad money and the attendant pressures on domestic prices and the exchange rate.

The extent to which government expenditure in 1990 was "excessive" can be determined by comparing actual expenditure with the level of expenditure that

---

fectiveness was severely constrained by the lack of instruments and the multiple and often conflicting roles it had to fulfill. Monetary policy was charged not only with bringing inflation under control, but also with a variety of sectoral and regional objectives, such as stimulating local production, promoting non-oil exports, and ensuring a proper distribution of credit. The most important handicap, however, was probably the Central Bank's lack of independence from the Federal Government, which gave the latter almost uncontrolled access to Central Bank credit and considerable influence over interest rate policy.

The Central Bank's inability to control the growth of money was to a large extent the result of fiscal policies, which relied heavily on central bank financing of large deficits. Monetary control was also complicated by the monetization of rising government oil revenues during 1989–90 (Table 7). Thus, strong money growth fueled inflationary pressures throughout most of the SAP period and placed increasing pressure on the exchange rate and interest rates. The inability to bring inflation under control contributed to the erosion of popular support for the SAP.

Credit Controls

The Central Bank relied on a system of direct credit controls, with bank-specific ceilings on credit

Stance of Fiscal Policy (Alternative Scenarios)
(In percent of GDP, unless otherwise indicated)

	1986	1987	1988	1989	1990
Actual outcome					
Aggregate price level (1986=100)[1]	100	129	163	195	214
Government expenditure (in billions of naira)[2]	13.0	15.5	24.4	28.3	41.3
Overall fiscal balance	−5.2	−11.7	−13.6	−7.0	−2.9
Primary fiscal balance	−0.5	0.9	−2.9	3.9	8.9
Targeted 20 percent inflation					
Aggregate price level (1986=100)[1]	100	120	144	173	207
Government expenditure (in billions of naira)[2]	13.0	13.3	19.5	23.1	39.2
Overall fiscal balance	−5.2	−9.7	−10.2	−4.7	−2.1
Primary fiscal balance	−0.5	2.9	0.5	6.2	9.7
Relative price stability[3]					
Aggregate price level (1986=100)[1]	100	102	105	108	113
Government expenditure (in billions of naira)[2]	13.0	9.3	9.3	8.1	11.2
Overall fiscal balance	−5.2	−6.0	−3.2	2.0	8.6
Primary fiscal balance	−0.5	6.6	7.5	12.8	20.5
Memorandum items:					
Consumer price index (average; 1986=100)	100	110	148	223	239
Average official exchange rate (naira/U.S. dollar)	1.75	4.02	4.54	7.36	8.04

[1] Non-oil GDP deflator.
[2] Excluding foreign interest payments.
[3] Inflation rate equal to consumer price inflation in partner countries.

would have been consistent with the Government's inflation objectives. Analytically, this involves solving equation (6) for government expenditure (G) under different assumptions of the price level (P), as shown by equation (7). The strong assumption of this analysis is that all the variables on the right-hand side of (7) are independent of government expenditure.

$$G = P*(y/v) - [NFACB_{t-1} + NDCG_{t-1} + NFAOB + NDCRE + (1-t)*XOIL + Z - DNBBG - OGR]. \quad (7)$$

As shown above, a more ambitious inflation target, e.g., with an inflation rate in line with trading partners, would have required much more restraint in government expenditure and growing primary fiscal surpluses.

expansion to the private sector. It also maintained guidelines on the sectoral and regional allocation of credit, which specified certain minimum shares of total bank lending to agriculture and other priority sectors and required commercial banks to maintain a minimum ratio of rural loans to rural deposits. In addition, it used minimum liquidity and cash reserve requirements, but not as active instruments of monetary policy. To reduce excess liquidity in the banking system, in November 1989 the Central Bank started an auction-based system for the issuance of treasury bills and certificates and introduced in August 1990 the so-called mandatory stabilization securities. The mandatory stabilization securities were issued selectively to banks on the basis of their liquidity positions and soundness.

In the aggregate, the credit ceilings proved largely ineffective in restraining the growth of bank credit to the private sector (Table 8), not only because of the relatively minor penalties for exceeding the stipulated ceilings, but also because of the rapid increase in new banks, which would have required frequent adjustments to individual bank ceilings.

Interest Rate Policy

Interest rate policy lacked consistency during the SAP, as periods of liberalization were intertwined

IV STRUCTURAL REFORM AND MACROECONOMIC POLICY, 1986–90

Box 6. Oil Revenue in Nigeria

Nigeria's fiscal revenue relies heavily on the oil sector. This reliance has continued unabated since the mid-1970s, despite numerous efforts to diversify the revenue base. As a share of total government revenue, oil revenue increased from 82 percent in 1986–89 to 84 percent in 1990–93, before dropping to 75 percent in 1994, largely on account of the fall in oil export prices and the introduction of the value-added tax. More important for 1994, the substantially overvalued official exchange rate affected oil revenue (in naira terms) significantly.

Oil revenues derive from the operations of the Nigerian National Petroleum Company (NNPC), and its joint venture partners. The NNPC's contribution to the budget consists of net export proceeds and the domestic retail sales of petroleum products. The joint venture partners pay a royalty to the Federal Government of 19.6 percent of total exports and a profit tax of 85 percent. They are permitted to withhold certain amounts from their net export proceeds in the form of "notional" costs and guaranteed profits, both of which are denominated in U.S. dollars per barrel. The partner companies settle their actual tax liability to the Federal Government at the end of each company's fiscal year.

Through the end of 1994, the NNPC was permitted to sell a specified number of barrels each day to cover its dollar-denominated costs ("dollar cash calls") and to help finance its capital budget ("dedicated oil"). A certain number of barrels per day were also sold on behalf of the Federal Government, which accrued directly to an offshore account. The NNPC's net export proceeds (excluding dollar cash calls and all dedicated oil) were deposited in the Central Bank's account at the Federal Reserve Bank of New York and the naira counterpart was deposited into the Federal Government's "Royalty Account" at the Central Bank. In addition, the NNPC generates revenue from the domestic retail sales of petroleum products and is expected to pay the Federal Government both a notional cost for the crude oil it uses for domestic refining (at a transfer price in 1994 of 183 naira per barrel) and operating profits. In the 1991–94 period, the NNPC incurred losses on its domestic operations, as a result of the low retail prices set by the Government, and did not pay the Federal Government for crude oil. In October 1994, the retail price of gasoline was raised substantially (from 3.25 naira to 11 naira per liter), and the NNPC has since been able to pay a higher transfer price (US$17 per barrel) to the Federal Government.

The system for collecting oil revenue was modified substantially in 1995, when the Federal Government closed the off-budget dedicated accounts and began depositing the total amount of NNPC export proceeds directly into a Federal Reserve Bank account. From this account, the Government's contribution to operating costs of the oil industry ("first charges" against the budget) are then deducted. Another change has been that profits from domestic sales have been transferred to a newly created Petroleum Trust Fund, which is managed outside the federal government budget. The Petroleum Trust Fund resources are being used for priority infrastructure and social sector projects.

---

with the reimposition of some forms of control. The liberalization of bank deposit and lending rates, with effect from August 1, 1987, had little impact on interest rate developments. The commercial banks followed the Central Bank's rediscount rate in adjusting their rates, even if the signals sent appeared to go in the wrong direction. This was particularly evident toward the end of 1987, when the CBN lowered its discount rate and the banks followed suit in the face of accelerating inflation. Responding to pressure from the private sector, the CBN reintroduced controls in November 1989 by imposing a maximum spread between lending and deposit rates and imposing a maximum lending rate. Real deposit and lending rates turned negative in early 1988 (Figure 4) and remained so until the beginning of 1990, when inflation temporarily abated. Negative real interest rates depressed financial savings, which dropped in 1988 and 1989 as a share of non-oil GDP; the currency-deposit ratio rose from an average of 30 percent in 1986–87 to 40 percent in 1988–89.

Financial Intermediation

The financial sector expanded rapidly during the SAP, with the number of commercial banks increasing from 29 in 1986 to 58 in 1990, and the number of merchant banks increasing from 12 to 49, respectively (Figure 5). During the same period, the number of commercial and merchant bank branches increased from 1,394 to 2,182. This rapid expansion occurred for a number of reasons. First, the Central Bank began issuing new banking licenses after a moratorium of several years. Second, the trade liberalization measures implemented under the SAP increased the demand for trade-related financing. Third, the emergence of a spread between the official exchange rate and the interbank rate (and later the foreign exchange bureau rate) made exchange rate arbitrage very profitable. Many of the emerging merchant banks were established almost solely for the purpose of participating in the Central Bank foreign exchange auctions, in which foreign exchange could be purchased at a growing discount relative to

Table 6: Structure of Federal Government Expenditures

	1986	1987	1988	1989	1990
	(In percent of total expenditure)				
Total expenditure and net lending	100.0	100.0	100.0	100.0	100.0
Of which: non-debt	(75.3)	(46.0)	(56.5)	(47.8)	(51.5)
Recurrent expenditure	54.8	70.8	62.7	68.9	64.8
Personnel costs	11.2	9.3	7.8	7.3	8.0
Overhead costs	18.9	7.4	11.5	9.4	8.3
Foreign interest due	7.1	33.1	29.0	35.2	32.9
Domestic interest due	17.7	15.0	11.7	12.9	13.3
Pre-SFEM payments	—	5.9	2.8	4.1	2.3
Capital expenditure	45.8	26.7	30.5	23.6	20.1
Of which: domestically financed	(17.6)	(15.1)	(23.9)	(12.0)	(11.6)
Net lending to state governments	−0.5	−0.6	−0.2	−1.0	−1.8
Supplementary/extrabudgetary outlays	—	3.2	7.0	8.5	16.9
	(In percent of GDP)				
Total expenditure and net lending	19.1	23.3	24.7	20.7	24.5
Of which: non-debt	(14.4)	(10.7)	(13.9)	(9.9)	(12.6)
Recurrent expenditure	10.5	16.5	15.5	14.3	15.9
Personnel costs	2.1	2.2	1.9	1.5	2.0
Overhead costs	3.6	1.7	2.8	2.0	2.0
Foreign interest due	1.4	7.7	7.1	7.3	8.1
Domestic interest due	3.4	3.5	2.9	2.7	3.2
Pre-SFEM payments	—	1.4	0.7	0.8	0.6
Capital expenditure	8.8	6.2	7.5	4.9	4.9
Of which: domestically financed	(9.1)	(3.5)	(5.9)	(2.5)	(2.8)
Net lending to state governments	−0.1	−0.1	—	−0.2	−0.5
Supplementary/extrabudgetary outlays	—	0.7	1.7	1.8	4.1
Memorandum items:					
	(In percent of non-oil GDP)				
Non-debt expenditure	16.9	14.3	18.0	15.5	19.1
Personnel	2.5	2.9	2.5	2.4	3.0
Overhead	4.2	2.3	3.6	3.1	3.1
Capital expenditure	10.3	8.3	9.7	7.7	7.5
Supplemental/extrabudgetary outlays	—	1.0	2.2	2.8	6.3

Sources: Data provided by the Nigerian authorities; and IMF staff estimates.

the interbank or foreign exchange bureau exchange rates. Fourth, the bank-specific credit ceilings provided an incentive for the establishment of new banks, rather than expanding lending activities at existing banks. Finally, the rapid growth in reserve money, arising from either Central Bank financing of government fiscal deficits or the monetization of rising official oil receipts, resulted in a strong expansion of the deposit base.

Notwithstanding the rapid growth in the number of commercial and merchant banks, only a few commercial banks dominated the industry. In 1985, three of the 28 commercial banks accounted for roughly one half of total deposits. By the end of 1990, this share had fallen to just below 40 percent, but the industry remained concentrated, with the top ten banks holding 63 percent of total deposits. While this concentration gave rise to concerns about the exploitation of monopoly power by the largest banks, especially in the Central Bank foreign exchange auctions, it contributed indirectly to sound banking practices, as the few dominant banks had extensive contacts with foreign institutions and followed international accounting standards. To encourage community-based savings and lending in the rural areas, community banking was introduced in 1990. In a similar vein, the People's Bank of Nigeria, which was established by the Government in 1989, provided services to small-scale private enterprises.

One of the central themes of the SAP was financial liberalization, while improving the confidence in Nigeria's financial system. As part of this effort, the Nigerian Deposit Insurance Corporation (NDIC)

IV STRUCTURAL REFORM AND MACROECONOMIC POLICY, 1986–90

Table 7. Monetary Targets and Outcomes
(Annual percentage change)

	1986	1987	1988	1989	1990
Net domestic credit					
Target	...	4.4	8.1	9.5	13.5
Outcome	11.1	13.9	33.0	–14.4	18.5
Credit to the private sector					
Target	...	8.4	13.3	10.7	15.8
Outcome	28.7	18.2	24.4	3.6	20.4
Net credit to the Federal Government					
Target	...	1.5	2.5	8.3	10.9
Outcome	–4.1	12.4	28.6	–33.7	15.1
Narrow money					
Target	...	11.8	15.0	14.6	13.0
Outcome	–6.0	15.8	55.5	20.0	47.8
Change in reserves (in millions of U.S. dollars)					
Target	...	...	300	200	300
Outcome	–851	–78	–331	1,272	2,508
Memorandum items:					
Broad money (actual)	2.7	22.7	43.3	7.2	42.3
Velocity (GDP/average broad money)	3.0	4.0	4.0	4.9	4.9

Sources: *Approved Budget of the Government of the Federal Republic of Nigeria*, various issues; Central Bank of Nigeria, *Annual Report and Statement of Accounts*, various issues; and IMF staff estimates.

was established in 1988 to protect depositors against bank failures and to instill greater confidence in the banking system. At the same time, the Central Bank addressed solvency concerns by increasing the minimum paid-up capital requirements for commercial and merchant banks. Subsequently, in 1990, it introduced minimum risk-weighted capital adequacy requirements, which were based on international standards, further raised the minimum paid-up capital requirements for banks, and introduced new accounting standards. International prudential guidelines were adopted by the CBN in 1990 to establish sound practices for asset classification, disclosure, and adequate provisioning for nonperforming assets. For the nonbank financial sector, a new *Securities and Exchange Commission (SEC) Decree* was approved in 1988, which repealed the decree of 1979 and gave the Commission broader powers to regulate and supervise the Nigerian capital market, including the power to revoke the registration of stockbrokers and disapprove the establishment of a new stock exchange in Nigeria. The role of the SEC was further expanded by the *Companies and Allied Matters Decree of 1990*, which gave the power to approve and regulate mergers and acquisitions.

The Nigerian Stock Exchange (NSE) has grown considerably since its establishment in 1960. A rapid expansion occurred during the oil boom in the early 1970s, fostered by the Government's indiginization program, and a further expansion during the SAP period. Responding to investors' increased confidence in the economy, as well as the introduction of the second-tier securities market (SSM) to assist small and medium-sized firms, activity on the exchange increased significantly in 1986, with the NSE all-share index increasing by 23 percent. However, activity in the stock market slowed in 1988 as alternative financial instruments, namely higher yield corporate bonds, increased as companies tried to escape the Central Bank's cap on credit to the private sector. The stock market again expanded rapidly in 1989 as higher interest rates brought firms back to the capital market and the Government's privatization program increased the volume of activity. The all-sector NSE equity price index rose from a base of 100 at the end of 1984 to 164 at the end of 1990,[19]

---

[19]The exchange included 217 securities at the end of 1990, including 131 equities, 43 government securities, and 43 industrial loans and preferred stocks. The market is heavily concentrated, with 20 stocks representing over 70 percent of the total equity capitalization during the same period.

Table 8. Credit Guidelines for Commercial Banks

	1986	1987	1988	1989	1990
	(Percent change)				
Loans and advances[1]					
Target	10.0	8.0	12.5	10.0	12.5
Actual	28.1	11.6	14.4	11.1	31.7
	(Percent of total credit)				
Allocation of credit					
Agriculture					
Target	15.0	15.0	15.0	15.0	15.0
Actual	11.8	12.9	15.3	15.3	15.9
Manufacturing					
Target	44.0	35.0	35.0	35.0	35.0
Actual	41.6	29.1	30.1	30.7	30.3
Other					
Target	41.0	50.0	50.0	50.0	50.0
Actual	46.6	58.0	54.6	54.0	53.8
	(Percent of rural deposits)				
Rural loans					
Floor	40.0	40.0	45.0	45.0	50.0
Actual	42.8	40.1	47.9	64.9	56.6
	(Liquid assets as a percent of deposit liabilities)				
Liquidity ratio[2]					
Floor	25.0	25.0	27.5	27.5	30.0
Actual	57.3	49.0	41.6	35.9	43.9
	(Cash reserves as a percent of deposit liabilities)				
Cash reserve ratio					
Actual	4.1	4.9	4.7	8.9	6.4

Source: Central Bank of Nigeria.

[1] Target applied to aggregate credit after 1989. Includes, in addition to loans and advances, investments, call money, certificates of deposit, bankers acceptances, commercial paper, bills discounted, and promissory notes.

[2] Total liquid assets less penalties and cash reserve requirements as a percent of total deposit liabilities.

boosted by the improved outlook for the economy during these years.

Public Enterprise Reform

State intervention in major sectors of the economy spread throughout the 1970s and early 1980s. Virtually all the country's largest enterprises were wholly government owned, including those in the petroleum, communications, transportation, banking, and steel, paper, and other manufacturing activities. Public enterprises posed a significant burden on the Federal Government's budget and contributed little to the budget in the form of dividends or debt repayments. In 1986, 33 percent of the Federal Government's domestically financed capital budget was allocated to investment in public enterprises, and they absorbed an estimated 40 percent of the Federal Government's nonsalary recurrent expenditure in the form of subsidies.

As part of the SAP, the commercialization and privatization program was announced in June 1986, but implementation did not commence until 1989. The Technical Committee on Privatization and Commercialization (TCPC) classified the parastatals it would deal with into four groups: those to be fully or partially privatized (50 enterprises), fully commercialized (9 enterprises), and partially commercialized (26 enterprises). The Government would fully divest itself of ownership of enterprises falling into the first category. Partially privatized enterprises were to be held to hard budget constraints and receive no financial support from the Federal Government. Fully and partially commercialized enterprises would continue to be wholly owned by the

IV STRUCTURAL REFORM AND MACROECONOMIC POLICY, 1986–90

Figure 4. Selected Interest Rates

Sources: IMF, *International Financial Statistics*; and Central Bank of Nigeria.

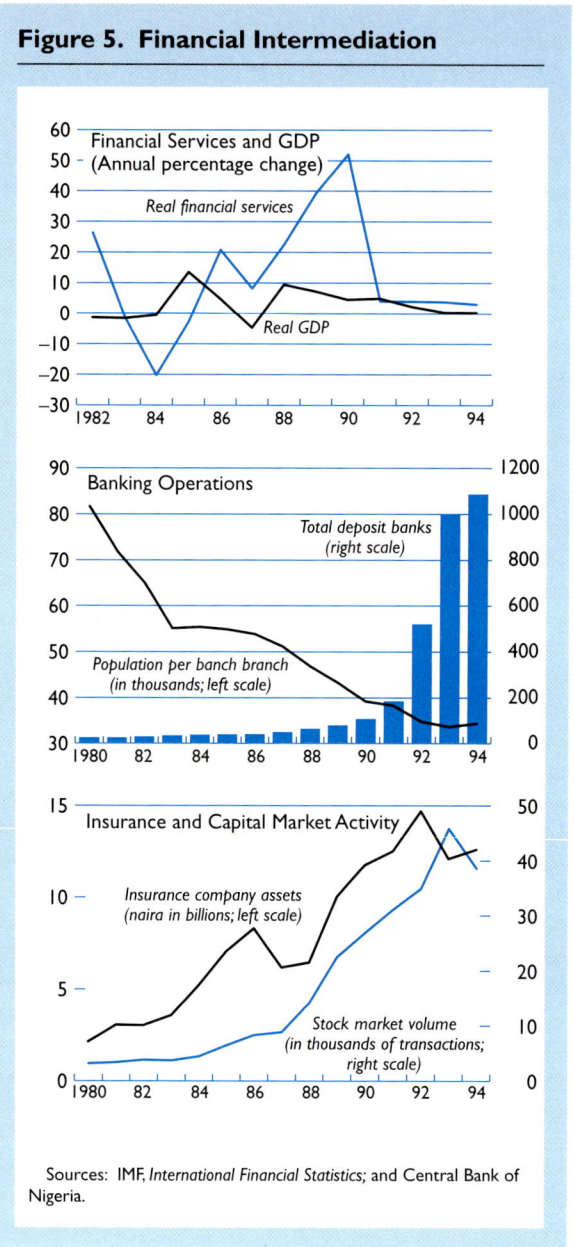

Figure 5. Financial Intermediation

Sources: IMF, *International Financial Statistics*; and Central Bank of Nigeria.

Federal Government. The former were to receive no budgetary support for either recurrent or capital expenditure, while the latter would receive support for both.

The TCPC privatized 16 federal public enterprises in 1989, comprising two oil companies, 13 insurance companies, and a flour mill, with a total market capitalization of about ₦130 million. Another five enterprises, with a capitalization of ₦116.5 million were privatized in 1990, including three cement companies. Little progress was made with respect to the commercialization of public enterprises. All the major wholly government-owned public enterprises continued to receive subventions from the federal budget, and none of the seven largest paid any dividends through 1990. Furthermore, while the proportion of the Federal Government's capital budget allocated for support of public enterprises fell from 33 percent in 1986 to 7 percent in 1990, actual lending deviated substantially from budgetary provisions. Total lending in 1990 amounted to ₦1.4 billion, compared with a budgeted ₦0.4 billion, and was nearly three times as large as in 1986.

V Adjustment and Growth, 1986–90

Market-oriented reforms under the SAP, coupled with relatively tight financial policies in the early years, prepared the ground for a substantial increase in output during the second half of the 1980s (Figure 6). The upsurge in growth during the SAP occurred despite the sharp deterioration in the terms of trade.[20] The liberalization of the economy and the substantial depreciation of the naira, on average 32 percent a year in real effective terms during 1986–90, masked many of the program's implementation shortcomings.

Sectoral Growth

Real GDP expanded by 5½ percent annually over the SAP period, compared with a decline of nearly 1 percent a year during 1981–85 (Table 9). The growth of real non-oil GDP was even more impressive, registering a 6 percent annual average growth, compared with less than ½ percent during the pre-SAP period. Excluding 1987, when a serious drought in important growing regions blighted crop production, real non-oil GDP expanded by over 7 percent annually.

Agricultural output rebounded significantly during the 1986–90 period, with crop production increasing by an annual average of 12 percent and food crops increasing by 13 percent, compared with average growth of 2 and 4 percent, respectively, during the pre-SAP period (Figure 7). Production improved significantly as well for export crops, as cocoa production increased from an average of 154,000 tons per year in 1981–85 to an average of 200,000 tons in the SAP period; rubber and palm kernel crops grew even more rapidly, increasing from an average of 88,000 and 316,000 tons in 1981–85 to 172,000 and 846,000 tons in the SAP period, respectively. Agricultural exports responded quickly and substantially to the improvement in export prices brought about by the devaluation of the naira, the elimination of the commodity boards, and the improvement in world market prices in 1986–88. The devaluation of the real effective exchange rate was found to be a significant factor in the improved export position of agricultural products.[21]

Net farmer income increased substantially over the SAP period.[22] Estimated gross margins for small-scale maize farmers widened from ₦87 per hectare in 1985 to ₦402 in 1989 in nominal terms; while for large-scale farmers, the gross margin per hectare rose from ₦608 to ₦1,311 (Table 10). For cocoa production, the turnaround in profitability was even more striking, from a loss of ₦105 per hectare in 1985 to a profit of ₦1,586 per hectare in 1989, despite the 40 percent fall in world market prices (in dollar terms) in 1989.

Manufacturing output also rebounded significantly, increasing by an annual average of 14 percent, compared with an average decline of 4 percent during the pre-SAP period (Figure 7). A key component of the Government's industrial policy was to encourage labor-intensive activities that could compete with high-cost imports and to discourage production in capital-intensive sectors with significant import content. The SAP reversed an eight-year decline in the capacity utilization rate in the manufacturing sector, with the rate increasing during each of the years from 1986 to 1989. Overall capacity utilization improved as well, with the utilization rate increasing from 38 percent in 1985 to 44 percent in 1989, before falling back to 40 percent in 1990 (Figure 8). A striking phenomenon was the growth in industries that could easily substitute domestic inputs for imported inputs, such as textiles, leather products, and sugar-based industries. These industries experienced a significant increase in capacity utilization: in the textile industry capacity rose from 45 percent in 1985 to 60 percent in 1989, and in the food sector it rose from 32 percent to 52 percent, respectively. On the other hand, the sectors that had

---

[20]Nigeria's external terms of trade declined by 9½ percent annually during 1986–90, compared with an annual average decline of 2½ percent during 1980–85.

[21]See Appendix III for an empirical analysis of the major factors influencing Nigeria's agricultural exports.

[22]See Central Bank of Nigeria (1991), *The Impact of SAP on Nigerian Agriculture and Rural Life.*

V ADJUSTMENT AND GROWTH, 1986–90

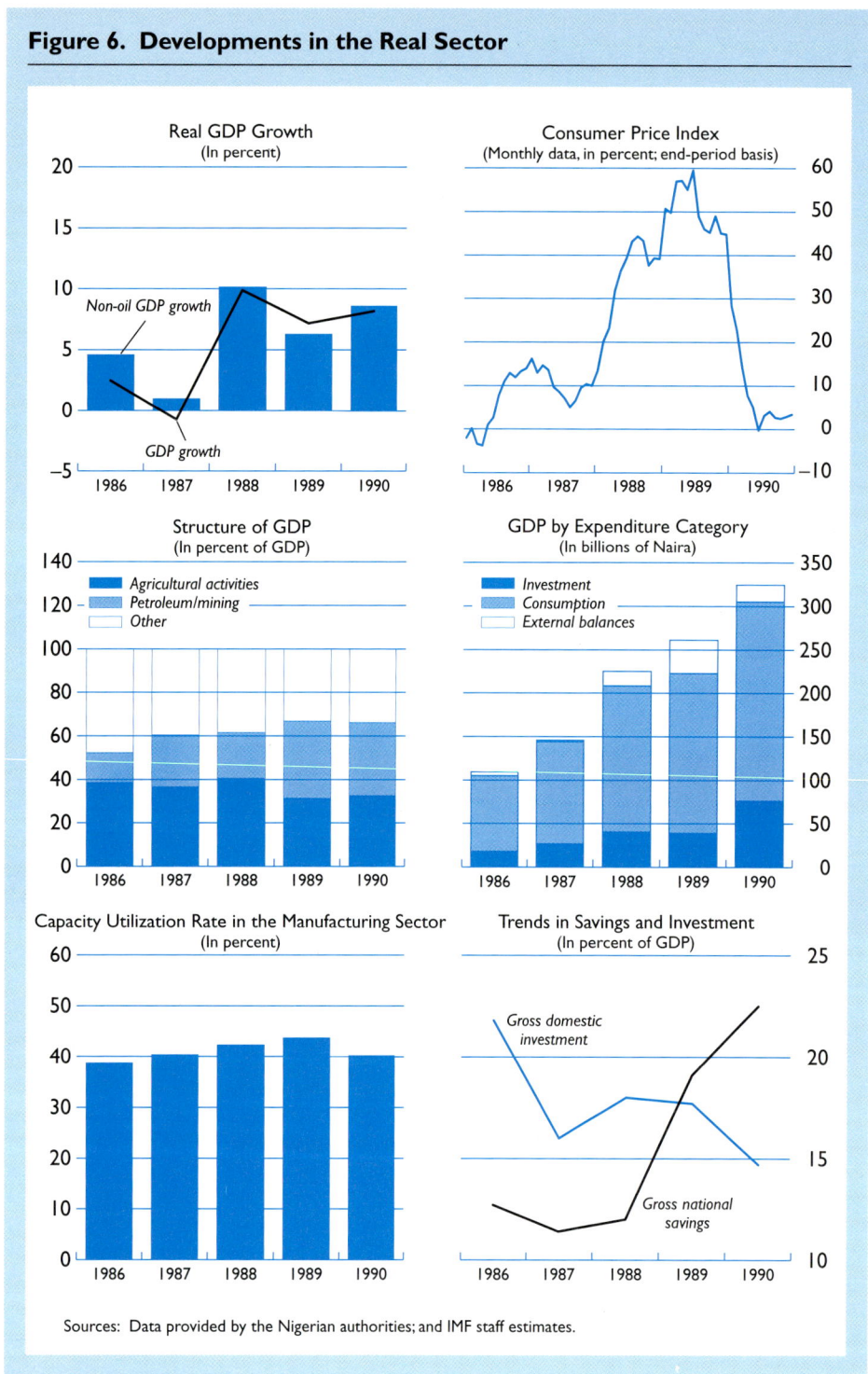

Figure 6. Developments in the Real Sector

Sources: Data provided by the Nigerian authorities; and IMF staff estimates.

been protected from competition and had benefited most from import and exchange controls in the early 1980s—motor vehicle assembly and steel—fared less well, and output and capacity utilization fell further as a result of the trade, exchange, and price reforms; thus capacity utilization fell from 26 percent in 1985 to 19 percent in 1989 for motor vehicles and from 37 percent to 24 percent for steel.

An important achievement of the SAP, resulting primarily from the substantial devaluation, was the

Table 9. Selected Economic and Financial Indicators, 1986–90

	1986	1987	1988	1989	1990	1981–85 Average	1986–90 Average
	(Annual percentage changes, unless otherwise indicated)						
National income and prices							
Real GDP (at 1984 market prices)	2.5	–0.7	9.9	7.2	8.2	–0.9	5.3
Oil GDP (at 1984 factor cost)	–5.2	–9.8	8.1	15.0	5.5	–6.4	2.3
Non–oil GDP (at 1984 factor cost)	4.6	1.0	10.2	6.3	8.6	0.4	6.1
Consumer prices (end of period)	13.6	9.7	39.0	44.7	3.5	16.7	21.0
Nominal GDP (in billions of naira)	73.1	108.9	145.2	224.8	260.6	57.6	297.9
Oil production volume (in m/b per day)	1.5	1.4	1.4	1.7	1.8	1.4	1.6
Average oil export price (U.S. dollars per barrel, f.o.b.)	14.3	17.2	14.9	18.5	24.3	31.1	17.8
Population (millions)	75.1	77.6	80.2	82.9	85.7	66.9	84.5
External sector							
Exports f.o.b. (in billions of U.S. dollars)	6.8	7.5	7.1	9.8	13.9	12.9	9.0
Of which: oil (in billions of U.S. dollars)	(6.4)	(7.0)	(6.5)	(9.4)	(13.5)	(12.6)	(8.6)
Imports f.o.b. (in billions of U.S. dollars)	–6.7	–5.8	–5.8	–5.9	–7.1	–12.4	–6.3
Non–oil export volume	10.8	16.0	14.0	–28.7	3.0	–11.3	1.5
Import volume	–27.9	–23.7	–6.4	2.5	9.2	–8.0	–10.4
Nominal effective exchange rate	–44.2	–69.9	–18.0	–33.0	1.6	2.0	–37.7
Real effective exchange rate	–45.4	–68.1	0.2	–10.7	–7.4	10.7	–32.1
Average official exchange rate (naira/U.S. dollar)	1.7	4.0	4.5	7.4	8.0	0.7	5.1
Terms of trade	–52.2	4.1	–16.1	22.6	18.5	–2.5	–9.5
Money and credit							
Net foreign assets	1.0	–38.6	805.3	126.2	93.7	–20.1	89.7
Net domestic assets	76.3	26.2	20.3	–33.1	–2.5	13.0	11.8
Net credit to the federal government	–4.1	12.4	28.6	–33.7	15.1	45.8	1.2
Credit to the rest of the economy	34.0	15.7	37.2	4.4	20.6	18.2	21.8
Broad money	2.7	22.7	43.3	7.2	42.3	13.6	22.5
Velocity (GDP/average broad money)	3.0	4.0	4.0	4.9	4.9	3.4	4.2
Savings deposit rate (end of period)	9.5	11.0	12.4	16.5	17.8	8.2	13.4
	(In percent of GDP)						
Investment and savings							
Gross national savings	12.7	11.4	12.0	19.1	22.5	14.9	15.5
Gross domestic investment	21.8	16.0	18.0	17.7	14.7	19.9	17.6
Federal Government budget							
Revenue	13.9	11.6	11.1	13.8	21.5	13.8	14.4
Expenditure and net lending	19.1	23.3	24.7	20.7	24.5	21.1	22.5
Current expenditure	10.5	16.5	15.5	14.3	15.9	9.6	14.5
Capital expenditure	8.8	6.2	7.5	4.9	4.9	11.5	6.5
Federal Government budget deficit	–5.2	–11.7	–13.6	–7.0	–2.9	–7.3	–8.1
External sector							
Current account balance	–9.1	–4.6	–6.0	1.3	7.8	–4.9	–2.1
Overall balance of payments	–20.1	–15.8	–15.3	–5.1	–1.8	–4.5	–11.6
External debt	58.9	104.5	94.1	102.9	104.0	18.0	92.9
	(In billions of U.S. dollars, unless otherwise indicated)						
Current account balance	–3.8	–1.2	–1.9	0.4	2.5	–3.9	–0.8
Overall balance of payments	–8.4	–4.3	–4.9	–1.5	–0.6	–3.5	–3.9
External public and publicly guaranteed debt	24.6	28.3	30.1	31.4	33.7	14.5	29.6
Gross international reserves (end of period)	0.9	0.8	0.3	1.6	4.1	2.2	1.5
(in months of imports of goods and nonfactor services)	1.3	1.4	0.5	2.5	5.3	1.6	2.2

Sources: Data provided by the Nigerian authorities; and IMF staff estimates.

substitution of local inputs for imported inputs. Local sourcing of industrial inputs increased from an estimated 33 percent in 1986 to 50 percent in 1990. The activities that could most effectively replace imports with local inputs fared better under the SAP. Unfortunately, toward the end of the SAP period, the domestic industries that had lost significant market share—such as motor vehicle assembly and steel—

V ADJUSTMENT AND GROWTH, 1986–90

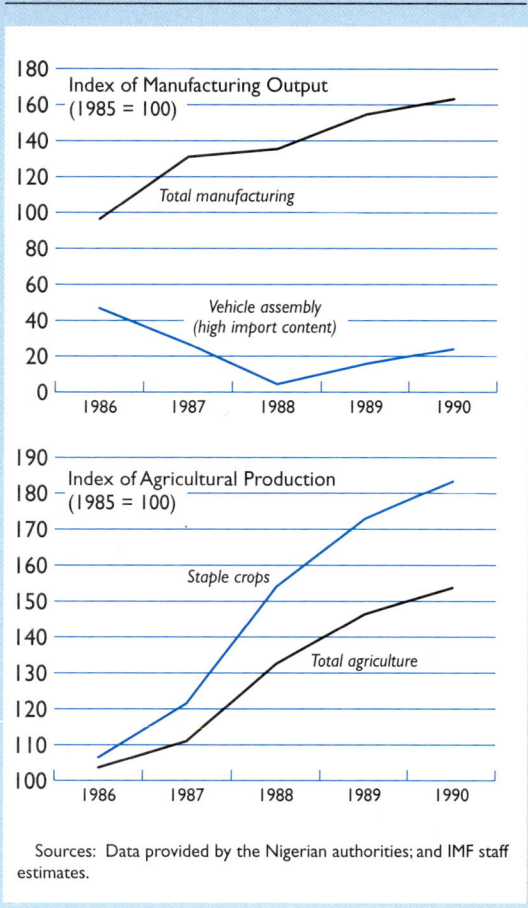

Figure 7. Manufacturing and Agricultural Output

Sources: Data provided by the Nigerian authorities; and IMF staff estimates.

Table 10. Farm Profitability Under the Structural Adjustment Program
(In naira)

	Pre-SAP 1985	SAP 1989	Percent Change
Maize production per hectare			
Output (700 kg)	525	1050	100
Costs	438	648	48
Seeds (14 kg)	9.8	21.0	114.3
Equipment	8	27	227
Labor (60 man-days)	420	600	43
Gross margin per hectare	87	402	362
Return to labor per man-day	1.4	6.7	378.6
Prices			
Maize producerp price (naira per kg)	0.8	11.5	1,337.5
Seeds (naira per kg)	0.7	1.5	114.3
Wage rate (per day)	7.0	10.0	42.9
Consumer price index	100.0	273.5	173.5
Cocoa production per hectare			
Output (350 kg)	525	2625	400
Costs	630	1265	101
Chemicals/Fertilizer	238	491	106
Equipment	22	34	55
Labor (74 man-days)	370	740	100
Gross margin per hectare	–105	1360	...
Return to labor per man-day	–1.8	22.7	...
Prices			
Cocoa producer price (naira per kg)	1.5	7.5	400.0
Insecticide (naira per liter)	20.0	45.0	125.0
Fertilizer (naira per 50 kg bag)	6.0	10.0	67.0
Wage rate (per day)	5.0	10.0	100.0
Consumer price index	100	273.5	173.5

Source: Central Bank of Nigeria (1991), The Impact of SAP on Nigerian Agriculture and Rural Life.

began to lobby successfully for reimposing protectionist trade and pricing policies.

Savings and Investment

The national savings rate increased markedly over the SAP period, from 15 percent of GDP in 1985 to 22½ percent in 1990, reflecting mainly the dramatic improvement in the Federal Government's fiscal position (Table 11).[23] During most of the 1980s, the Federal Government's savings balance (as a share of GDP) closely tracked changes in Nigeria's external terms of trade (primarily oil prices), underscoring the authorities' inability to insulate the revenue base from exogenous shocks (Figure 9); private sector savings more closely paralleled changes in underlying economic conditions; increasing from 8 percent of GDP in 1985 to 16½ percent in 1989, before falling temporarily in 1990 to 14 percent.

Gross investment fell over the SAP period, from 22 percent of GDP in 1986 to 14 percent in 1990, largely as a result of the Government's efforts to reduce extrabudgetary expenditures and inefficient capital outlays in 1987–89. Public investment decreased from an average of 16 percent of GDP in 1981–85 to 10½ percent during 1986–90. However, this reduction did not

---

[23]Estimates of savings and investment balances for the public and private sectors are based on official GDP data and Fund staff balance of payments and fiscal estimates.

Inflation

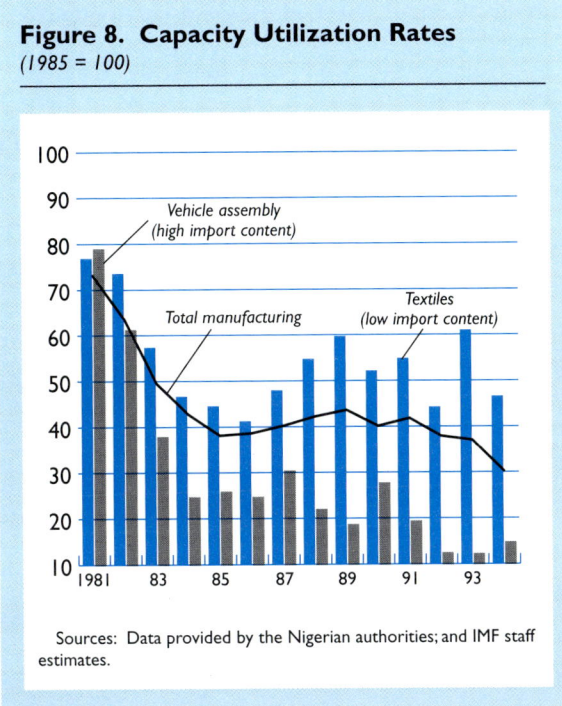

Figure 8. Capacity Utilization Rates
(1985 = 100)

Sources: Data provided by the Nigerian authorities; and IMF staff estimates.

hinder the resurgence of growth, as a large share of public investment was in unproductive import-substitution projects and employment-generating activities that might have been more appropriately classified as

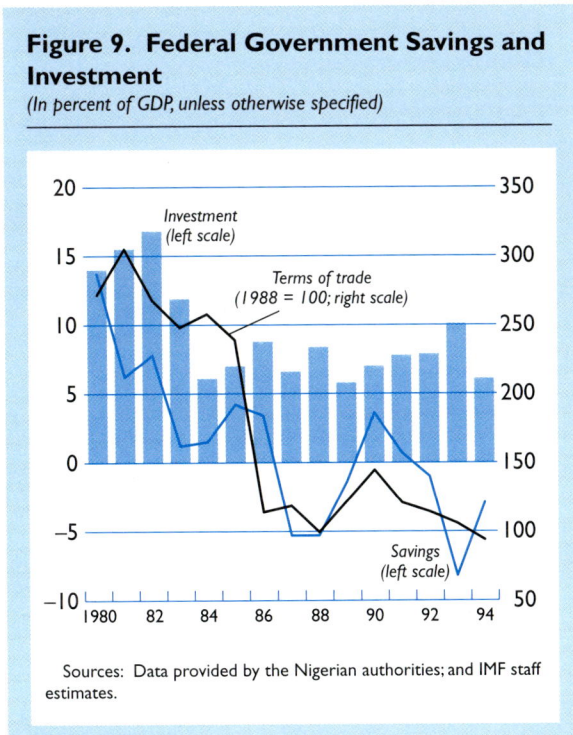

Figure 9. Federal Government Savings and Investment
(In percent of GDP, unless otherwise specified)

Sources: Data provided by the Nigerian authorities; and IMF staff estimates.

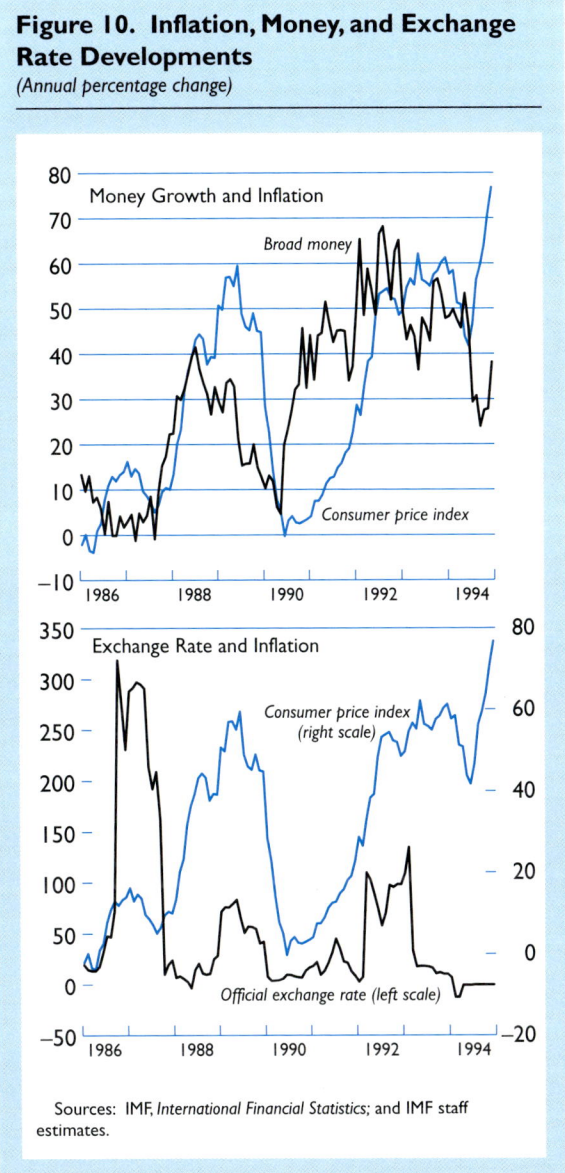

Figure 10. Inflation, Money, and Exchange Rate Developments
(Annual percentage change)

Sources: IMF, *International Financial Statistics*; and IMF staff estimates.

consumption. Private investment, on the other hand, rose from an average of 4 percent of GDP during 1981–85 to 7 percent during the SAP period.

Inflation

The authorities' success at bringing inflation under control was mixed. Their off-again, on-again tightening of financial policies was reflected in substantial fluctuations in the inflation rate, which rose from an annual average of 19 percent in 1981–85 to 20 percent in 1986–90 (Figure 10). The reform

V ADJUSTMENT AND GROWTH, 1986–90

process started with a tight fiscal and monetary stance, which helped to contain the initial impact of substantial trade and price liberalization on inflation. Consequently, inflation was limited to 5 percent in 1986 and to 10 percent in 1987, despite the substantial devaluations in 1986 and 1987 (97 percent and 130 percent, respectively, in local currency terms) (Box 7).

In early 1988, financial policies became increasingly expansionary, leading to the buildup of domestic liquidity and inflationary pressures. The overall fiscal deficit more than doubled in one year, to 12 percent of GDP in 1987, and increased further to 14 percent in 1988; broad money growth surged from 3 percent in 1986 to 23 percent in 1987 and 43 percent in 1988. As a result, inflation increased to 35 percent in 1988. In an attempt to rein in aggregate demand, the Government implemented a tight fiscal and monetary program in 1989. Nonetheless, inflation continued to accelerate owing to the cumulative impact of the monetary overhang resulting from the expansion in 1988 and the sizable devaluation in 1989.

During the first half of 1990, fiscal adjustment continued and the overall budget deficit was contained within the programmed range. The economic outlook improved significantly in August 1990, when oil prices rose rapidly during the Middle East crisis. Unfortunately, as in the past, the Government was unable to temper the impact of the oil price rise. Despite the establishment of an oil windfall account, in which US$1 billion was temporarily accumulated, the Government did not adhere to its expenditure budget and much of the windfall oil

---

Box 7. Main Determinants of Inflation

The rate of inflation in Nigeria has increased steadily and markedly since independence in 1960. During the period following independence (1965–75), Nigeria's rate of inflation was about equal to that of its trading partners, averaging 10 percent annually. In the ensuing decade (1975–85), the respective rates of inflation diverged dramatically, as Nigeria's average annual rate nearly doubled, to 18 percent, while that of the trading partners narrowed significantly, to 4 percent. These trends continued between 1985 and 1990, as Nigeria's annual average inflation rose to 24 percent, while the trading partners posted an average rate of 13 percent. More recently, since late 1990, Nigeria has experienced a period of stagflation. By the end of 1994, inflation had reached 57 percent and real per capita income growth had stalled.

The rate of inflation in Nigeria is based on a composite urban and rural consumer price index (CPI), with food items representing 69 percent of the total market basket. Consequently, factors affecting food prices dominate movements in the CPI. These factors include agroclimatic conditions, wages, domestic inputs, and import prices, with rainfall playing a key role. Subsistence agriculture, which is not included in marketed production, plays an important role in marginal supply and demand during periods of drought or abundant rainfall. Imports, while important in the economy as a whole, have tended to have less influence on the CPI since household consumption, which is predominantly food related, has a low import content.

On the basis of a monetary model of inflation, the key factors influencing the rate of inflation (money, income, and exchange rates) were analyzed. (See Appendix I for a detailed discussion of the model and empirical results.) The results of the analysis confirm the findings of earlier studies, namely that monetary growth, driven mainly by expansionary fiscal policies, explains to a large degree the inflationary process in Nigeria. It was also found that the depreciation of the naira affected inflation significantly, but its impact could be moderated with appropriately tight fiscal and monetary policies. Given the considerable role of food in the CPI, agroclimatic conditions (rainfall) were also found to be important.

Consumer Price Index Market Basket
(In percent)

Commodity	CPI Weights Combined urban and rural centers	All urban centers	All rural centers
Food	69.1	65.4	69.9
Drinks, tobacco, and cola	4.7	3.6	5.0
Clothing and footwear	4.7	4.3	4.8
Accommodation, fuel, and light	11.9	14.0	11.5
Household goods	3.6	3.4	3.6
Health-related	1.1	1.2	1.1
Transportation	2.4	5.0	1.8
Recreation, education, and entertainment	1.4	1.9	1.3
Other services	1.2	1.3	1.2
All items	100.0	100.0	100.0

Source: Nigerian Federal Office of Statistics, based on the 1985/86 National Consumer Survey.

Inflation

Table 11. Savings and Investment[1]
(In percent of nominal GDP)

	1980	1981	1982	1983	1984	1985	1986	1987	1988	1989	1990	1991	1992	1993	1994 (Estimated)
Gross domestic savings	25.2	19.6	19.9	15.5	13.5	18.4	18.4	19.9	19.1	25.3	29.4	29.4	29.1	20.3	20.0
General government	18.6	12.7	14.0	6.0	3.0	7.0	5.2	−1.5	−3.0	2.4	8.4	7.4	5.4	−3.9	0.3
Federal	13.7	6.2	7.8	1.2	1.5	4.2	3.4	−5.3	−5.3	−1.4	3.6	0.7	−1.0	−8.2	−2.9
Other	4.9	6.5	6.2	4.8	1.5	2.8	1.7	3.8	2.2	3.8	4.8	6.8	6.4	4.3	3.3
Private sector	6.5	6.9	5.9	9.4	10.5	11.5	13.2	21.4	22.1	22.9	21.0	21.9	23.8	24.2	19.7
Gross national savings	23.2	18.1	17.9	13.1	10.4	15.2	12.7	11.4	12.0	19.1	22.5	23.5	22.6	13.9	15.2
General government	18.6	12.7	14.0	6.0	3.0	7.0	5.2	−1.5	−3.0	2.4	8.4	7.4	5.4	−3.9	0.3
Federal	13.7	6.2	7.8	1.2	1.5	4.2	3.4	−5.3	−5.3	−1.4	3.6	0.7	−1.0	−8.2	−2.9
Other	4.9	6.5	6.2	4.8	1.5	2.8	1.7	3.8	2.2	3.8	4.8	6.8	6.4	4.3	3.3
Private sector	4.6	5.4	3.9	7.0	7.4	8.2	7.5	12.9	15.0	16.7	14.2	16.0	17.3	17.8	14.9
Foreign savings	−4.7	7.4	9.4	6.3	1.3	0.3	9.1	4.6	6.0	−1.3	−7.8	−0.1	1.9	2.9	2.4
Gross investment	18.5	25.5	27.3	19.4	11.7	15.5	21.8	16.0	18.0	17.7	14.7	23.4	24.5	16.8	17.7
General government	18.4	23.0	23.8	17.0	7.4	8.3	10.8	9.6	12.1	9.4	10.8	11.6	12.4	13.6	8.8
Federal	14.0	15.5	16.8	11.9	6.1	7.0	8.8	6.6	8.4	5.8	7.0	7.8	7.9	10.1	6.1
Other	4.4	7.5	7.0	5.0	1.3	1.3	2.1	3.0	3.7	3.6	3.8	3.7	4.4	3.5	2.7
Private sector	0.1	2.5	3.5	2.4	4.3	7.2	10.9	6.3	5.9	8.3	3.9	11.8	12.1	3.2	8.8
Savings–investment balance	4.7	−7.4	−9.4	−6.3	−1.3	−0.3	−9.1	−4.6	−6.0	1.4	7.8	0.1	−1.9	−2.9	−2.4
General government	0.2	−10.3	−9.8	−10.9	−4.4	−1.4	−5.7	−11.1	−15.1	−7.0	−2.4	−4.1	−7.0	−17.5	−8.5
Federal	−0.3	−9.3	−9.0	−10.8	−4.6	−2.8	−5.3	−11.9	−13.6	−7.2	−3.4	−7.2	−9.0	−18.3	−9.1
Other	0.5	−0.9	−0.8	−0.2	0.2	1.4	−0.3	0.7	−1.5	0.2	1.0	3.0	2.0	0.8	0.6
Private sector	4.5	2.9	0.5	4.6	3.1	1.1	−3.4	6.5	9.1	8.4	10.2	4.2	5.1	14.6	6.0

Sources: Data provided by the Nigerian authorities; and IMF staff estimates.
[1]Estimates of savings and investment balances for the public and private sectors are provisional IMF staff estimates, based on official GDP data and IMF staff balance of payments and fiscal estimates.

Box 8. Macroeconomic Policies and Growth: A Quantitative Analysis, 1980–94

The overall impact of the SAP on the economy has continued to be sharply debated in Nigeria. Opposition to the adjustment effort intensified over the SAP period as the macroeconomic situation deteriorated and inflation accelerated, resulting in the derailment and, in a number of areas, reversal of key policy measures. Subsequently, the further economic and financial deterioration since 1990 has been blamed on the policies adopted under the SAP, particularly the sizable devaluation of the naira. This tentative analysis reviews the impact of macroeconomic policies on economic growth during the 1980–94 period.

Background and Model

Nigeria has experienced a prolonged period of internal and external imbalances. Inappropriate policies have caused the misallocation of resources, lowering the optimal level and productivity of capital and labor supplied to the economy, leading to lower growth and employment. In addition, macroeconomic instability placed a further cost on growth by reducing investor confidence in the economy.

Appropriate macroeconomic policies, which provide a stable macroeconomic environment, would be expected to enhance economic growth in Nigeria by improving the allocation of resources, increasing domestic savings, attracting foreign investment and advancing technological progress. The relationship between stabilization policies and growth has been studied extensively, with recent papers by Fischer (1991, 1993) and Hadjimichael and others (1995) confirming, as one would expect, a significant and positive link between economic growth and improved macroeconomic performance, as measured by reduced inflation, lower budget deficits, and a competitive real exchange rate.

Policies undertaken during the SAP to improve the allocation of resources in Nigeria included trade, price, and interest rate liberalization; the restructuring of the public sector; and the improvement in external competitiveness through exchange rate adjustments. In addition, the SAP aimed at establishing macroeconomic stability through appropriately tight fiscal and monetary policies. In line with other recent empirical surveys, this analysis assesses the impact of exchange rate policies (represented by a change in the real effective exchange rate), consumer price inflation, public investment, and the budget deficit on growth. In addition, one exogenous factor, rainfall, was included in the analysis as it was thought to have an important role in explaining real growth in the short to medium term. Thus:

$$\Delta GDP = f(\Delta \overline{REER}, \overline{INFLAT}, \overline{BUDDEF}, \overset{+}{PUBINV}, \overset{+}{PSINV}, \overset{+}{\Delta RAIN}, \overset{+}{\Delta TOT}) \quad (1)$$

where ΔGDP represents real GDP growth, $\Delta REER$ is the percentage change in the real effective exchange rate, $INFLAT$ is the annual average change in the consumer price index, $BUDDEF$ the overall fiscal deficit to GDP ratio, $PUBINV$ the ratio of public investment to GDP, $PSINV$ the ratio of private sector investment to GDP, and $\Delta RAIN$ is the percentage change in average rainfall.[1]

A depreciation of the real effective exchange rate is expected to have an unambiguously positive impact on growth. In the short to medium term, increased demand for tradable goods will augment output while increased profitability will lead to rising investment and thus an increase in productive capacity in the longer term. The ultimate impact of the rate of inflation on growth is ambiguous in the literature. Early growth models assumed higher inflation will lead to increased output through a shift away from money balances (as real interest rates fall) toward real capital accumulation, while "cash-in-advance" models posit that inflation will raise the cost of capital, thereby reducing the rate of capital accumulation and growth. In addition, inflation will increase the cost of transactions due to information constraints. Recent empirical studies on sub-Saharan Africa support the "cash-in-advance" assumption regarding the negative impact of inflation on growth. Accordingly, we expect persistent inflation to have a negative impact. The budget deficit is also included as a separate explanatory variable on the grounds that increased public sector borrowing raises real interest rates, and, therefore, crowds out private investment. The level of public and private investment (as a share of GDP) is expected to contribute positively to growth, both in terms of the increase in the stock and an improvement in efficiency. Finally, since Nigeria's economy is heavily dependent on foreign exchange generated by the oil sector and agricultural output, both terms of trade shocks and rainfall are included as potential additional explanatory variables.[2]

Equation (1) above was estimated for the economy as a whole and separately for the agriculture sector, which represents the largest single sector of the economy—and the lion's share of employment— and which was expected to benefit substantially from the macroeconomic reforms under the SAP.

Empirical Results

The following estimatable form of equation (1) was developed for real GDP:

$$\Delta GDP_t = a_0 + \sum_{i=0}^{n} [\alpha_{1i}(\Delta REER_{t-i}) + \alpha_{2i}(INFLAT_{t-i}) + \alpha_{3i}(BUDDEF_{t-i}) + \alpha_{4i}(PUBINV_{t-i}) + \alpha_{5i}(PSINV_{t-i}) + \alpha_{6i}(\Delta TOT_{t-i}) + \alpha_{7i}(\Delta RAIN_{t-i}) + \alpha_{8i}(\Delta GDP_{t-1-i})] + e_t, \quad (2)$$

where Σ represents the sum of the expression over the period $i=0$ to n. The most parsimonious lag structure

---

[1]This approach is based on the analysis of correlations and expected causality between the right-hand side and dependent variables and should not be interpreted as a reduced-form structural model.

[2]The terms of trade were not found to have a significant impact on real growth.

was determined by appropriate F-tests. The lag of the GDP variable was also included as an additional explanatory variable, as it is believed that the production cycle is an important component of current period growth. Estimation of the dynamic model yielded (with the *t*-statistics in parentheses):[3]

$$\Delta RGDP_t = 17.77 - 0.07(\Delta REER_{t-3})$$
$$(4.96) \quad (3.11)$$
$$- 1.29(PUBINV_{t-1}) + 0.08(\Delta RAIN_t). \quad (3)$$
$$(4.11) \quad\quad\quad (1.50)$$

Sample: 1980–94 Adjusted $R^2 = 0.81$
DW = 2.51 S.E.R. = 2.04

The estimated equation performed well in terms of explaining the impact of macroeconomic policies on overall economic growth for the period 1980–94, with the independent variables explaining 81 percent of the change in real GDP.[4] While the data analyzed are for an admittedly short period of time, the provisional results largely confirm the a priori assumptions stated above. In particular, the role of a competitive exchange rate in the improvement of growth prospects is confirmed. A 10 percent depreciation in the real effective exchange rate was found to lead to a 1 percentage point increase in real GDP growth after three years. The empirical results above suggest that the response to changes in relative prices is delayed and, consequently, should be considered when designing a reform program. While the coefficients on the inflation and budget deficit variables had the appropriate signs, they were not found to be significant factors in explaining movements in GDP growth over the period.

Somewhat surprising was the negative relationship between public investment and output growth, although it appears to support the contention that inefficient public investment crowded out more productive private investment. As the Government substantially reduced public investment during the SAP period—while it implemented, at the same time, a market-oriented liberalization program—the private sector was able to increase productive investment. Some recent reviews of the Government's public investment program concluded that a not unimportant part of public investment consisted of ill-chosen projects. Private sector investment proved not to be a significant explanatory factor, although the sign on the coefficient was positive as expected.

The role of rainfall in short-run growth dynamics was confirmed as expected, with a 10 percent increase in rainfall over the prior year leading to a 1 percentage point increase in the current rate of growth.

Agriculture

The impact of macroeconomic policies and exogenous shocks on agricultural growth was studied based on annual crop production (CROPPRO).[5] Equation (2) was reestimated with crop production as the dependent variable. The estimated regression for crop production (with the *t*-statistics in parentheses below the variables) performed quite well, explaining 85 percent of the change in crop production over the period:[6]

$$\Delta CROPPRO_t = 9.757 - 0.076(\Delta REER_{t-2})$$
$$(3.14) \quad\quad (3.10)$$
$$- 0.150(INFLAT_{t-2}) - 0.3120(PUBINV_{t-1})$$
$$(3.32) \quad\quad\quad\quad (2.14)$$
$$+ 0.133(\Delta RAIN_t)$$
$$(3.97)$$
$$+ 0.434(\Delta PSINVGDP_t). \quad (4)$$
$$(1.76)$$

Sample: 1980–94 Adjusted $R^2 = 0.851$
DW = 2.37 S.E.R. = 2.01

A 10 percent depreciation in the real effective exchange rate was found to increase crop production by about 1 percent after two periods, while a 10 percent decrease in the rate of inflation leads to a 2 percent increase in crop production after two periods. An increase in public investment (as a percent of GDP) was again found to be negatively correlated with agricultural output over the period studied. It is interesting to note that while public investment was found to have a negative impact, an increase in private investment was found to lead to a significant increase in real growth. The model above suggests that a 1 percentage point increase in the ratio of public investment to GDP in the previous period would be expected to decrease real growth by 0.3 percent in the current period while the same increase in private investment would lead to a 0.4 percent increase in growth in the same period.

As expected rainfall was a key factor affecting crop production. A 10 percent increase in average rainfall over the previous period was found to boost crop production by 1 percent in the current period. In addition, while the coefficients on the budget deficit and terms of trade variables were found to have the appropriate signs, they were not significant and dropped from the model.

---

[3]The statistical significance and relative explanatory factors were tested using two-stage least squares. Instrumental variables included lagged independent variables and lagged GDP. The lag structure of the explanatory variables were investigated, based on broad to specific specification search.

[4]The constant and public investment coefficients were significant at the 1 percent level; the real effective exchange rate coefficient was significant at the 5 percent level; and the rainfall variable was significant at the 20 percent level.

[5]Crop production data are believed to be a more reliable indicator of agricultural activity than estimates of agricultural GDP.

[6]The statistical significance and relative explanatory factors were tested using standard ordinary least squares (OLS) estimation techniques. Inflation and rainfall were significant at the 1 percent level; the real effective exchange rate and constant were significant at the 5 percent level; public investment was significant at the 10 percent level; and private investment was significant at the 15 percent level.

V ADJUSTMENT AND GROWTH, 1986–90

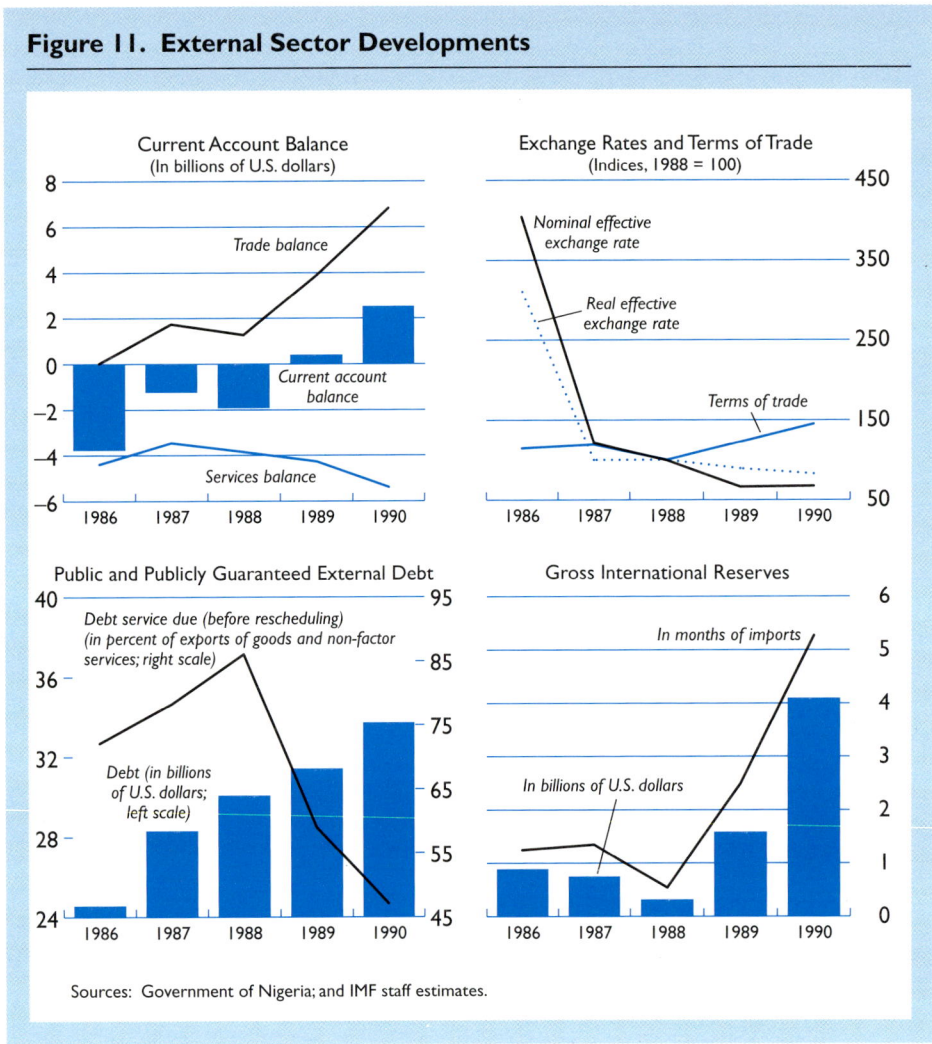

Figure 11. External Sector Developments

Sources: Government of Nigeria; and IMF staff estimates.

revenue was spent. Thus, during the last three months of the year, there was a significant reversal of the progress recorded in 1989 and early 1990 (See Box 8, above, and Box 9). The monetization of increased oil revenues, combined with a sizable credit expansion, led to broad money growth of 42 percent. Nonetheless, the cautious budgetary and monetary policies of late 1989 and early 1990 helped to hold down inflationary pressures in 1990, as domestic prices rose by only 7½ percent, well below the targeted 13½ percent.

External Sector

External sector developments were dominated by the drop in world oil prices in 1986 and their subsequent increase in 1989/90 (Figure 11). Oil prices fell from an average of US$26.9 per barrel in 1985 to US$14.3 in 1986, recovering again temporarily in 1990 to US$24.3 per barrel. In order to compensate partially for lower prices, the Government boosted the level of oil exports by an average of 4.4 percent annually during the SAP. Nonetheless, oil export earnings fell from an annual average of US$12.6 billion during the pre-SAP period to US$8.6 billion during the SAP. Non-oil exports, however, grew substantially during the 1986–88 period, owing largely to improved profitability resulting from the devaluation of the naira and the liberalization of prices. Non-oil exports increased from US$363 million in 1985 to US$613 million in 1988, but fell to US$406 million in 1989 as export prices for food and beverages declined sharply.

With the fall in oil revenues, Nigeria was forced to cut imports substantially in 1986 and 1987. Yet, the current account deficit increased considerably; the fall in oil revenue, coupled with the drying up of

Box 9. Inefficient Public Investment

Over the past two decades, Nigeria has undertaken a large public investment program, which focused on ill-defined infrastructure projects in the 1970s, industrial plants (refineries, electric power, steel, aluminum, and petrochemicals) and the new federal capital territory in the 1980s and early 1990s. A number of these projects were funded outside the budget process and most of them lacked a rigorous analysis of economic viability, leading to inappropriate choices of technology, location, and size. Overcharging by foreign suppliers and a lack of transparency in the accounting of the funds further undermined the integrity of the process. During the period 1973–90, the Government spent an estimated US$115 billion on public investment projects, representing about two thirds of total investment.

A recent study of Nigeria's public investment program (Ishrat Husain and Rashid Faruqee, eds., *Adjustment in Africa* (World Bank 1994)) found that project costs in Nigeria were some 25 percent higher than the norm for sub-Saharan Africa and infrastructure projects were generally more than twice the size needed to meet foreseeable demand. As a result, many public sector investment projects have not been economically viable from the start, with actual capacity utilization rates estimated at about 30 percent against planned rates of 80 percent. The overcharging and oversizing of public investment projects has led to excessive costs in the range of 50 percent of the total investment. Based on these estimates, an efficient and effective public investment program could have yielded the same output results for about US$58 billion, resulting in financial savings of the same order, which if invested at an annual rate of return of 5 percent would have yielded almost US$3 billion in annual revenue for the Government, or some 40 percent of total government revenue in 1991.

Specific examples of public investment projects with low or negative rates of return include:
- The Ajaokuta steel complex: By end-1990, the project had already cost over US$3 billion and was expected to need an additional US$2–3 billion to complete. The new complex, when completed, will have an annual production capacity of 2 million tons of steel. The existing Delta steel complex is currently meeting domestic demand while running at only 50 percent capacity. Based on present world market prices, Ajaokuta is not economically viable as its production costs are estimated to be four times the industry average.
- The new federal capital area of Abuja has proved to be a very costly investment. It is estimated that the Government spent some US$10 billion constructing the new capital city over the past decade, and will require an additional US$2–4 billion to complete it.
- The aluminum smelter plant at Ikot Abasi, with an estimated cost of US$1.4 billion, will cost about 60 percent more than the industry standard.
- Investments in the oil and gas sector by the Nigerian National Petroleum Corporation have been both inefficient and ill planned. The lack of transparency in NNPC's investment portfolio and decision-making process have led to mismanagement and overcharging in many of its projects.

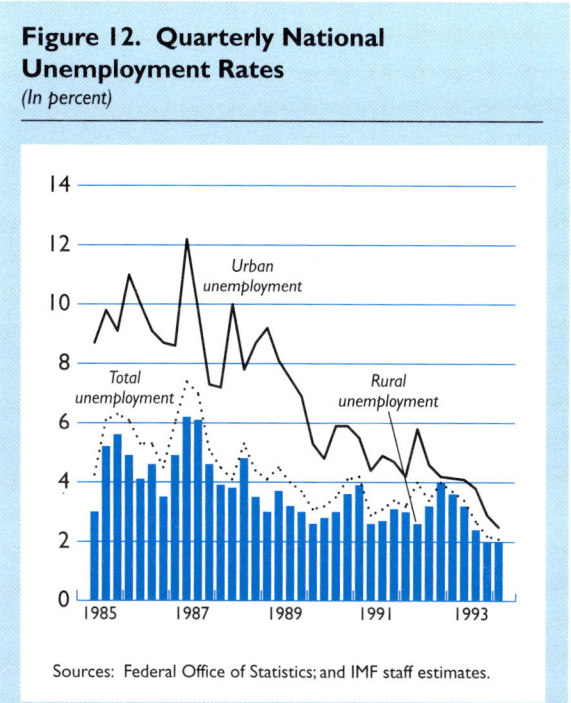

Figure 12. Quarterly National Unemployment Rates
(In percent)

Sources: Federal Office of Statistics; and IMF staff estimates.

capital inflows, led to higher overall balance of payments deficits, which were financed by the accumulation of external arrears and the drawdown of reserves through 1988. These adverse trends were then interrupted as the increase in world oil prices in 1989 and 1990 boosted exports substantially, leading to a notable, though temporary, improvement in the external current account balance and international reserves.

Employment and Wages

Officially recorded unemployment fell sharply during the SAP period,[24] compared with 1980–85, primarily as a result of the improved profitability of the private sector (particularly in agriculture) and increased investment, which spurred job creation (Figure 12). Although labor statistics are weak, broad trends can be detected. Employment opportunities increased substantially over the SAP period, with urban unemployment (on an annual average basis) dropping from an average rate of 10 percent in 1986

---

[24]The official unemployment statistics exclude a significant share of the labor force that is underemployed or not actively seeking employment.

V ADJUSTMENT AND GROWTH, 1986–90

to 6 percent in 1990. Rural unemployment also followed a similar path, decreasing from an average of 5 percent in 1986 to 3 percent in 1990. There are also indications that the reduction in indirect subsidies to the urban sector and the freeing up of agricultural prices slowed, and may have reversed, the urban migration trend. In the event, despite the shake-out in the manufacturing sector and the retrenchment in the civil service, overall unemployment fell from an average of 6 percent in 1986 to 3 percent in 1990.

More interesting than movements in the overall unemployment rate is the change in the rate of underemployment estimated by the Government's Federal Office of Statistics. During the pre-SAP period, underemployment increased from 35 percent in 1980 to 42 percent in 1985, while during the SAP period it declined significantly, to 26 percent in 1990.

VI Post-Adjustment Decline, 1991–94

Despite the relatively favorable developments under the SAP, as reflected in robust growth, moderating inflation, and improved external conditions, popular support for the liberalization policies never took hold and adjustment fatigue started setting in. The rapid depreciation of the exchange rate in the past few years and the persistent inflationary pressures, which affected large segments of the population, were blamed on the SAP. Voices to abandon market-oriented reforms and return to government controls became stronger.

The decline in oil export prices put pressures on fiscal resources, without prompting the Government to adjust expenditure policies. Thus mounting fiscal deficits, financed by central bank credit, led to a strong monetary expansion, which in turn caused an acceleration of inflation, a sharp loss of international reserves, a further depreciation of the exchange rate, and a slowing of real GDP growth. As the Government was unwilling to bring the budget under control, the policy response to emerging pressures was ad hoc and signaled a retreat from the reforms it had implemented under the SAP. Thus, the country's economic downturn was exacerbated in 1994 by the reversal of key market-based economic policies, specifically the elimination of the free market for foreign exchange, the imposition of interest rate controls, and the reinforcement of mandatory credit allocation schemes. Figure 13 vividly shows the overall downturn in the economy in the 1990–94 period.

The post-adjustment decline in economic performance was severe. Real GDP growth, which averaged more than 5 percent a year during 1986–90, fell to 1 percent by 1994 (Table 12). Inflation, which averaged 20 percent during 1986–90, doubled in the post-SAP period and reached 57 percent in 1994. The external current account balance moved from a surplus equivalent to 8 percent of GDP in 1990 to a deficit of more than 2 percent in 1994; international reserves dropped from the equivalent of more than five months of imports to one month in the same period; and external payments arrears reached US$9 billion, equivalent to 22 percent of GDP.

Fiscal Deterioration

The deterioration in the fiscal position can be traced in large part to a decline in oil revenue and a rapid increase in nondebt expenditures. As a share of GDP, federally retained revenue fell a full 11 percentage points of GDP over 1990–94, while nondebt expenditure fell by only 1 percentage point. The peak of the fiscal imbalances was reached in 1993, when the overall fiscal deficit reached 18 percent of GDP, and the primary fiscal deficit amounted to 6 percent of GDP, compared with a surplus of 9 percent in 1990.

Important elements in the surge of nondebt expenditures between 1990 and 1993 were the substantial rise in the Government's wage bill and the rapid increase in extrabudgetary expenditure by ½ and 7½ percentage points of GDP, respectively. Meanwhile, extrabudgetary expenditure rose by more than 600 percent, from 33 percent of nondebt expenditure in 1990 to 53 percent in 1993, before falling to 5 percent in 1994. While little information is available on the use of extrabudgetary expenditure, it is believed that a large share of the resources was directed toward the support of nonperforming parastatals and activities surrounding the national elections in 1992 and 1993.

Monetary Expansion and Interest Rates

Monetary developments during the post-SAP period were dominated by the monetization of the rising federal government deficits, despite the Central Bank's effort to contain the expansion of domestic credit through direct credit controls and, after mid-1993, open market operations. The average annual growth rate of net credit to the Federal Government amounted to 82 percent in 1991–94, compared with 1 percent in 1986–90. As a result, private sector credit was crowded out and average broad money growth almost doubled, to 42 percent in 1991–94. Fiscal behavior and the constraints placed on monetary policy instruments during most of the period undermined the effectiveness of central bank interventions. The introduction of open market operations in

VI POST-ADJUSTMENT DECLINE, 1991–94

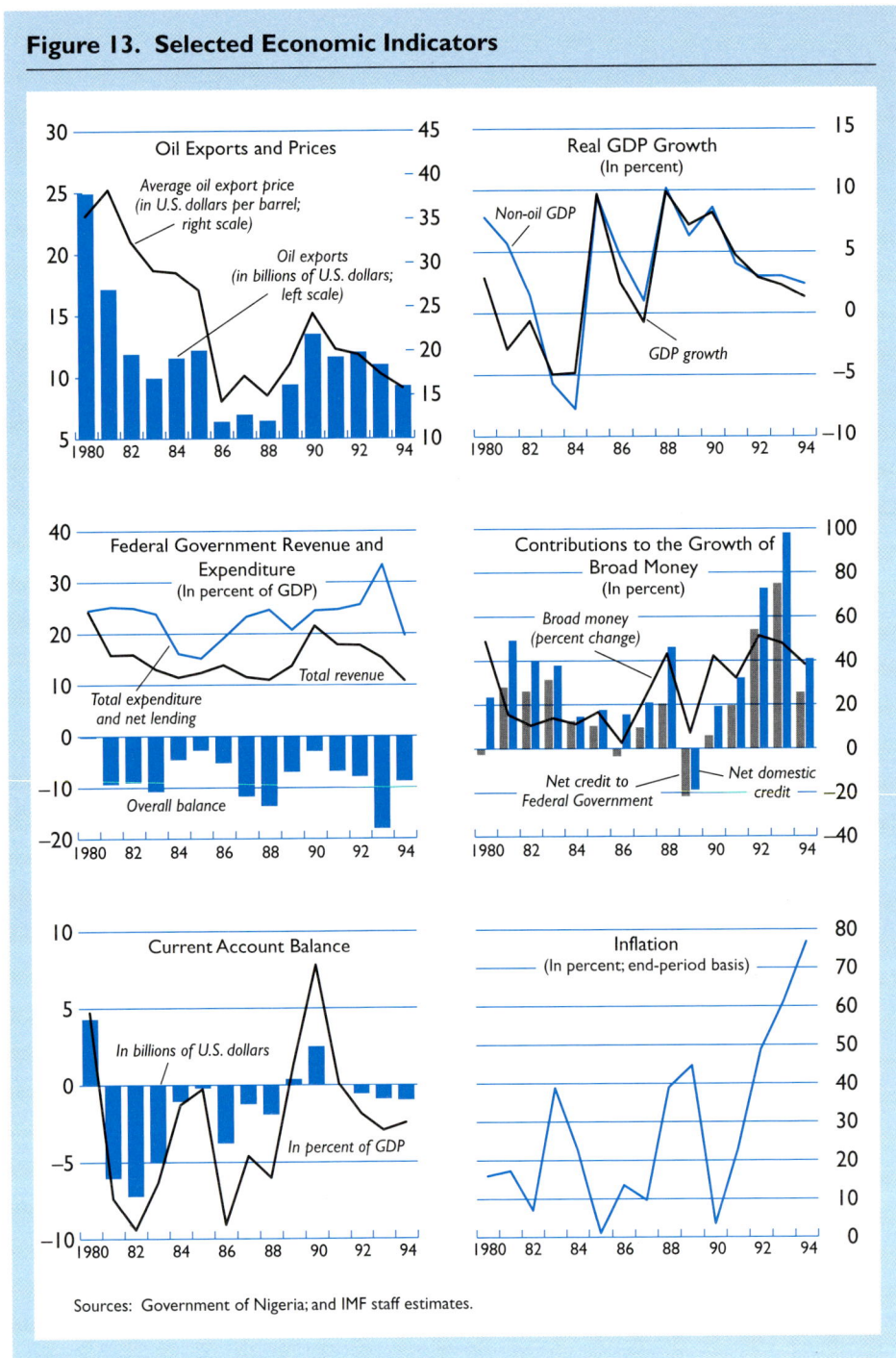

Figure 13. Selected Economic Indicators

Sources: Government of Nigeria; and IMF staff estimates.

July 1993, together with the suspension of the use of mandatory stabilization securities, would have provided the instruments for an effective control of credit, if properly utilized (Box 10).

Real interest rates turned positive in 1990 for the first time in a number of years, as inflation declined precipitously, from 60.4 percent in June 1989 to 0.3 percent in June 1990. The resulting increase in real lending rates, to more than 20 percent, evoked strong protests from the manufacturing sector and interest rate controls were reimposed in January 1991. The maximum lending and minimum deposit

Table 12. Selected Economic and Financial Indicators, 1990–94

	1990	1991	1992	1993	1994	1981–85 Average	1986–90 Average	1991–94 Average
(Annual percentage changes, unless otherwise indicated)								
National income and prices								
Real GDP (at 1984 market prices)	8.2	4.8	2.9	2.3	1.3	–0.9	5.3	2.8
Oil GDP (at 1984 factor cost)	5.5	9.2	2.7	–2.6	–6.0	–6.4	2.3	0.7
Non-oil GDP (at 1984 factor cost)	8.6	4.1	3.0	3.0	2.4	0.4	6.1	3.1
Consumer prices (end of period)	3.5	23.0	48.8	61.3	76.8	16.7	21.0	51.2
Nominal GDP (in billions of naira)	260.6	324.0	549.8	697.1	897.5	57.6	297.9	617.1
Oil production volume (in m/b per day)	1.812	1.894	1.956	2.038	2.007	1.370	1.567	1.974
Average oil export price (U.S. dollars per barrel, f.o.b.)	24.3	20.2	19.6	17.4	15.8	31.1	17.8	18.2
Population (millions)	85.7	88.5	91.4	94.3	97.1	66.9	84.5	92.8
External sector								
Exports f.o.b. (in billions of U.S. dollars)	13.9	12.1	12.3	11.3	9.5	12.9	9.0	11.3
Of which: oil (in billions of U.S. dollars)	(13.5)	(11.7)	(12.0)	(11.0)	(9.3)	(12.6)	(8.6)	(11.0)
Imports f.o.b. (in billions of U.S. dollars)	–7.1	–7.9	–8.7	–8.1	–6.7	–12.4	–6.3	–7.9
Non-oil export volume	3.0	19.0	–39.8	–5.5	–26.9	–11.3	1.5	–16.1
Import volume	9.2	11.5	7.3	–3.4	–20.1	–8.0	–10.4	–2.0
Nominal effective exchange rate	1.6	–17.5	–35.4	–22.3	33.0	2.0	–37.7	–13.9
Real effective exchange rate	–7.4	–15.7	–17.2	9.1	83.3	10.7	–32.1	8.7
Average official exchange rate (naira/U.S. dollar)	8.04	9.91	17.30	22.05	22.00	0.73	5.14	17.8
Terms of trade	18.5	–16.4	–5.5	–7.3	–11.2	–2.5	–9.5	–10.2
Money and credit								
Net foreign assets	93.7	31.2	–33.9	47.4	0.1	–20.1	89.7	6.3
Net domestic assets	–2.5	35.0	339.5	3.3	54.4	13.0	11.8	75.4
Net credit to the Federal Government	15.1	61.0	138.3	121.6	27.8	45.8	1.2	81.6
Credit to the rest of the economy	20.6	23.4	36.8	50.3	32.7	18.2	21.8	35.4
Broad money	42.3	32.3	51.3	48.0	38.4	13.6	22.5	42.3
Velocity (GDP/average broad money)	4.9	4.3	5.1	4.3	4.4	3.4	4.2	4.5
Savings deposit rate (end of period)	17.8	14.0	16.1	16.7	12.3	8.2	13.4	14.8
(In percent of GDP)								
Investment and savings								
Gross national savings	22.5	23.5	22.6	13.9	15.2	14.9	15.5	18.8
Gross domestic investment	14.7	23.4	24.5	16.8	17.7	19.9	17.6	20.6
Federal Government budget								
Revenue	21.5	17.9	17.8	15.3	10.9	13.8	14.4	15.4
Expenditure and net lending	24.5	24.7	25.6	33.3	19.6	21.1	22.5	25.8
Current expenditure	15.9	14.5	14.7	17.7	13.5	9.6	14.5	15.1
Capital expenditure	4.9	5.2	3.8	4.4	5.8	11.5	6.5	4.8
Federal Government budget deficit	–2.9	–6.8	–7.9	–18.1	–8.8	–7.3	–8.1	–10.4
External sector								
Current account balance	7.8	0.1	–1.9	–2.9	–2.4	–4.9	–2.1	–1.8
Overall balance of payments	–1.8	–7.0	–24.2	–10.6	–6.1	–4.5	–11.6	–12.0
External debt	104.0	103.2	90.7	94.2	76.4	18.0	92.9	91.1
(In billions of U.S. dollars, unless otherwise indicated)								
Current account balance	2.5	0.0	–0.6	–0.9	–1.0	–3.9	–0.8	–0.6
Overall balance of payments	–0.6	–2.3	–7.7	–3.3	–2.5	–3.5	–3.9	–4.0
External public and publicly guaranteed debt	33.7	33.7	28.8	29.8	31.2	14.5	29.6	30.9
Gross international reserves								
(end of period)	4.1	4.2	0.8	0.7	0.9	2.2	1.5	1.7
(in months of imports of goods and nonfactor services)	5.3	4.8	0.9	0.8	1.3	1.6	2.2	2.0

Sources: Data provided by the Nigerian authorities; and IMF staff estimates.

rates were set at 21 percent and 13½ percent, respectively. As inflation began to accelerate once again in early 1991, real interest rates began to fall, eventually turning negative toward the end of the year.

Interest rate ceilings were lifted once again in January 1992. However, the Government made it clear that banks were to look to the Central Bank discount rate in setting their own interest rates. In his annual

VI POST-ADJUSTMENT DECLINE, 1991–94

> **Box 10. Monetary Policy Targets and Outcomes**
>
> The Central Bank set targets for money growth, total domestic credit, and credit to the private sector, based on the Federal Government's budget and external sector policies. As shown below, outcomes deviated significantly from targets in recent years. The growth of narrow money consistently exceeded targets by large margins, as did domestic credit expansion.
>
> | | 1991 | | 1992 | | 1993 | | 1994 | |
> | --- | --- | --- | --- | --- | --- | --- | --- | --- |
> | | Target | Outcome | Target | Outcome | Target | Outcome | Target | Outcome |
> | | (Percentage change) | | | | | | | |
> | Narrow money | 14.6 | 31.5 | 24.3 | 57.1 | 20.0 | 51.3 | 21.4 | 46.5 |
> | Broad money | ... | 32.3 | 26.8 | 51.3 | 18.0 | 48.0 | 14.8 | 38.4 |
> | Net domestic credit | 10.6 | 37.3 | 13.2 | 81.2 | 17.5 | 91.3 | 9.4 | 29.4 |
> | Credit to Government (net) | — | 61.0 | 7.7 | 138.3 | 14.5 | 121.6 | — | 27.8 |
> | Credit to private sector | 16.0 | 24.2 | 17.7 | 36.9 | 20.0 | 51.1 | 32.6 | 32.8 |
>
> Sources: Central Bank of Nigeria; and IMF staff estimates.

budget address, the President stated that the formal lifting of the ceilings did "not imply that banks could indiscriminately... raise their interest rates... [and] that the banks will adhere strictly to the market signals as monitored and transmitted to them by the Central Bank."[25] As the Central Bank raised its discount rate infrequently and by very little, real interest rates continued to become increasingly negative. By the end of 1993, real lending and deposit rates had fallen to –25 percent and –38 percent, respectively. Nonetheless, as nominal rates surged toward the end of the year, with the interbank market rate temporarily reaching almost 100 percent, the Government once again responded by imposing interest rate ceilings in January 1994.

Over 1992–94, distress in the banking system spread considerably. By the end of 1994 the number of technically insolvent commercial and merchant banks had risen to 34 and an additional 8 banks were deemed illiquid. Combined, these distressed banks accounted for about 10 percent of the deposit liabilities of the banking system. More than two thirds of the aggregate loans and advances extended by these banks were nonperforming. Distress in the system has been traced, in part, to the rapid—and largely uncontrolled—expansion in the sector following the liberalization measures in the late 1980s and the substantial arbitrage profits available in the foreign exchange markets in recent years. Audits of the distressed banks by the Nigeria Deposit Insurance Corporation and the Central Bank identified serious management weaknesses or malfeasance as critical factors in the banks' poor performance. In response to this, the Federal Government issued a decree in 1994, supporting the investigation of banking abuse and providing penalties for malpractice in banking.[26]

Foreign Exchange Market

After the introduction of foreign exchange bureaus in August 1989, there were virtually two separate markets for foreign exchange in Nigeria. The foreign exchange bureaus—where the exchange rate was close to the parallel rate for much of the period—were allowed to deal in foreign currency notes and, to a limited extent, in traveler's checks, but they were prohibited from opening demand deposit accounts and from sourcing foreign exchange from the domestic banking system. Most of the country's foreign currency receipts, including oil export earnings, were allocated by the Central Bank to the banking system. Initially the allocation was based on the relative size of banks measured in terms of paid-in capital. In mid-December 1990 the guaranteed quota were removed and a Dutch auction system was instituted.

During 1991 and early 1992, as inflationary pressures mounted, the spread between the official and

---

[25] *Approved Budget of the Federal Republic of Nigeria*, 1992, p. xxiii.

[26] *Failed Banks (Recovery of Debts) and Financial Malpractices in Banks Decree,* November 9, 1994.

foreign exchange bureau rates widened, from 16 percent in December 1990 to 78 percent in February 1992. The official exchange rate vis-à-vis the U.S. dollar depreciated by 17 percent, whereas the bureau rate depreciated by 80 percent over the same period.

On March 5, 1992, the foreign exchange auction system was replaced by an interbank system, under which the official exchange rate of the naira was freely determined in the interbank market. Consequently, the official exchange rate depreciated by some 57 percent, from ₦10.56 to ₦18.48 per U.S. dollar. The spread between the official and bureau exchange rates narrowed from 83 percent at the beginning of March to less than 5 percent immediately thereafter. With heavy interventions by the Central Bank, the official exchange rate remained stable through end-August 1992, but depreciated subsequently to ₦19.75 per U.S. dollar at the end of December 1992. The spread between the official and bureau rates widened to around 15 percent in December.

Following several interruptions of foreign exchange sales owing to the inability to meet demand, the Central Bank reintroduced a Dutch auction system for the allocation of foreign exchange to authorized dealers in February 1993. The exchange rate depreciated by 22 percent to ₦24.9 per U.S. dollar for the first auction, and further to ₦30 in the second. The rapid depreciation of the currency prompted the Central Bank to peg the exchange rate, initially at ₦24.9 per U.S. dollar, and to allocate foreign exchange on a pro rata basis. The rate was subsequently revalued to ₦21.9 per U.S. dollar in April 1993. The pegging of the exchange rate in the face of rising inflation caused the spread between the official and foreign exchange bureau rates to increase to 112 percent by the end of 1993, from 20 percent a year earlier.

In 1994 the authorities took an even more drastic step by eliminating the free market for foreign exchange and pegging the exchange rate at a highly overvalued rate (US$1 = ₦22). It was believed that the stabilization of the exchange rate was necessary to control inflation. As a result, pressures in the official foreign exchange market mounted. The demand for foreign exchange at the official rate was a multiple of the official supply, which declined from roughly US$3 billion in 1993 to US$2 billion in 1994, prompting the authorities to reduce the frequency of the allocation sessions from every fortnight to every three weeks. Measures in midyear to divert part of the demand to the foreign exchange bureaus by allowing them a margin of 10 percent above the official rate did not have their intended results, and the spread between the official and parallel market exchange rates widened to around 300 percent by the end of 1994, compared with 100 percent at the beginning of the year. In real effective terms, the exchange rate appreciated by 83 percent in 1994.

Domestic Petroleum Prices

To improve the profitability of the downstream petroleum operations and increase revenue, the Government raised domestic prices of petroleum products three times during the post-SAP period. The first increase came in March 1991, when price increases ranged from 10 percent for diesel fuel to 150 percent for liquefied petroleum gas. The price of gasoline was increased by 17 percent, raising the ratio of the domestic price to the world price of gasoline from 37 percent in 1990 to 42 percent in 1991. On November 8, 1993, the Interim National Government raised domestic retail prices of petroleum products by about 600 percent. However, on November 22 the new military Government partially rolled back the price increases, in response to mounting civil unrest, with the result that they were contained within a range of 364 percent for premium gasoline and 450 percent for kerosene. This increase pushed the ratio of the domestic price to the world price to 122 percent at the official exchange rate. However, when measured at the parallel exchange rate, the domestic price of gasoline was still far below import parity. The Government increased pump prices again in October 1994, with the effect of raising the retail price of gasoline to the world market wholesale price measured at the then prevailing parallel market exchange rate. The action had the effect of both substantially improving the profitability of the petroleum parastatal and increasing the net revenue to the Federal Government.

Privatization

Privatization picked up steam during 1991–93, with another 35 public enterprises fully privatized, bringing the total to 55 since the inception of the program and leaving another 11 still scheduled for privatization. The program stalled in 1994 as the authorities began to reassess their progress and look at alternative approaches. While the Government focused on the smaller, less viable public enterprises, it was unwilling to address the key problems of the largest enterprises, mainly the oil sector, utilities, the steel mills, the airline, and the railways. This resulted in a continued drain on the budget during the post-SAP period and an alarming deterioration in the quality of public services as many of the public utilities were approaching insolvency while tariffs were frozen or held substantially below market rates. Total privatization proceeds amounted to ₦3.7 bil-

VI POST-ADJUSTMENT DECLINE, 1991–94

lion by the end of 1993 but represented less than 3 percent of the Government's total investment in the public enterprise sector as of the end of 1987.[27] Despite these sales, the Government's equity in public enterprises has continued to grow substantially since 1987. A partial listing of 40 public enterprises, including the seven largest parastatals showed a federal equity holding of ₦19.3 billion as of the end of 1993, compared with a total of ₦11.5 billion at the end of 1987.

---

[27]More current data on government equity in and loans to public enterprises are not available on a comprehensive basis.

VII Concluding Observations

In the preceding chapters an attempt has been made to analyze Nigeria's key economic policies and performance during a period that was characterized by bold attempts to introduce market-oriented reforms and stabilize the economy. The country's homegrown SAP, which effectively covered 1986–90, brought about a reorientation of economic policies, in which deregulation and liberalization of the economy were the guiding principles. In terms of results, and despite reversals and setbacks, the analysis shows that the SAP paid off; economic growth accelerated, and the improvement in economic conditions contrasted rather sharply with the pre- and post-adjustment periods. Nonetheless, adjustment fatigue set in quickly in Nigeria, and one wonders why the reform efforts could not be sustained. There are several possible explanations, but the inability to bring inflation effectively under control certainly played a major role in the erosion of support for the reforms. The attendant substantial depreciation of the naira fed the popular belief that the introduction of a market-determined exchange rate, one of the most difficult decisions the authorities faced, and the ensuing rapid depreciation of the currency was the driving force behind rising domestic prices. Unfortunately, the fundamental role of fiscal policy in the inflation process, particularly in an oil economy, was never fully appreciated in the internal debate on what went wrong during the SAP. The consequences of an expansionary fiscal policy stance could have been corrected by a countervailing monetary policy, if it would have been allowed to act. Obviously, this would have shifted the burden of adjustment to the private sector, which would have been difficult to pursue without a fundamental change in fiscal policy on the horizon.

One of the most striking aspects of economic policy making in Nigeria is its distaste for gradualism. Measures are almost always taken in a big way, whether it is an adjustment of domestic gasoline prices, a tightening of fiscal policy, or a reform in the exchange system. As a result, these policies often generated internal shocks that translated into an extreme volatility in economic and financial variables, which not only had a profound impact on the domestic economy, but also affected the region in a major way. The erratic and often unpredictable nature of the policies discouraged the private sector from responding as promptly as would have been expected given the direction of the reform.

What lessons can be drawn from Nigeria's experience with structural adjustment? First, sustainable reform requires continuity and coherence in economic policies, in which the achievement of macroeconomic stability is a sine qua non for raising the productivity of human and physical capital. The lack of effective coordination of fiscal, monetary, and exchange rate policies undermined the realization of the broader reform agenda and brought the adjustment process to a halt. Second, important sectors of the economy were left outside the scope of reforms. In particular, the reform of the public finances with a view to reducing reliance on oil revenue never took place, with the effect that fiscal policy was driven by the volatility in oil revenue. On the expenditure side, sizable resources were wasted on unviable projects, such as steel, or were spent on subsidies that did not reach the targeted groups. The deterioration in social indicators in Nigeria testifies to the neglect of policies aimed at the development of human capital through education and health services. In addition, the reform needed to focus on the agricultural sector, which was the primary source of non-oil growth and employment in the economy. Third, the deteriorating physical infrastructure reflected in large measure the extremely poor functioning of public utilities, which increasingly failed to deliver basic services to the population. The privatization of the national oil company and commercialization of the public utilities early on should have been a priority in the SAP. Finally, the weak economic governance, as reflected inter alia in the lack of transparency in the management of the country's oil wealth, contributed to a distrust in government and prevented a broad-based support for fundamental economic reforms.

Appendix I   Determinants of Inflation in Nigeria

Gary Moser

The rate of inflation in Nigeria has increased steadily and markedly since independence in 1960. During the period following independence (1965–75), Nigeria's rate of inflation was about equal to that of its trading partners, averaging 10 percent annually (Figure 14). In the next decade (1975–85), the respective rates of inflation diverged dramatically, as Nigeria's average annual rate nearly doubled, to 18 percent, while that of the trading partners narrowed significantly, to 4 percent. These trends continued between 1985 and 1990, as Nigeria's annual average rose to 24 percent while its trading partners posted an average rate of 13 percent. More recently, since late 1990, Nigeria has experienced a period of stagflation. By the end of 1993, inflation had reached 60 percent and real per capita income growth had stalled.

This study reviews previous empirical studies of the determinants of inflation in Nigeria, analyzes the dominant factors influencing inflation, presents the empirical results of an error correction model, and discusses the policy implications of the empirical results.

Consumer Price Index

The official consumer price index (CPI) is based on a composite of urban and rural price data compiled monthly by the Federal Office of Statistics (FOS)[28] and reflects household expenditure patterns in the 1985/86 National Consumer Survey.[29]

Composite food prices dominate the CPI, representing 69 percent of the total market basket (Table 13), with staple food commodities alone representing 42 percent. Consequently, factors affecting food prices dominate movements in the CPI (Figure 14). These factors include agroclimatic conditions, wages, domestic inputs, and import prices, with rainfall playing a key role. Subsistence agriculture, which is not included in marketed production, is important in marginal supply and demand during periods of drought or abundant rainfall. Imports, while significant in the economy as a whole, have tended to be less significant in influencing the CPI since household consumption, which is predominantly food related, has a low import content.

Inflation During 1985–93

The rate of inflation dropped sharply in 1985 and 1986, as favorable weather conditions led to abundant crop production and tight fiscal and monetary policies substantially reduced excess liquidity in the economy (Figure 15). Anchored by a tight fiscal and monetary policy stance, and aided by favorable weather, the devaluation of the naira in 1986 (96 percent in domestic currency terms) had virtually no impact on that year's rate of inflation. Inflation increased moderately in 1987, averaging 10 percent, with the onset of the 1987–88 drought and the lagged impact of the substantial devaluation in 1986. Table 14 presents data since the mid-1980s on some of the factors that have influenced inflation in Nigeria.

A severe drought in key growing regions of the country in 1987 and 1988, combined with fiscal and monetary expansion, led to a virtual doubling of food prices in 1988. Consequently, the rate of inflation jumped to 55 percent in 1988. While food prices actually fell during the second half of 1989 as rains and production improved, the average rate of inflation remained above 50 percent, primarily as a result of the cumulative impact of broad money growth and the sizable devaluation of the naira in 1989.

Inflation slowed considerably in 1990, to an average annual rate of 7.4 percent, largely reflecting the contractionary fiscal and monetary policies implemented during late 1989 and early 1990 and the improved harvests in 1989 and 1990 resulting from ex-

---
[28]Price data are collected for 256 items in 83 urban towns and 312 rural centers on a weekly or monthly basis. The FOS compiles the data monthly to prepare a CPI for each of the 21 states and an aggregate rural and urban CPI as well as the national composite CPI.

[29]The FOS completed a new National Consumer Survey during the period April 1992 to March 1993. A preliminary analysis suggests that expenditure on food items is broadly in line with the data from the 1985/86 national survey.

Appendix I

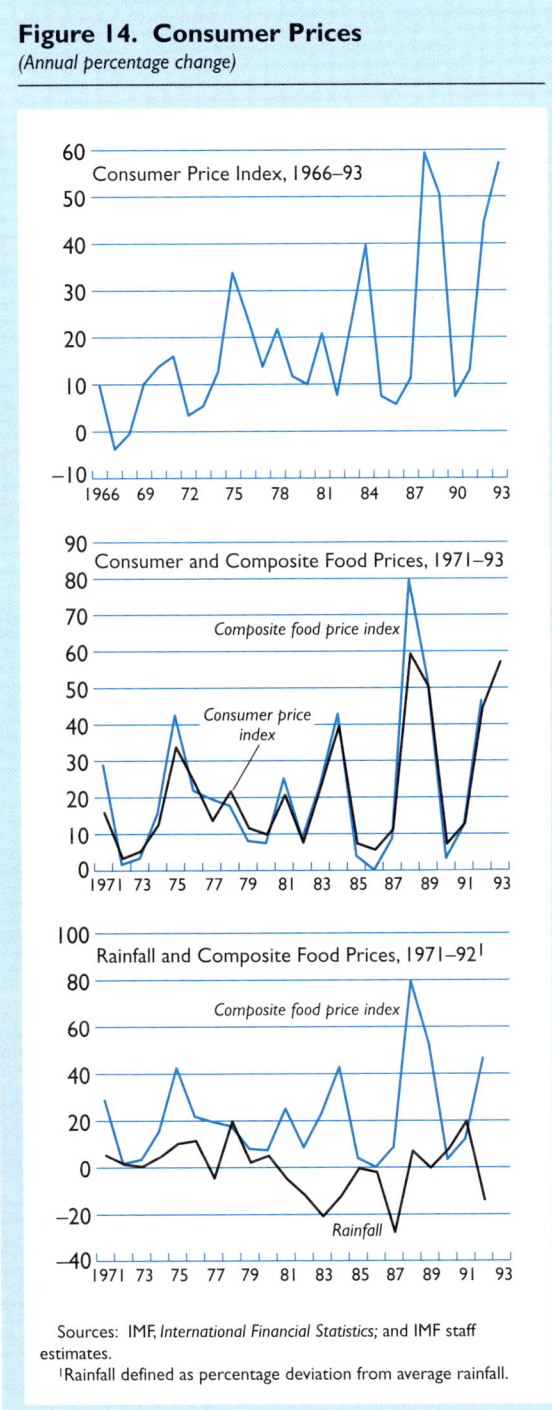

Figure 14. Consumer Prices
(Annual percentage change)

Sources: IMF, *International Financial Statistics*; and IMF staff estimates.
¹Rainfall defined as percentage deviation from average rainfall.

Table 13. Consumer Price Index Market Basket
(In percent)

	CPI Weights¹		
Commodity	Combined urban and rural	All urban centers	All rural centers
Food	69.1	65.4	69.9
Drinks, tobacco, and cola	4.7	3.6	5.0
Clothing and footwear	4.7	4.3	4.8
Accommodation, fuel, and light	11.9	14.0	11.5
Household goods	3.6	3.4	3.6
Health-related	1.1	1.2	1.1
Transportation	2.4	5.0	1.8
Recreation, education, and entertainment	1.4	1.9	1.3
Other services	1.2	1.3	1.2
All items	100.0	100.0	100.0

Source: Nigerian Federal Office of Statistics; based on the 1985/86 National Consumer Survey.
¹Figures may not add due to rounding.

cellent rains. As a result, the increase in food prices was held to 3 percent in 1990. Toward the end of 1990, fiscal and monetary policies loosened considerably, which led to the upward movement in inflation in 1991 to 13 percent. The depreciation of the naira by 23 percent during 1991 also added to the upward pressure on prices.

The rate of inflation increased markedly in 1992, to 45 percent on an annual average basis, as a result of substantial excess liquidity in the economy brought about by the continued monetization of the growing fiscal deficit, which increased to 8 percent of GDP in 1992. The sharp devaluation of the naira (75 percent in local currency terms) during this expansionary period put further upward pressure on prices.

Inflation accelerated further in 1993, to an estimated 57 percent annually, reflecting the sharp increase in the fiscal deficit, to 18 percent of GDP. The devaluation of the official exchange rate (28 percent in local currency terms) also added upward pressure on the rate of inflation, but this pressure was tempered somewhat by the estimated 4 percent decline in the index of foreign prices.

Quantitative Analysis

Factors Influencing Inflation

Recent studies on inflation in Nigeria broadly agree on the key factors influencing the rate of inflation: money growth, income growth, and exchange rate movements. These factors are presented for period averages in Table 15. It is noteworthy that, as the table indicates, the widening of the differential between do-

APPENDIX I

Table 14. Matrix of Factors Influencing Inflation

	Budget Deficit (In percent of GDP)	Broad Money Growth	Exchange Rate Devaluation[1]	Real GDP Growth	Rainfall	Current Year Inflation
1986	5.2	2.7	96.3	2.5	Good	5.7
1988	13.6	43.3	13.0	9.9	Drought	54.5
1990	2.9	32.7[2]	9.1	8.2	Good	7.4
1993	18.1	51.9	27.5	2.3	Below average	57.2

Sources: International Monetary Fund, *International Financial Statistics*; and IMF staff estimates.
[1]End-of-period basis.
[2]Broad money rose sharply during the second half of the year.

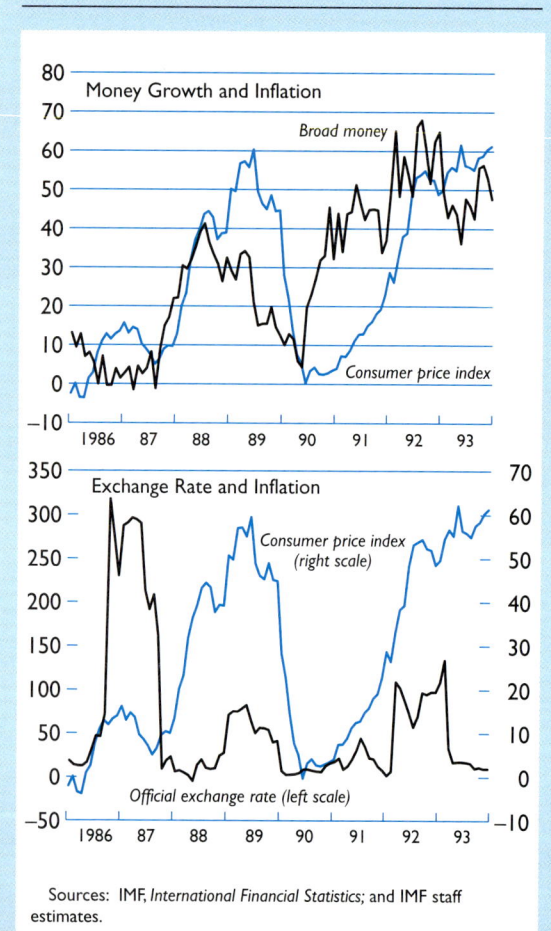

Figure 15. Inflation, Money, and Exchange Rate Developments
(Annual percentage change)

Sources: IMF, *International Financial Statistics*; and IMF staff estimates.

mestic and foreign inflation has generally occurred during periods of rapid monetary expansion, while the impact of exchange rate movements on inflation is less clear. However, recent empirical studies do not concur on the relative importance of each of these factors as determinants of inflation. Most of them conclude that excess domestic demand, generated by expansionary fiscal and monetary policies, has been the principal factor underlying the rising inflation rate in Nigeria.[30] Others suggest that cost-push inflation resulting from excessive devaluations and wage increases has been the primary impetus for the upward inflationary spiral.[31]

Broad money growth has been found to be a fundamental determinant of inflation in many of the studies, while the impact of exchange rate movements on inflation has been less clear. This ambiguity is most likely the result of the time periods studied. During the 1960s and 1970s, when the official exchange rate was stable, there were numerous periods of high inflation. Subsequently, in the 1980s and early 1990s, the considerable devaluation of the naira occurred during a period of increasing price instability and rising inflationary pressures and most likely added to the upward movement in inflation. As the magnitude of the impact of exchange rate movements on inflation is unclear, it will be tested empirically below.

Many of the studies also reported that real income growth played a significant deflationary role by increasing the demand for real money balances. In addition, some studies reported a significant and negative relationship between agricultural production and

---
[30]See, for example, Darrat (1985), Ojameruaye (1988), Ekpo (1992), and World Bank (1993).
[31]See, for example, Adamson (1989) and Aigbokhan (1991).

Appendix I

Table 15. Selected Price, Money, and Exchange Rate Indicators
(Average annual change)

	1965–75	1975–85	1985–90	1990	1991	1992	1993
Inflation	9.6	17.7	24.0	7.4	13.0	44.6	57.2
Broad money	24.0	19.1	20.0	32.7	37.4	62.5	51.9
Exchange rate (naira/U.S. dollar)[1]	–1.5	3.8	55.2	9.1	23.3	74.6	27.5
Foreign inflation[2]	8.0	4.0	12.6	16.4	3.5	7.2	–4.4

Sources: International Monetary Fund, *International Financial Statistics*; and IMF staff estimates.
[1]End-of-period basis.
[2]Weighted average of trading partner prices (in U.S. dollar terms).

inflation. While this latter result is intuitive, the linear relationship between the income and production variables may have led to spurious results since agricultural production has accounted for such a large share of total production.

Derivation of the Inflation Equation

To measure the impact of relevant explanatory variables discussed above and predict the likely inflationary outcome of a specific mix of policy measures and exogenous factors, an equation for inflation is derived and analyzed below. The overall price level (P) is a weighted average of the price of tradable goods (P^T) and nontradable goods (P^N), and can be represented in log-linear form as

$$\log P = \alpha(\log P^N) + (1 - \alpha)(\log P^T), \quad (1)$$

where α represents the share of nontradable goods in total expenditure. The price of tradable goods (P^T) is determined exogenously in the world market and, in domestic currency terms, can be represented by foreign prices (P^f) and the exchange rate (e):

$$\log P^T_t = \log e_t + \log P^f_t. \quad (2)$$

Both an increase in the exchange rate (in domestic currency terms) and an increase in foreign prices will lead to an increase in the overall price level.

The price of nontradable goods (P^N) is assumed to be set in the money market, where demand for nontradable goods is assumed, for simplicity, to move in line with demand in the economy overall. As a result, the price of nontradable goods is determined by the money market equilibrium condition, real money supply (M^s/P) equals real money demand (m^d), which yields the following equation for nontradable goods prices:

$$\log P^N = \beta(\log M^s - \log m^d), \quad (3)$$

where M^s represents the nominal stock of money, m^d is the demand for real money balances, and ß is a scale factor representing the relationship between economy-wide demand and demand for nontradable goods. The demand for real money balances (m^d) is assumed to be a function of real income, inflationary expectations, and foreign interest rates:

$$m^d_t = f(y_t, \pi_t, r_{t+1}), \quad (4)$$
$$+ \; - \; -$$

where y_t represents real income, π_t represents expectations formed in period $t-1$ of inflation in period t, and r_{t+1} is the expected nominal foreign interest rate in period $t+1$ adjusted by the expected change in the exchange rate in period $t+1$.[32] According to money demand theory, an increase in the stock variable (real income) will stimulate money demand, whereas an increase in the domestic opportunity cost variable (expected inflation) will lead to a decline. The expected rate of inflation in period t is assumed, based on adaptive expectations, to be equal to

$$\pi_t = d_1(\Delta \log P_{t-1}) + (1 - d_1)\pi_{t-1}, \quad (5)$$

where $\Delta \log P_{t-1}$ represents actual inflation in period $t-1$ and π_{t-1} is the expected rate of inflation in period $t-1$. In this analysis, we assume that $d_1 = 1$, leading to the following reduced-form inflation equation:

$$\pi_t = \Delta \log P_{t-1}. \quad (6)$$

Moreover, based on similar assumptions regarding the formulation of expectations, we assume that the expected foreign interest rate (r_{t+1}), corrected for the expected change in the exchange rate, is equal to the observed rate in period t:

$$E(r_{t+1}) = r_t. \quad (7)$$

---
[32]As a result of fixed interest rates over most of the period, domestic interest rates were not included as they do not add significant additional information.

APPENDIX I

An increase in expected future foreign interest rates ($r_t + 1$) is assumed to lead to a decrease in current real money demand as a result of substitution effects. Substituting equations (6) and (7) into equation (4) yields the following log-linear money demand function:

$$\log m_t^d = c_2 \log y_t - c_3 \Delta \log P_{t-1} - c_4 r_t. \tag{8}$$

Substituting equation (8) into equation (3) yields

$$\log P_t^N = \beta(\log M_t - c_2 \log y_t + c_3 \Delta \log P_{t-1} + c_4 r_t). \tag{9}$$

Equations (2) and (9) can then be substituted into equation (1), where

$$\log P_t = \alpha\beta(\log M_t - c_2 \log y_t + c_3 \Delta \log P_{t-1} + c_4 r_t) + (1 - \alpha)(\log e_t + \log P_t^f). \tag{10}$$

As discussed above, based on casual observation, the independent role of rainfall in influencing the predominantly food-related consumer price index appears to be substantial. Accordingly, rainfall (Z) is investigated below as a potential additional explanatory variable.

Based on the underlying assumptions discussed above, the following a priori assumptions can be made regarding the signs of the explanatory variables:

$$P_t = f(M_t, y_t, e_t, r_t, \Delta P_{t-1}, P_t^f, Z_t), \tag{11}$$
$$\quad\;\; +\;\; -\;\; +\;\; +\;\;\;\;\; +\;\;\; +\;\; -$$

where an increase in nominal broad money, the naira/U.S. dollar exchange rate, expected nominal foreign interest rates adjusted for the expected change in the exchange rate, expected inflation, or foreign prices leads to an increase in prices in period t, while an increase in real income or rainfall leads to a fall in prices.

Econometric Methods and Results

This appendix adopts a time-series approach to the development of an econometric price model to address the criticism of potentially spurious results encountered in most recent studies of inflation in Nigeria, based on the nonstationarity of the data series, and to analyze the short-run, dynamic structure of the relationship. Engle and Granger (1987) suggest a two-step approach. First, the existence of a cointegrating relationship among the variables in equation (10) is determined based on standard cointegration techniques. If the variables are cointegrated, a stable long-run relationship can be estimated using standard ordinary least squares (OLS) techniques. Second, the information in the error term of the long-run relationship is used to create a dynamic error correction model. According to Engel and Granger (1987), this error correction model produces consistent results even when the right-hand-side variables are not completely exogenous. The error correction model is then used to analyze the impulse response of inflation to a stimulus in the explanatory variables in a dynamic setting.

Testing for Cointegration

Testing for cointegration requires information on the order of integration of the variables, as vectors with multiple orders of integration require multiple-stage testing.[33] Accordingly, the stationarity of the vector of variables was analyzed based on appropriate unit root tests, and the order of integration of the P, M, y, e, and Z variables (all in log form) was determined based on standard Dickey-Fuller (DF) and augmented Dickey-Fuller (ADF) statistics.[34] All the variables were found to be integrated of order 1, I(1).

A cointegrating relationship was confirmed for the P, M, y, e, and Z variables. The DF and ADF test statistics rejected the hypothesis of the existence of a unit root in the error term of the regression of the variables, with P as the dependent variable, confirming that the error term was stationary.

Estimation of the long-run relationship yielded (with the T-statistic in parentheses)

$$P_t = -3.028 + 0.689 M_t - 0.561 y_t + 0.254 e_t + 0.191 Z_t + u_t. \tag{12}$$
$$\quad\;\;(1.97)\;\;(30.13)\;\;\;(9.24)\;\;\;(7.64)\;\;(1.15)$$

Sample: 1960–1993 $R^2 = .996$ SE = 0.095 CRDW = 1.24

The model performed well in terms of explaining the price level as a function of money, income, and the exchange rate. All the coefficients had the appropriate signs with the exception of the rainfall variable. The rainfall variable, though, was found to be insignificant in the long run, consistent with one's intuition.

Dynamic Model

The dynamic version of the long-run relationship estimated in equation (12) can be specified as an error correction model:

$$\Delta P_t = \beta_0 + \sum_{i=0}^{\eta} (\beta_{1i}\Delta M_{t-i} + \beta_{2i}\Delta y_{t-i} + \beta_{3i}\Delta e_{t-i} + \beta_{4i}\Delta Z_{t-i}) + \sum_{i=1}^{\eta} (\beta_{5i}\Delta P_{t-i}) + \beta_6 EC_{t-1} + v_t, \tag{13}$$

where Δ represents the first difference operator, EC_t the error correction term, and v_t a disturbance term.

The error correction model utilizes information in the error term of the long-run model to approximate deviations from the equilibrium and represent the short-run response necessary to move the system back toward its equilibrium. The error correction term is calculated as

$$EC_t = P_t - \hat{P}_t, \tag{14}$$

where P_t is the actual value of P in period t and $\hat{P}_t$ is the fitted value of P_t estimated in equation (12).

Equation (13) was used to estimate the short-run model, with the most parsimonious formulation of

---

[33] See Engle and Granger (1991).
[34] The inflation, foreign interest rate, and foreign prices variables were dropped from the analysis as they were found in earlier versions of this paper to be insignificant.

the model presented below, based on a simplification search with η = 2:

$$\Delta P_t = 0.019 + 0.356\Delta M_t - 0.294\Delta y_t + 0.191\Delta e_{t-1}$$
$$ (0.025) \ (0.082) \quad\ (0.102) \quad\ (0.064)$$
$$ - 0.230\Delta Z_{t-2} + 0.333\Delta P_{t-1} - 0.508 EC_{t-1}. \quad (15)$$
$$\ (0.107) \qquad\ (0.118) \qquad\ (0.153)$$

$R^2 = 0.691 \quad SE = 0.075 \quad DW = 2.342$

The model was estimated using standard OLS estimation techniques on annual data for 1963–93. It performed well in terms of the expected signs on the coefficients of the explanatory variables and in terms of its explanatory power, with an adjusted coefficient of determination (R^2) value of 0.69.[35] When the error correction model was fitted against historical inflation data, it performed well in terms of tracking the cyclical nature of price movements in Nigeria (Figure 16).

The presence of serial correlation, or more general forms of autocorrelation, were rejected based on the Breusch-Godfey and Box-Pierce Q statistic. The Jargue-Bera test statistic confirmed normality, and the ARCH test rejected up to fourth-order heteroskedasticity in the disturbance term. The presence of a general specification error was rejected based on the results of the Ramsey RESET(1) test.

The estimated error correction model was found to be stable over the period studied based on the Chow breakpoint test. Four years were selected for the Chow F-test as possible breakpoints (1977, 1979, 1982, and 1985), consistent with previous empirical studies, representing years of pronounced structural reform or exogenous shocks. The CUMSUM recursive residuals test also confirmed the structural stability of the model. Figure 17 plots the CUMSUM cumulative recursive residuals, with deviations outside the 5 percent critical line implying structural instability.

Impulse Responses and Policy Implications

The impact of changes in the exogenous variables on the inflation path can be studied using the dynamic structure of the error correction model above. More specifically, the impulse response of inflation to each of the explanatory variables can be calculated based on the dynamic multipliers. Figure 18 shows the impulse response of inflation (ΔP_t) over time to a permanent 1 percent increase in each of the right-hand-side variables in equation (15).

---

[35]All the coefficients were significant at the 1 percent level with the exception of the constant term, which was insignificant at the 10 percent level.

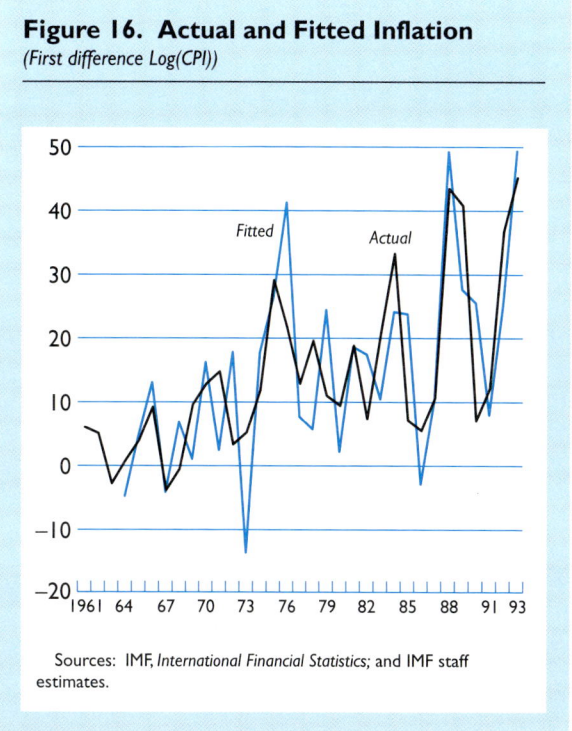

Figure 16. Actual and Fitted Inflation
(First difference Log(CPI))

Sources: IMF, *International Financial Statistics*; and IMF staff estimates.

Based on the multipliers, a permanent 1 percent increase in the rate of money growth would yield a 0.36 percent increase in inflation in the initial year, increasing to 0.53 percent by the fourth year, moving toward a long-run increase in inflation of 0.69 percent. At the same time, a permanent 1 percent increase in the exchange rate (devaluation) would lead to an increase of only 0.19 percent in inflation by the second year, with no impact in the initial year, and an increase of 0.25 percent in the long run.

A permanent 1 percent increase in real GDP would be expected to reduce inflation by 0.29 percent in the first year, with a decrease of 0.44 percent after four years, moving toward a long-run decrease of 0.56 percent. Improved rainfall also reduces inflation. A 1 percent increase in rainfall would be expected to decrease inflation by 0.23 percent after two years, decreasing to 0.34 percent by the sixth year.

In addition to confirming that inflation is directly linked to growth in the money supply, the model also suggests that the Nigerian authorities could use appropriately tight financial policies to reduce the inflationary impact of a devaluation. Conversely, the model predicts that a devaluation during a period of excessively expansionary fiscal and monetary policies will have substantial inflationary consequences, as the impact of the monetary growth further adds to the inflationary pressures. Moreover, the inflationary

APPENDIX I

Figure 17. Structural Stability of Price Equation

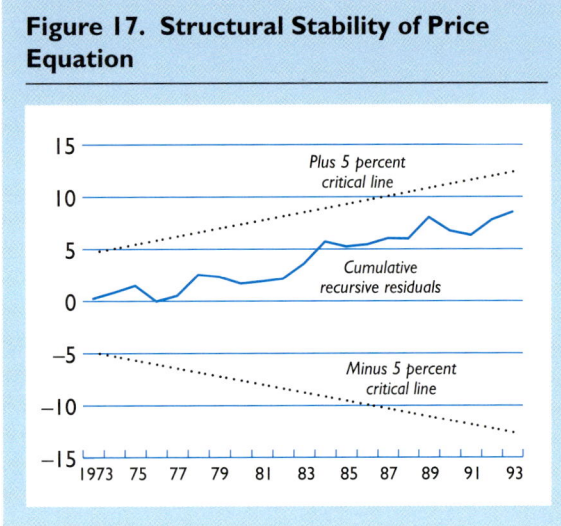

impact of a devaluation during a period of loose financial policies would be especially strong if the country were in the midst of, or just pulling out of, a long period of drought.

Conclusions

Nigeria's rate of inflation has increased markedly over the past two and a half decades. The results of this analysis confirm the basic findings of earlier studies, namely, that monetary expansion, driven mainly by expansionary fiscal policies, explains to a large degree the inflationary process in Nigeria. Other important factors were the devaluation of the naira and agroclimatic conditions.

It was found that concurrent fiscal and monetary policies had a major influence on the impact of the

Figure 18. Dynamic Response of Inflation

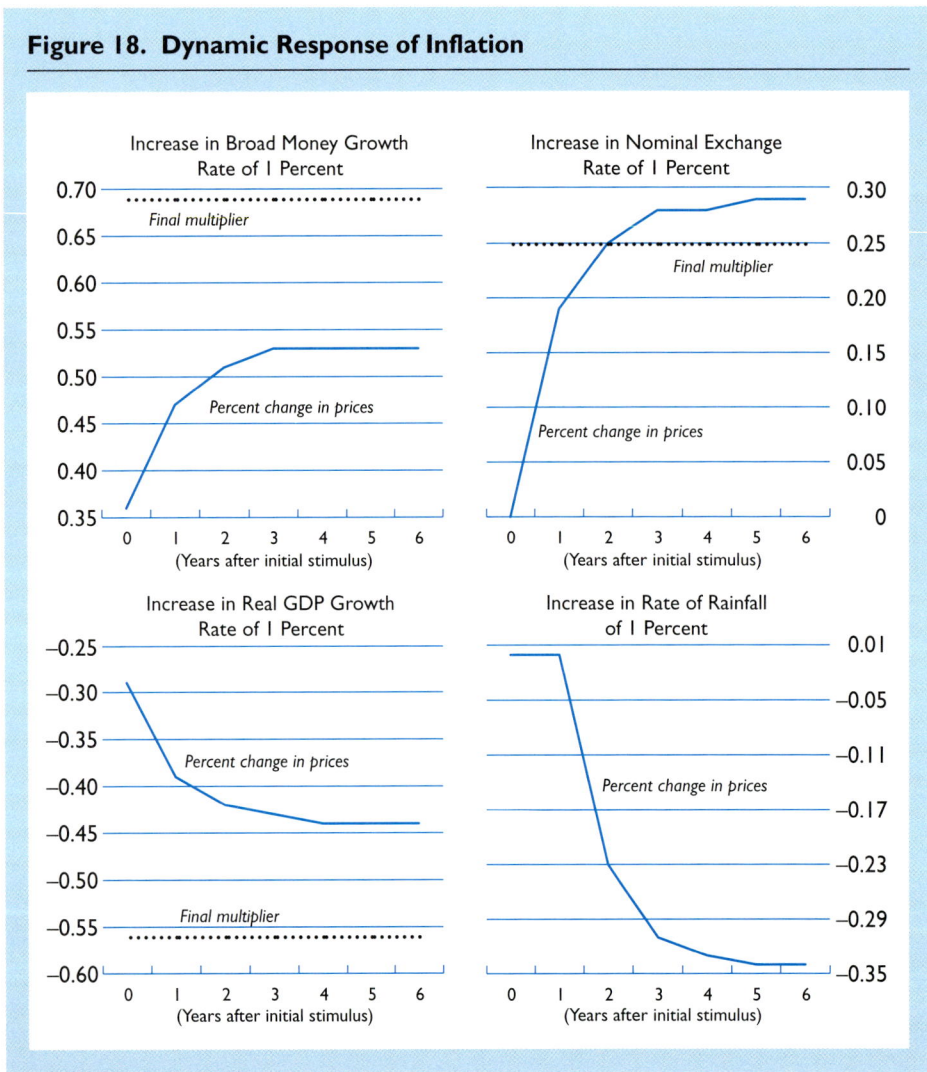

Table 16. Inflation Database
(In millions of naira, unless otherwise specified)

	Naira/U.S. dollar Exchange Rate Index	Broad Money	Gross Domestic Product	Consumer Price Index	Rainfall[1]
1960	80.04	296	2,400	6.85	1,558
1961	80.04	314	2,378	7.28	1,362
1962	80.04	333	2,516	7.66	1,494
1963	80.04	362	2,946	7.45	1,459
1964	80.04	431	3,145	7.52	1,217
1965	80.04	469	3,361	7.82	1,519
1966	80.04	520	3,614	8.58	1,359
1967	80.04	454	2,951	8.26	1,345
1968	80.04	522	2,878	8.22	1,320
1969	80.04	663	3,851	9.06	1,509
1970	80.04	979	5,621	10.30	1,346
1971	79.87	1,042	7,098	11.95	1,406
1972	73.72	1,204	7,703	12.37	1,352
1973	73.72	1,370	11,199	13.03	1,339
1974	70.46	2,592	18,811	14.69	1,394
1975	68.97	4,035	21,779	19.66	1,471
1976	70.22	7,608	27,572	24.44	1,487
1977	72.23	7,675	32,747	27.82	1,273
1978	71.17	7,521	36,084	33.86	1,597
1979	67.54	9,849	43,151	37.82	1,362
1980	61.24	14,390	50,849	41.60	1,400
1981	68.78	15,239	50,749	50.25	1,269
1982	75.44	16,694	51,709	54.12	1,176
1983	81.07	19,034	57,142	66.68	1,056
1984	85.64	21,243	63,608	93.08	1,170
1985	100.00	23,153	72,355	100.00	1,327
1986	150.91	23,605	73,062	105.72	1,306
1987	449.00	28,895	108,885	117.65	966
1988	502.32	38,406	145,243	181.79	1,426
1989	824.37	43,371	224,797	273.53	1,330
1990	900.07	57,554	260,637	293.67	1,436
1991	1,105.30	79,067	324,011	331.87	1,596
1992	1,828.54	128,522	553,154	479.85	1,149
1993	2,439.00	195,220	770,718	754.32	1,149

Sources: International Monetary Fund, *International Financial Statistics*; and IMF staff estimates.
[1] In millimeters per year.

depreciation of the naira on inflation. The devaluation increases prices but the impact can be counteracted by implementing appropriate financial policies. As shown in 1986 and 1990, a tight fiscal and monetary policy stance during and shortly after a devaluation substantially reduces the impact of the devaluation on domestic prices, while a devaluation during a period of excessive expansionary financial policies magnifies the impact on inflation, as was seen in 1992.

Agroclimatic conditions were also found to be a factor influencing the rate of inflation. Given the considerable role of food commodities in the CPI, agroclimatic conditions (rainfall) have a significant influence on overall movements in prices, as was shown in 1988/89 and 1990/91.

Data Sources

The estimates were based on annual data from *International Financial Statistics (IFS)* for 1960–93 (Table 16). The *IFS* data were supplemented as necessary with staff estimates for 1992 and 1993. Real income is derived by deflating nominal GDP by the consumer price index.

Broad money is defined as the sum of narrow money plus quasi-money, and the official naira/U.S. dollar exchange rate index is used for the exchange rate variable. The Fund's estimate of the exchange-weighted inflation rate of partner countries is used as the proxy for the foreign inflation variable and the U.S. three-month treasury bill rate is used to proxy foreign interest rates.

The rainfall variable was based on annual rainfall data (in millimeters). The source of the data for the period 1970–92 was *The Central Bank of Nigeria Statistical Bulletin* (June 1993) while the data for the period 1960–69 were compiled from the *World Weather Database*.

References

Adamson, Yahya K., 1989, "Structural Disequilibrium and Inflation in Nigeria: A Theoretical and Empirical Analysis of the Causes and Effects of Inflation in a Developing Economy," *Center for Economic Research on Africa*, Research Publication No. 89.5 (Upper Montclair, New Jersey: Montclair State College, Center for Economic Research on Africa).

Aigbokhan, Ben E., 1991, "The Naira Exchange Rate Depreciation and Domestic Inflation," *The Indian Journal of Economics,* Vol. 71 (April), pp. 507–17.

Asogu, J.O., 1991, "An Econometric Analysis of the Nature and Causes of Inflation in Nigeria," *Central Bank of Nigeria Economic and Financial Review,* Vol. 29, No. 3 (September).

Central Bank of Nigeria, 1993, *The Central Bank of Nigeria Statistical Bulletin* (June).

Darrat, Ali F., 1985, "Monetary Explanation of Inflation: The Experience of Three Major OPEC Economies," *Journal of Economics and Business,* Vol. 37 (August), pp. 209–21.

Ekpo, Akpan H., 1992, "Unemployment and Inflation Under Structural Adjustment: The Nigerian Experience," *East Africa Economic Review,* Vol. 8 (December), pp. 102–13.

Engle, Robert F., and C.W.J. Granger, 1987, "Cointegration and Error Correction: Representation, Estimation and Testing," *Econometrica,* Vol. 55 (March), pp. 251–76.

―――, eds., 1991, *Long-Run Economic Relationships, Readings in Cointegration* (Oxford; New York: Oxford University Press).

Granger, C.W.J., 1986, "Developments in the Study of Cointegrated Economic Variables," *Oxford Bulletin of Economics and Statistics,* Vol. 48 (August), pp. 213–28.

Hendry, David F., 1986, "Econometric Modelling with Cointegrated Variables: An Overview," *Oxford Bulletin of Economics and Statistics,* Vol. 48 (August), pp. 201–12.

Ikhide, Sylvanus I., 1993, "Financial Liberalization and the Inflationary Process: Is There a Link in Adjusting Developing Countries?" *Rivista Internazionale di Scienze Economiche è Commerciali,* Vol. 40 (February), pp. 157–70.

Khan, Mohsin S., and Malcolm D. Knight, 1991, "Stabilization Programs in Developing Countries: A Formal Framework," in *Macroeconomic Models for Adjustment in Developing Countries,* ed. by Mohsin S. Khan, Peter J. Montiel, and Nadeem U. Haque (Washington: International Monetary Fund), pp. 38–85.

Lahiri, Ashok K., 1991, "Money and Inflation in Yugoslavia," *Staff Papers,* International Monetary Fund, Vol. 38 (December), pp. 751–88.

Ojameruaye, E.O., 1988, "Analysis of the Determinants of the General Price Level in Nigeria," *Research for Development,* Vol. 5 (January), pp. 80–96.

Pinto, Brian, 1989, "Black Market Premia, Exchange Rate Unification, and Inflation in Sub-Saharan Africa," *World Bank Economic Review,* Vol. 3 (September), pp. 321–38.

World Bank, 1993, "Nigeria—Structural Adjustment Program: Policies, Implementation, and Impact," Report No. 12366-UNI (Washington: World Bank, October).

World Weatherdisk Associates, 1994, *World Weather Database* (World Weatherdisk Associates).

Appendix II Money Demand in Nigeria, 1970–94

Gary Moser

The demand for money is commonly described in terms of its ability to facilitate transactions and store wealth. Money demand functions typically include a scale variable (income or wealth) as a proxy for transactions demand and opportunity cost variables (including interest rates and/or the rate of inflation) as proxies for the return on financial and nonfinancial assets.[36] In line with most recent studies of money demand in developing countries, this analysis uses real income as the scale variable, which is expected to positively influence money demand through both transactions and wealth considerations. In addition, the real exchange rate is included as a potential explanatory variable based on the assumption that economic agents in Nigeria's oil-dominated economy desire to hold foreign currencies to expedite transactions and as a hedge against a real depreciation. Consequently, a real depreciation of the exchange rate (in terms of naira per U.S. dollar) is expected to reduce demand for real naira balances.

Expected inflation is included as an opportunity cost variable and is assumed to negatively influence the desire to hold real money balances. The expected rate of interest, which could have a positive or negative influence on money demand, depending on the definition of money and the competing transactions and wealth effects, is also included as an opportunity cost variable.

Accordingly, the proposed formulation of the long-run money demand equation, along with the expected signs on the coefficients of each of the variables, is

$$(M^d/P)_t = f(y_t, \varepsilon_t, \pi_{t+1}, r^*_{t+1}), \qquad (1)$$
$$+\ -\ -\phantom{\pi_{t+1},}\ ?$$

in which: M^d is the nominal demand for money, P is the price level, y denotes real income, ε the average real exchange rate, π expected inflation, and r^* expected nominal return on money.[37] The money, price, income, and exchange rate variables are in log form. Expected inflation is defined as the rate of inflation expected to prevail in period $t+1$ based on information in period t, and the expected real rate of return on money balances is defined in a similar fashion. The equation for money demand can subsequently be written in log-linear form as

$$m_t = \alpha_1 + \alpha_2 y_t + \alpha_3 \varepsilon_t + \alpha_4 \pi_{t+1} + \alpha_5 r^*_{t+1}, \qquad (2)$$

where m equals M^d/P.

The expected rate of inflation in period $t+1$ is assumed, based on adaptive expectations, to be equal to

$$\pi_{t+1} = \lambda_1 (\Delta P_t) + (1 - \lambda_1) \pi_t, \qquad (3)$$

where ΔP_t represents actual inflation and π_t is the expected rate of inflation in period t. The coefficient λ_1 represents the adjustment lag and, for this analysis, is assumed to equal 1, leading to

$$\pi_{t+1} = \Delta P_t. \qquad (4)$$

In a similar fashion, we assume that the expected return on money in period $t+1$, based on information (I) in period t, is equal to the observed rate in period t:

$$E[r^*_{t+1}|I_t] = r_t. \qquad (5)$$

Substituting equations (4) and (5) into equation (2) yields

$$m_t = \alpha_1 + \alpha_2 y_t + \alpha_3 \varepsilon_t + \alpha_4 \Delta P_t + \alpha_5 r_t. \qquad (6)$$

In addition to the explanatory variables discussed above, three dummy variables will be included and investigated, based on the review of financial markets developments: one for 1974–75, covering the impact of the first oil shock; one for the 1989 period, when all deposits of the public enterprises were transferred to the Central Bank; and a variable representing financial market intermediation (the number of bank branches). The first two dummy variables represent sizable, though temporary, shocks to the financial system, while the third variable represents the broader expansion of financial services over the period.

Equation (6) assumes that actual money holdings adjust instantaneously and without cost to changes in money demand while, in reality, adjustments reflect a trade-off between the speed and cost of ad-

---

[36]See, for example, Laidler (1993) for a detailed discussion of money demand models.

[37]Interest rates were controlled and significantly negative in real terms over much of the period. Real interest rates were tested as a possible opportunity cost variable but were not found to have significant explanatory power. Future empirical work could investigate real curb rates as an alternative opportunity cost variable.

APPENDIX II

justment, as well as confusion as to whether a shift is permanent or transitory in nature. To embody this concept, and study the short-run impact of policy measures, a dynamic version of the model can be specified. While most recent studies of money demand in sub-Saharan Africa have utilized a standard partial adjustment mechanism to estimate the speed of adjustment, a more general error correction model is employed here. The error correction model fully utilizes the available information in the residual term of the long-run equilibrium model (equation (6)) to develop consistent short-run parameter estimates.

Econometric Methods and Results

Cointegration

A cointegration time series analysis is undertaken in this section to confirm the presence of a long-run equilibrium relationship between money and the explanatory variables. According to Granger and others, equation (6) represents a long-run equilibrium, and can be estimated using standard OLS estimation techniques, if a cointegrating relationship between the nonstationary (I(1)) variables exists.[38] In the absence of such a relationship Granger found that OLS estimation is inappropriate and could lead to spurious results, given the presence of nonstationary series. Further, first differencing the I(1) time series to achieve stationarity could lose important information. In practical terms, a long-run relationship can be confirmed if the residual term of the undifferenced I(1) process is stationary.

After confirming that equation (6) represents a cointegrating relationship, the second step is to develop an error correction model to study the short-run dynamics of the relationship:[39]

$$\Delta m_t = \beta_0 + \sum_{i=1}^{n}(\beta_{1i}\Delta y_{t-i} + \beta_{2i}\Delta^2 P_{t-i} + \beta_{3i}\Delta\varepsilon_{t-i} + \beta_{4i}\Delta r_{t-i})$$
$$+ \sum_{i=1}^{n}(\beta_{5i}\Delta m_{t-i}) + \beta_6 EC_{t-1}, \quad (7)$$

where a change in real money balances in period t is a function of the current and/or lagged changes in real income, expected inflation, exchange rate, expected domestic interest rates, and lagged real money balances. The appropriate lag structure of the equation will be analyzed, based on standard general-to-specific simplification search procedures. In addition, the lagged error correction term (EC) from equation (6) is included, and is calculated as

$$EC_t = m_t - \underline{m}_t, \quad (8)$$

where m_t is the actual value of real money in period t and $\underline{m}_t$ is the fitted value of m_t from equation (6).[40] This variable approximates deviations from long-run equilibrium real money balances and represents the short-run response necessary to move money demand toward its long-run equilibrium level. When the coefficient of the error correction term is significant and negative, convergence is assured. If β_6 is less than 1 in absolute value, the adjustment process is stable and m_t will adjust toward its long-run value. The closer β_6 is to 1, the faster the adjustment process.

Summary of Main Findings

The existence of a true long-run equilibrium relationship was tested for each of three definitions of money (broad money, narrow money, and currency) based on the Johansen cointegration test.[41] To do so, the stationarity of each of the time series was first analyzed, with the order of integration for each of the variables ascertained on the basis of appropriate unit root tests. The money, income, price, exchange rate, and nominal interest rate variables were found to be integrated of order 1, I(1), based on the augmented Dickey-Fuller (ADF) unit root test (constant, no trend) at the 5 percent confidence level.[42]

The Johansen maximum likelihood cointegration test was employed to confirm the presence of cointegrating vectors for each of the money demand equations. The Johansen test provides information on all possible cointegrating vectors in the multivariate model, an improvement over the Engle-Granger cointegration tests.[43] A review of the cointegrating vectors found a unique vector with the appropriate signs for each of the equations. In addition, the significance and the appropriate sign of the error correction term provides additional evidence/confirmation of the existence of cointegration among the various monetary aggregates and the explanatory variables.[44] The long-run money demand equations were then estimated, using standard ordinary least squares (OLS)

---

[39]See Engle and Granger (1987).
[38]That is, if a linear combination of the I(1) variables is stationary, or I(0).

[40]See Engle and Granger (1987 and 1991) for a detailed discussion of error correction models. See Lahiri (1991), Tseng and Corker (1991), and Tseng and Khor (1994) for recent examples of error correction cointegration models applied to money demand.
[41]See Johansen (1988 and 1991) for a detailed discussion of the Johansen test.
[42]The ADF test for the income variable excludes both a constant and trend term.
[43]See Appendix III and IV of Tseng and Khor (1994) and Reinhart (1995) for a detailed discussion of the mechanics of using the Johansen test.
[44]See Kremers and others (1992) on the superiority of this test over the conventional tests of cointegration. Harris (1995) also provides an excellent discusison of this. Kremers and others argue that htis test is more pwoerful than the ADF test, as it uses the inofrmation *scope* efficiently.

Appendix II

Table 17. Long-Run Real Money Demand

	Real Income Elasticity (y_t)	Real Exchange Rate Elasticity (ε_t)	Interest Rate Semi-elasticity (r_t)	Dummy1	Dummy2	Cointegration Test Status[1]
Currency (1970–94)	0.74* (0.14)[2]	–0.24* (0.05)	0.02* (0.00)	–0.22*** (0.11)	–0.25* (0.16)	Yes
Narrow money (1970–94)	1.05* (0.12)	–0.36* (0.04)	0.01** (0.00)	–0.22** (0.09)	–0.21 (0.13)	Yes
Broad money (1970–94)	1.01* (0.12)	–.038* (0.04)	0.01* (0.00)	–.025** (0.09)	–0.21** (0.13)	Yes

* Represents significance at 1 percent level.
** Represents significance at 5 percent level.
*** Represents significance at 10 percent level.
[1]Johansen's maximum likelihood unit root test and significance of error correction term in partial adjustment model, as described by Kremers and others (1992) and Banerjee and others (1993).
[2]Numbers in parentheses below coefficients represent the standard error.

estimation techniques on annual data for the period 1970–94, and performed well in terms of the expected signs on the coefficients of the explanatory variables and in terms of explanatory power.

Long-Run Equations

The estimated long-run elasticity of real money demand with respect to real income ranged from 0.7 for currency, to approximate unit elasticity for narrow and broad money (1.1 and 1.0, respectively, Table 17). The signs and magnitudes of the coefficients were in line with the a priori assumptions, although they do not support an assumption of a high degree of monetization over the period. The estimated income elasticities are significantly below those that were reported in a recent Central Bank of Nigeria (CBN) study,[45] although the CBN empirical results are based on a partial adjustment model and exclude the influence of the exchange rate.

The long-run elasticity of real broad money balances with respect to the real exchange rate was estimated in the range of –0.36 to –0.38 for narrow and broad money, confirming our assumption of the negative impact of an expected real devaluation on the demand for real naira balances. The elasticity was lower for currency, at –0.24, suggesting that the impact of an expected devaluation is more likely to affect portfolio balances demand than transactions demand. The inclusion of the exchange rate variable in the long-run model, an innovation in this study, is supported by its significant impact on the desire to hold real naira balances, and suggests that the increasing role of hard currency in the economy as a means of transactions and a store of wealth should not be excluded in the Nigerian context. The long-run nominal interest rate semi-elasticity of real money balances was estimated at 0.01 for narrow and broad money and somewhat higher, at 0.02, for currency. This result is consistent with one's intuition regarding the broader money definitions, with a nominal interest rate hike (under a largely fixed rate regime) increasing positive, or decreasing negative, real interest rates.

The inflationary expectations variable was not included in the estimated equations, as it was not found to provide significant additional information in the long run. The previously discussed two dummy variables, including the 1974–75 oil price shock and 1989 transfer of public enterprise deposits to the Central Bank, were found to be significant and were included in the final long-run specification, while the financial deepening variable, represented by the number of bank branches, was not significant and was dropped from the model.

Dynamic Model

The short-run error correction models performed well in terms of their explanatory power and statistical properties, with adjusted R^2 values of 0.70, 0.67, and 0.75 for currency, narrow money, and broad money, respectively (Table 18). The presence of serial correlation, as well as higher order autocorrelation, was rejected in each of the equations based on the

---
[45]See Oresotu and Mordi (1992). The CBN study estimated an income elasticity of 2.03 in the long run for real broad money based on a partial adjustment model.

APPENDIX II

Table 18. Short-Run Real Money Demand

	C	Real Income (Δy_t)	Real Exchange Rate ($\Delta \varepsilon_{t-2}$)	Nominal Interest Rate (Δr_t)	(Δr_{t-1})	(Δr_{t-2})	Inflation[1] ($\Delta^2 P_{t-1}$)	Lagged Dependent Variable (Δm_{t-1})	(Δm_{t-2})	Error Correction Term (EC_{t-1})
Currency (1972–94)	−0.13* (0.05)[2]	0.35* (0.12)	−0.38* (0.10)	0.12*** (0.01)	−0.05* (0.02)	0.05** (0.02)	0.19 (0.19)	0.49* (0.17)	0.34** (0.15)	−1.31** (0.26)
Period: 1973–94		Adj. R² = 0.70	S.E.R. = 0.08							
Narrow money (1972–94)	−0.04 (0.03)	0.75* (0.22)	−0.32* (0.11)	...	0.03*** (0.02)	...	0.50** (0.23)	0.38** (0.14)	...	−0.80** (0.31)
Period: 1972–94		Adj. R² = 0.67	S.E.R. = 0.11							
Broad money (1972–94)	−0.03 (0.03)	0.71* (0.16)	−0.33* (0.10)	...	0.02*** (0.01)	...	0.55* (0.20)	0.34* (0.12)	...	−0.91* (0.22)
Period: 1972–94		Adj. R² = 0.75	S.E.R. = 0.10							

* Represents significance at 1 percent level.
** Represents significance at 5 percent level.
*** Represents significance at 10 percent level.
[1] Inflation coefficient enters currency equation with no lag.
[2] Numbers in parentheses below coefficients represent the standard error.

Breusch-Godfrey and Ljung-Pierce Q-tests. The Jarque-Bera test confirmed normality and the ARCH test rejected heteroskedasticity in the disturbance terms. The RESET(1) and RESET(4) tests accepted the null hypothesis of no general misspecification in the models.

While the dynamic structure of the short-run models is complex, particularly with respect to currency, the results strongly support our a priori assumptions regarding the direction of the relationship between the right-hand-side variables and money demand, with the exception of inflation. When corrected to include the lagged impact of the dependent variable, the income coefficients in the short-run equations were not substantially different than in the long run. The real exchange rate and nominal interest rate variables were again found to be significant, with appropriate signs in the short-run model, while the inflation variable entered with the opposite sign than expected. The sum of the interest rate effect in the currency equation was positive, entering with a complicated lag structure. The positive impact of a change in inflation on real money demand may be explained by the increased transactions demand in the short run, as households increase commodity purchases in response to an increase in expected inflation. The significant impact of the error correction term in each of the models confirms that the short-run relationship adjusts toward its long-run equilibrium, adjusting quickly for narrow and broad money, while the coefficient for currency, which is greater than 1 in a absolute value, suggests that the short-run model may not be stable.

Stability

The long-run stability of the money demand functions was confirmed on the existence of a cointegrating relationship for each of the equations. The stability of the short-run money demand equations was tested on the basis of the Chow Forecast F-test and the results supported the assumption of stability. Three subperiods were selected on the basis of their potential for presenting a structural change in the economy, including the beginning of the debt crisis (1982); the introduction of the structural adjustment program (1986); and the end of the intensive phase of the adjustment effort (1990).

The stability of the models was also confirmed based on the recursive residuals test, which uses one-step-ahead forecast errors (recursive residuals) for increasingly large sample sizes. If the model is stable, the recursive residuals are expected to have a zero mean and constant variance. No residuals fall outside the band of two standard errors.

Policy Implications

The short-run forecasting models performed reasonably well in terms of explaining the changes in real money growth over the 1970–94 period, as shown in Figure 19. To review the policy implications of the

Appendix II

Figure 19. Actual and Fitted Money Demand
(First difference of the log value)

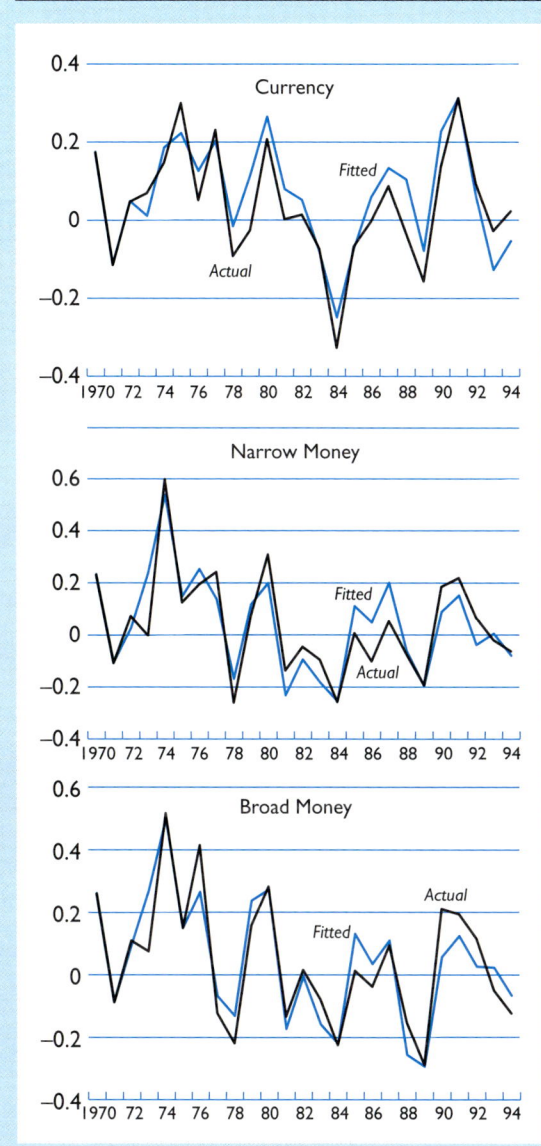

Figure 20. Dynamic Response of Broad Money

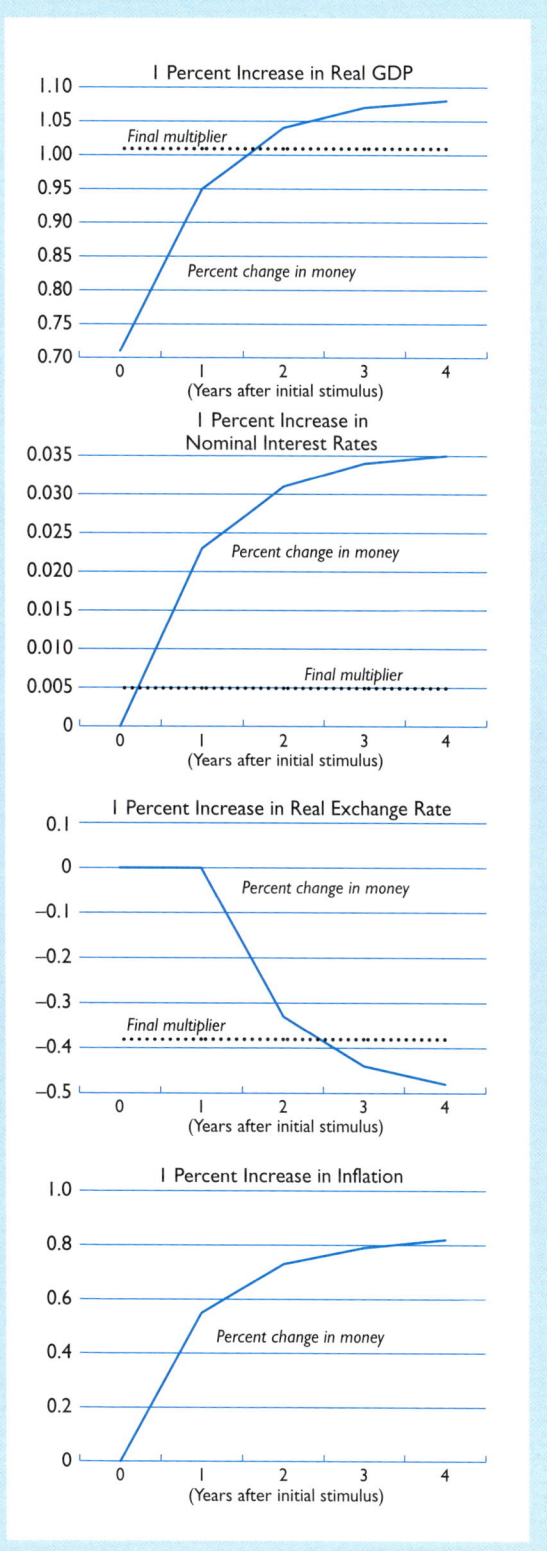

models, the impulse response of money demand to changes in the exogenous variables was analyzed. The impulse response functions for the narrow and broad money demand equations are provided in Figures 20 and 21. (The currency model was dropped from this analysis because of the complexity of the lag structure and the possibility of instability suggested by the error correction term.) One interesting result is that the cumulative impact of short-run models suggests that there is an over-shooting of long-run equilibrium in

APPENDIX II

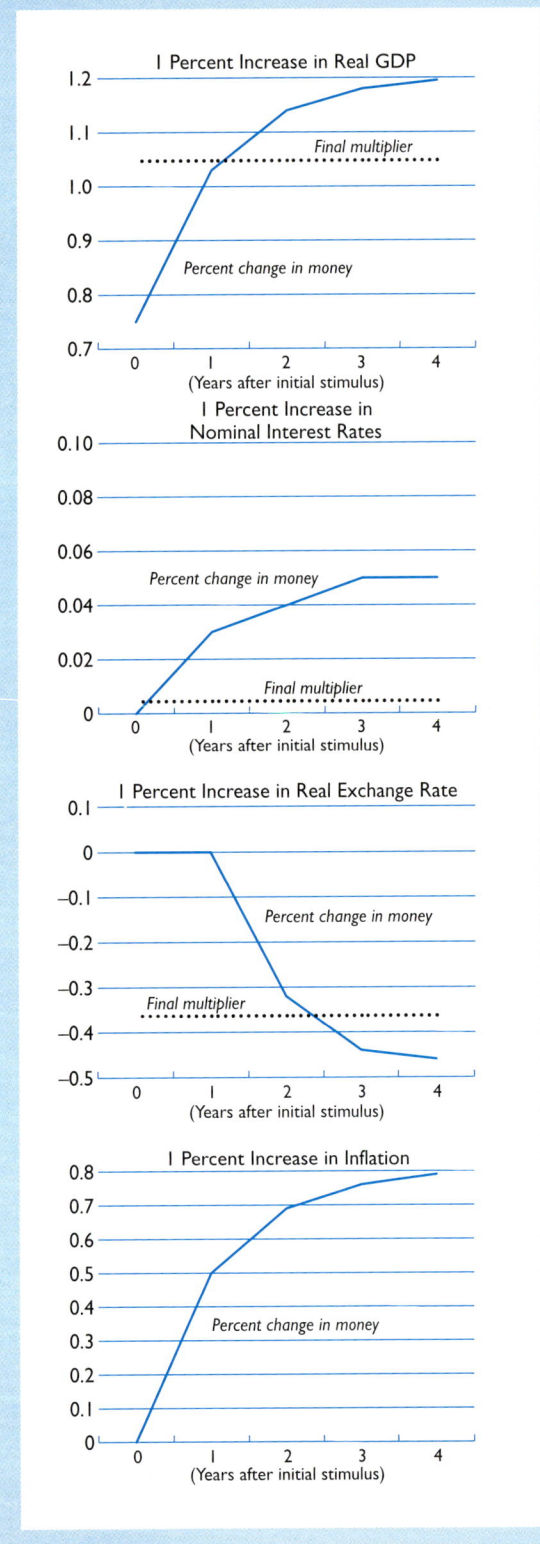

Figure 21. Dynamic Response of Narrow Money

most cases. This suggests that the return toward the long-run path, in fact, takes more time than indicated by the error correction term.

A 1 percent permanent increase in real income was found to increase real narrow money by 0.75 percent in the initial period, rising to 1.20 percent after the fourth period, and to increase real broad money by 0.71 percent in the initial period and 1.08 percent after the fourth period. Both the narrow and broad money impulse responses trend toward the long-run income multiplier after four periods.

The impact of a 1 percent increase in the real exchange rate on narrow and broad money is not felt until after the second year of stimulus, though the dynamic response converges toward the long-run multiplier fairly quickly. A 1 percent permanent increase in the real exchange rate leads to 0.32 percent and 0.33 percent decreases in real narrow and broad money, respectively, with money demand stabilizing above the long-run multiplier after the fourth period.

The impulse response function shows that the impact of a 1 percent increase in the rate of inflation leads to about a 0.5 percent increase in real narrow and broad money demand after two periods, increasing further before stabilizing after the fourth period. As discussed earlier, this unanticipated outcome may result from increased transactions demand in the short run.

In addition to confirming the central role of real income growth in money demand, the empirical results show importantly that, with a stable money demand function, the Nigerian authorities can effectively use monetary policy to pursue broader inflation objectives. More specifically, with additional work on the relationship between base money and broader monetary aggregates and the monthly seasonality of demand, the authorities can effectively use indirect monetary policy to target central bank balance sheet aggregates to meet broader monetary objectives.

Conclusions

The demand for real money balances in Nigeria has been shown to be a stable function in the long run of real income, the real exchange rate, and nominal domestic interest rates. The empirical results confirm the outcome of a number of previous studies of money demand in Nigeria, in terms of the sizable role of real income in money demand but also confirm the central role of the exchange rate in the demand for real naira balances. The income elasticity of demand for narrow and broad money was found not to be significantly different than unity, consistent with our expectations, although it was lower than that found in previous studies in Nigeria.

Appendix II

Table 19. Database
(In millions of naira unless otherwise specified)

	Gross Domestic Product	Consumer Price Index	Currency	Broad Money	Narrow Money	Nominal Interest Rate	Real Exchange Rate Index
1970	5,621	10.3	342.4	979.3	642.6	3.00	776.7
1971	7,098	11.9	354.5	1,041.9	670.1	3.00	668.2
1972	7,703	12.4	385.2	1,204.2	747.3	3.04	596.2
1973	11,199	13.0	435.9	1,370.1	788.1	3.00	565.6
1974	18,811	14.7	569.8	2,592.2	1,619.3	3.00	479.7
1975	21,779	19.7	1,030.8	4,035.1	2,463.0	3.00	350.8
1976	27,572	24.4	1,351.2	7,607.7	3,728.4	2.67	287.3
1977	32,747	27.8	1,940.8	7,675.3	5,420.1	2.83	259.6
1978	36,084	33.9	2,157.3	7,521.0	5,100.6	4.15	210.2
1979	43,151	37.8	2,350.8	9,848.8	6,146.7	4.47	178.6
1980	50,849	41.6	3,185.9	14,389.9	9,226.7	5.27	147.2
1981	50,749	50.3	3,861.9	15,238.9	9,744.7	5.72	136.9
1982	51,709	54.1	4,222.5	16,693.5	10,048.6	7.60	139.4
1983	57,142	66.7	4,842.8	19,034.2	11,282.5	7.41	121.6
1984	63,608	93.1	4,883.6	21,242.7	12,204.1	8.25	92.0
1985	72,355	100.0	4,909.9	23,153.0	13,227.4	9.12	100.0
1986	73,062	105.7	5,177.9	23,605.2	12,662.9	9.24	142.8
1987	108,885	117.7	6,298.6	28,895.4	14,906.1	13.09	381.6
1988	145,243	181.8	9,413.6	38,405.8	21,446.3	12.95	276.3
1989	224,797	273.5	12,124.4	43,370.9	26,664.1	14.68	301.4
1990	260,637	293.7	14,950.9	57,553.6	34,540.1	19.78	306.5
1991	324,011	331.9	23,120.6	79,067.3	48,707.6	14.92	333.1
1992	549,808	479.8	36,766.0	128,522.0	75,407.0	18.04	381.1
1993	697,095	754.1	56,261.0	192,459.0	116,391.0	23.24	327.7
1994	897,498	1,184.3	90,492.0	267,760.0	172,005.0	13.09	208.1

A short-run forecasting model was estimated for the period 1970–94, providing a reliable one-step-ahead forecast for money demand. The short-run error correction model confirmed the presence of a prolonged adjustment process in returning the system to equilibrium after a shock, particularly with regard to currency demand.

The analysis confirmed a stable money demand function over the short and long term, providing robust results for the development of more market-oriented indirect monetary programming in Nigeria. With an appropriate interest rate structure and the continued expansion of the financial sector, the monetary authorities should be able to use a wider range of monetary instruments under the auspices of open market operations to meet specific annual and quarterly targets for monetary aggregates.

Data Sources

The data are based on annual observations from *International Financial Statistics* (*IFS*) for the period 1970–94 and have been supplemented as necessary with IMF staff estimates (Table 19). Real income and real exchange rate variables are derived by deflating the nominal variables by the consumer price index. Broad money is defined as narrow money plus quasi money as shown in the *IFS*.

References

Banerjee, A., Dolado, J.J., Galbraith, J.W., and D.F. Hendry, 1993, "Co-integration, Error-Correction, and the Econometric Analysis of Non-Stationary Data," *Advanced Texts in Econometrics* (Oxford: Oxford University Press).

Dotsey, Michael, 1988, "The Demand for Currency in the United States," *Journal of Money, Credit, and Banking* (February).

Engle, Robert F., and C.W.J. Granger, 1987, "Co-integration and Error Correction: Representation, Estimation and Testing," *Econometrica*, Vol. 55 (March), pp. 51–76.

———, eds., 1991, *Long-Run Economic Relationships, Readings in Cointegration* (Oxford: New York: Oxford University Press).

Granger, C.W.J., 1986, "Developments in the Study of Cointegrated Economic Variables," *Oxford Bulletin of Economics and Statistics,* Vol. 48 (August), pp. 213–28.

―――, and Paul Newbold, 1986, *Forecasting Economic Time Series* (Orlando: Academic Press).

Harris, Richard I.D., 1995, *Using Cointegration Analysis in Econometric Modelling,* (Englewood Cliffs, New Jersey: Prentice Hall/Harvester Wheatsheaf).

Hendry, David F.. 1986, "Econometric Modelling with Cointegrated Variables: An Overview," *Oxford Bulletin of Economics and Statistics,* Vol. 48 (August), pp. 201–12.

Ikhide, Sylvanus I., 1993, "Financial Liberalization and the Inflationary Process: Is there a Link in Adjusting Developing Countries?," *Rivista Internazionale di Scienze Economiche è Commerciali* (February).

Johansen, Soren, 1988, "Statistical Analysis of Cointegration Vectors," *Journal of Economic Development and Control,* Vol. 12 (June–September), pp. 231–54.

―――, 1991, "Estimation and Hypothesis Testing of Cointegration Vectors in Gaussian Vector Autoregressive Models," *Econometrica,* Vol. 59 (November), pp. 551–80.

Kallon, Kelfala M., 1992, "An Econometric Analysis of Money Demand in Ghana," *The Journal of Developing Areas* (July).

Khan, Moshin S., and Malcolm D. Knight, 1991, "Stabilization Programs in Developing Countries: A Formal Framework," in *Macroeconomic Models for Adjustment in Developing Countries,* ed. by Mohsin S. Khan, Peter J. Montiel, and Nadeem U. Haque (Washington: International Monetary Fund).

Kremers, J.J.M., Ericsson, N.R. and J. Dolado, 1992, "The Power of co-integration Tests," *Oxford Bulletin of Economics and Statistics,* Vol. 54, pp. 325–48.

Lahiri, Ashok K., 1991, "Money and Inflation in Yugoslavia," *Staff Papers,* International Monetary Fund, Vol. 38 (December), pp. 751–88.

Laidler, David E.W.,1993, *The Demand for Money: Theories, Evidence and Problems* (New York: Harper Collins College Publishers).

Moser, Gary G., 1995, "The Main Determinants of Inflation in Nigeria," *Staff Papers,* International Monetary Fund, Vol. 42 (June), pp. 270–89.

Ojameruaye, E.O., 1988, "Analysis of the Determinants of the General Price Level in Nigeria," *Research for Development* (January).

Oresotu, F. O., and Charles N. O. Mordi, 1992, *The Demand for Money Function in Nigeria: An Empirical Investigation*, Central Bank of Nigeria Research Department Occasional Paper No. 3 (July).

Reinhart, Carmen M., 1995, "Devaluation, Relative Prices, and International Trade: Evidence from Developing Countries," *Staff Papers,* Vol. 42 (June), pp. 290–312.

Tseng, Wanda, and Robert Corker, 1991, *Financial Liberalization, Money Demand, and Monetary Policy in Asian Countries,* IMF Occasional Paper 84 (Washington: International Monetary Fund).

Tseng, Wanda, and Hoe Ee Khor, 1994, *Economic Reform in China: A New Phase,* IMF Occasional Paper 114 (Washington: International Monetary Fund).

World Bank, 1993, "Nigeria–Structural Adjustment Program: Policies, Implementation, and Impact." Report No. 12366-UNI (October).

Appendix III Nigeria's Non-Oil Exports: Determinants of Supply and Demand, 1970–90

Inutu Lukonga

The weakening of the world oil market in the early 1980s and Nigeria's ensuing payment difficulties rekindled the urgency for diversifying the country's export base. To promote non-oil exports, Nigeria introduced in 1986, as part of its structural adjustment program, a number of measures that included reform of the exchange rate system, elimination of export licensing, abolition of commodity marketing boards, and other export promotion initiatives.[46]

The overall success of the export promotion strategy depends, inter alia, on what factors constrain export growth and on the responsiveness of producers to changes in the exchange rate and relative prices. Accordingly, a better understanding is desirable of the determinants of past export performance and of the direction and magnitude of the relevant elasticities. This study, therefore, reviews the performance of Nigeria's non-oil exports and investigates the price responsiveness of export supply, using data for 1970–90.

This appendix is organized as follows. It first synopsizes Nigeria's export performance since 1970 and reviews the factors underlying Nigeria's dismal export performance. Then it delineates a methodological framework to quantify the determinants of Nigeria's exports and estimate supply elasticities. Its principal conclusions follow. Definitions of the data used in the estimation and the sources of these data are given in an annex.

Developments in Non-Oil Exports, 1970–90

Composition and Structure of Non-Oil Exports

Agricultural products dominate Nigeria's non-oil export trade, accounting for nearly 70 percent of the value of non-oil exports. (For the composition of Nigeria's trade, see Statistical Appendix, Tables 39–47.) Agro-manufactures and semi-manufactures have remained relatively insignificant, averaging 7.9 percent over the period under review. Miscellaneous and other manufactures, including tin metal, textiles, and fertilizer, account for the remainder. Small quantities of minerals, predominantly columbite, were exported during the 1970s, but exports of this mineral virtually disappeared in the 1980s (see Figure 22).

Of the agricultural products, cocoa beans are the single most important export commodity, representing more than half the total value of non-oil exports since 1975. Rubber and palm kernels have been of limited importance, with each accounting for less than 10 percent of the total value of agricultural exports. Coffee exports have been small and erratic. Other agricultural commodities, such as hides and skins, groundnuts, groundnut oil, palm oil, and timber, were of great importance in the early 1970s, but have greatly diminished in significance since then because of restrictions governing their export.[47] Since 1988, several agricultural products—including pineapples, cashew nuts, spices, fish, and shrimp—have been exported, albeit in small quantities.

Agro-manufactures consist mainly of processed cocoa products, including cocoa butter, powder, cake, and paste. Exports of groundnut cake diminished after 1976. Manufactured exports have been dominated by tin metal, while textiles and fertilizer have been exported only recently and account for a minute proportion.

The countries of the European Community absorb more than 70 percent of Nigeria's non-oil exports. Germany, the Netherlands, and the United Kingdom represent the country's major export markets. The share of the United States has been constant at about 10 percent and exports to Japan have remained below 3 percent. Despite efforts to stimulate inter-African trade through the creation of the 16-member Economic Community of West African States (ECOWAS) and other treaties, exports to African countries constitute only 3 percent of Nigeria's non-oil exports.

---

[46]For a detailed account of the incentives proffered, see Central Bank of Nigeria, *Annual Report and Statement of Accounts,* and *Export (Incentives and Miscellaneous Provisions) Decree 1986.*

[47]A chronological account of quantitative restrictions on exports is provided below.

APPENDIX III

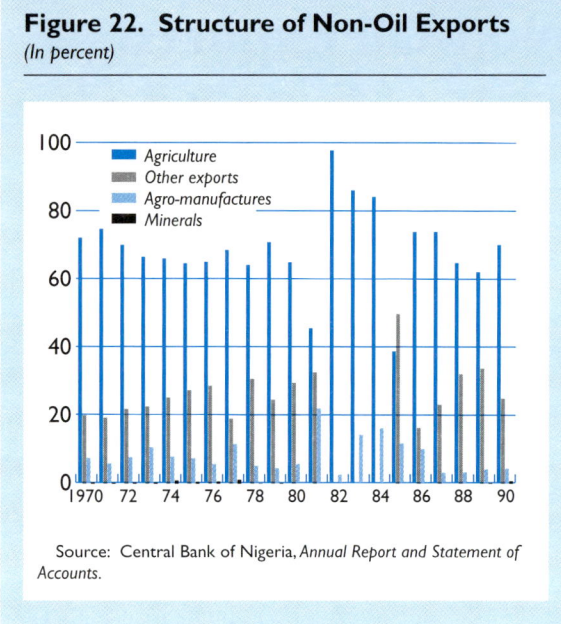

Figure 22. Structure of Non-Oil Exports
(In percent)

Source: Central Bank of Nigeria, *Annual Report and Statement of Accounts.*

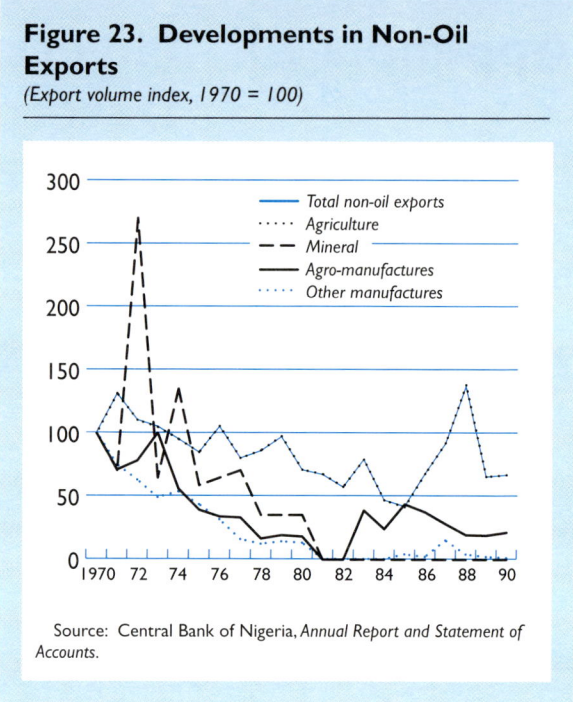

Figure 23. Developments in Non-Oil Exports
(Export volume index, 1970 = 100)

Source: Central Bank of Nigeria, *Annual Report and Statement of Accounts.*

Performance of Non-Oil Exports

Several indicators of performance show that non-oil exports fared poorly during 1970–90. The share of non-oil exports in total exports diminished from 40 percent in 1970 to less than 5 percent for much of the 1980s, while the contribution to GDP declined from 6.5 percent in 1970 to 0.4 percent by 1984, and only recovered somewhat thereafter, reaching 1.3 percent by 1990. In international markets, Nigeria lost market shares in all commodities, except palm kernels.

Although the diminishing importance of non-oil exports in the Nigerian economy was inevitable because of the colossal increase in oil exports, non-oil exports also declined in absolute terms, particularly during the 1980s. A composite volume index for non-oil exports shows that by 1980 exports were one third below the level obtained in 1970, and no major improvement was registered in the subsequent decade, except for the aberration in 1988, which was caused by the exceptional surge in cocoa exports (Figure 23). Virtually all commodities contributed, in varying magnitudes, to the decline. Cocoa exports showed a continual decline except in 1988, while palm kernels and rubber exports were virtually halved after 1978. Exports of cotton, hides and skins, timber, groundnuts, palm oil, and groundnut oil disappeared by the close of the 1970s. The value of non-oil exports exhibited a similar trend because world prices of most commodities were weak throughout most of the 1980s.

The decline in Nigeria's exports contrasts markedly with trends in world trade. It is also at variance with income growth in industrial countries during 1970–90. Comparative figures on export growth rates show that, with the exception of palm kernels, world trade of corresponding commodities grew, while Nigeria's exports declined (Table 20). Real GDP of industrial countries, Nigeria's major trading partners, also grew on average by 2.8 percent between 1970 and 1990.

Determinants of Past Export Performance

A dominant theme in studies that examined the erosion of Nigeria's agricultural and other non-oil exports is that unfavorable domestic terms of trade for exports, declining agricultural output, a loss in international competitiveness, and increasing domestic demand are the principal contributors to the dismal performance.[48] These developments, in large measure, reflect the interaction of the oil boom and inappropriate domestic policies.

The oil boom created disincentives for agricultural exports through its impact on relative product and factor prices, including the appreciation of the exchange rate, the enhanced profitability of investments in nontradable commodities and services, and rising wages in the public sector, which drained labor from rural areas and put an upward pressure on

---

[48]See for instance Olayide and Olatunbosun (1970), Ojo (1977), Scherr (1989), Okonkwo (1989), Oyejide (1986), and Nigeria's Ministry of Agriculture (1988).

Table 20. Comparative Growth Rates of Selected Commodities[1]

	Nigeria	World
Cocoa	−2.1	2.3
Palm kernels	−6.6	−8.8
Rubber	−0.5	1.8
Groundnuts	−40.2	0.2
Coffee	−9.1	1.6
Cotton	−15.9*	1.3
Hides and skins	−21.8	7.7
Palm oil	−14.6*	8.2
Groundnut oil	−16.9*	2.3

Sources: Central Bank of Nigeria, *Annual Report and Statement of Accounts*; and UNCTAD, *Commodity Year Book*.

[1]These growth rates were obtained using the semi-log growth model, and therefore reflect trends that are not unduly influenced by exceptional values. Asterisks indicate that the outcome was not statistically significant, either because there is no discernible trend or available observations were insufficient.

rural wages. Nigeria's real effective exchange rate appreciated by 63 percent between 1970 and 1980 and by a further 84 percent between 1980 and 1984.[49] Concurrently, labor costs increased at an annual rate of 20.7 percent during 1970–82, compared with an average annual increase of the consumer price index of 17.5 percent, indicating that wages rose in real terms.[50] The price-cost squeeze, resulting from a real effective appreciation of the naira and the rising unit labor costs, adversely affected the profitability and competitiveness of exports.[51]

Another corollary of the oil boom is the high level of effective demand that it induced, which grossly curtailed exportable output. The oil boom during the 1970s enabled Nigeria's real per capita GDP to increase at an annual average of 1.2 percent between 1973 and 1980, while the population grew at an average annual rate of 2.4 percent between 1970 and 1990. In the absence of changes in population characteristics, such increases in per capita income accelerate the average per capita growth in demand for domestically consumed crops beyond that prescribed by the population growth rate, particularly for crops with an income elasticity of more than 1.[52] Increases in incomes that are not matched by output increases lead to inflationary pressures that raise profit margins on domestic sales in relation to exports, and goods may be diverted to the home market, leading to a fall in export surpluses. The restrictive effect of increasing domestic demand on exports is pronounced in Nigeria's case, because most export commodities enter directly or indirectly into domestic consumption.

The overall growth in domestic demand and the increase that is attributable to the growth in per capita income are difficult to quantify in the absence of information on the size of the income elasticities of the commodities. However, to the extent that domestic demand, at a given period in time, is equivalent to domestic production and imports net of exports, developments in the magnitudes of these variables are indicative of the trends. Available data on exports and output show that, with few exceptions, domestic demand for consumption or industrial use exceeded output growth, resulting in a decline in the export-to-output ratio of most export commodities. In extreme cases, exports were completely eliminated, and imports were increased to supplement domestic output. For example, the expansion of Nigeria's textile industry in the early 1970s led to the elimination of cotton exports and the growth of cotton imports from US$25,700 in 1970 to US$45 million in 1984.[53] Similarly, increasing domestic demand for derivatives of oilseeds resulted in the elimination of groundnut and groundnut oil exports, a decline in the export-to-output ratio of palm kernels from 62 percent in 1970 to 10 percent by 1990, a colossal increase in imports of oilseeds, nuts, and kernels, and the increase in imports of complementary products, including soybean oil and other vegetable oils. Imports of oilseeds, nuts, and kernels increased from almost nothing in 1970 to US$26.7 million by 1984, while soybean oil and other vegetable oils increased from US$40,000 and US$204,000 in 1970 to US$26.2 million and US$75 million in 1984, respectively.[54]

The adverse impact of increasing domestic demand was amplified by the stagnation in agricultural

---

[49]During the 1970s, exchange rate policy in Nigeria aimed at maintaining a stable nominal exchange rate in order to moderate the impact of external inflation on the domestic economy. This policy stance was reinforced by the presumption that cheap imports were essential to political stability, and that the benefits of higher agricultural exports were modest (Scherr (1989)).

[50]No official data on rural wages are available. These estimates were computed by Duncan and Rouis (World Bank (1985), pp. 21–22).

[51]There is evidence that wages in Nigeria's oil palm subsector were well above average wages in other oil palm producing countries, including Brazil, Cameroon, Côte d'Ivoire, Ghana, Indonesia, and Malaysia. Assuming that these wages are representative of the agriculture sector in general, it is clear that Nigeria's agricultural exporters had a competitive disadvantage vis-à-vis their competitors. (See World Bank (1981); also quoted in World Bank (1982) Report No. 3771-UNI, p.12).

[52]The growth in demand for a commodity is expressed as $D = GZ + P$, where D = growth rate in demand, Z = income elasticity, G = GNP per capita growth rate, and P = population growth rate.

[53]Disaggregated trade statistics were available for the years 1970 to 1984 only.

[54]The import figures were obtained from *Nigeria Trade Summary*, an annual publication of the Federal Office of Statistics of Nigeria.

output. Although it is not possible to provide generally accepted figures that demonstrate the structure and performance of agriculture in a definitive way,[55] there is general consensus that the trend in the output of export commodities has been declining. Available data show that aggregate crop production increased at an annual rate of 3.5 percent between 1975 and 1990, and cash crops averaged 2.6 percent a year, but the principal export crops generally grew at a lower rate than the population.[56] Cocoa, the major export commodity, declined at an average rate of 2.3 percent whereas groundnuts declined by 0.96 percent a year. Production of rubber, palm oil, and palm kernels increased at respective annual rates of 0.18, 0.64, and 3 percent.

The sluggish performance of agriculture exports also reflects the cumulative effect of the Nigerian Government's agricultural policies, including the explicit taxation of agriculture exports in the early 1970s, unfavorable marketing and pricing of agricultural exports by marketing boards, the "exportable surplus" approach to trade enforced primarily by export bans, and the relative neglect of the sector in Nigeria's overall development planning, particularly during the 1970s. Government intervention in Nigeria's agricultural marketing and pricing system makes a distinction between export and food crops, even though a number of agricultural commodities belong to both categories. Between 1970 and 1975, agricultural exports were taxed at rates ranging between 15 percent and 30 percent for cocoa, palm kernels, groundnuts, and cotton, while the marketing and pricing of export crops were determined by marketing boards (until their abolishment in 1986). With the exception of palm kernels, domestic producer prices were far below their export parity prices for much of the 1970s, thus encouraging the smuggling of export commodities to neighboring countries.[57]

Restrictions on the export of selected commodities have been a recurrent phenomenon in the country's trade policy in a bid either to avoid domestic shortages or to promote local processing that would permit export of higher value-added items. The export of groundnuts, groundnut oil, palm oil, and timber was first banned in February 1976 to ensure an adequate supply for domestic use, while hides and skins were subsequently prohibited in April 1978 in order to promote the domestic tanning industry. In 1986, most bans were eliminated as part of the structural adjustment program, but were soon reintroduced. Commencing with the ban on the export of timber in 1988, the export of maize, rice, cassava, yams, beans and derivatives, and all imported foods was subsequently banned in 1989. Most recently, the list of prohibited exports was expanded to include raw hides and skins (in 1990) and unprocessed palm kernels (in 1991).[58]

Finally, nonprice factors also play an important role in the determination of Nigeria's export performance. Insufficient productive investment in agriculture, unreliable supply of inputs, poor or nonexistent extension services, inadequate infrastructure, lack of well-developed credit institutions, and the traditional system of land tenure have all contributed somewhat to the below-potential performance of the sector. The predominance of agricultural exports in the basket of non-oil exports also renders their export performance vulnerable to the vagaries of climate, while the long lags between acreage adjustment and output supply, characteristic of tree crops, delay the export response. The Sahelian drought adversely affected the overall performance of the agricultural sector in the early 1970s. For Nigeria, climatic conditions returned to more normal levels only after 1983. These problems have been compounded by the deteriorating age structure in existing stocks, and other crop-specific problems, including the black pod disease that affected cocoa.

Econometric Analysis of Export Performance

To assess the relative importance of the individual factors discussed above, econometric techniques are applied to quantify important economic variables that are presumed to affect the export behavior of Nigeria's nonpetroleum products. We begin by examining the main methodological issues in the specification of export supply functions, and we discuss the variables that ought, in theory, to be included and the choices and compromises that have to be made in

---

[55]Nigeria's official production figures for exportable crops relate to purchases of commodity boards, and may therefore be underestimated, because the share of crops that are domestically consumed is not known with a reasonable degree of certainty.

[56]Estimates of growth were computed using the log-linear model, and are based on the index of agricultural production reported by the Central Bank of Nigeria. Estimating the average growth by the compound method produced lower estimates of 2.05 for aggregate crops and 2.1 for cash crops.

[57]No reliable estimates of the volume of smuggling are available, but there is evidence of large-scale smuggling of cocoa and other manufacturing exports, particularly to neighboring countries, part of which serves as capital flight. In 1985, the Nigerian Cocoa Board estimated that more than 20,000 metric tons of cocoa were smuggled out of Nigeria yearly, fueled by delays in the payment of farmers by licensed buying agents. Efforts to curb the illicit trade flows by closing the country's land borders from mid-1984 to March 1986 only terminated official trade with Nigeria's neighbors, while falling short of its objective.

[58]The ban on the export of cocoa beans announced in January 1991 was rescinded only because of opposition from domestic producers and exporters who pointed out that domestic processing capacity fell short of bean production.

the measurement of the variables. We then derive a model that specifies both demand and supply side determinants of exports, measures the responsiveness of export volumes to these determinants, and distinguishes the long-term developments from short-term fluctuations.

Methodological Issues

There is general consensus on the empirical forms of the demand and supply function of exports,[59] even though the theoretical modeling of export supply still raises controversial issues, particularly in connection with the transparency of its microeconomic foundations.[60] The standard approach for specifying and estimating foreign trade equations is the imperfect substitutes model, in which the key assumption is that exports are not perfect substitutes for domestic goods. In this model, export demand is hypothesized to vary positively with world economic activity, and inversely with the export prices of the exporting country relative to the prices of foreign substitutes, while the export supply function is specified to depend positively on the price of exports, negatively on input prices, and positively on productive capacity.[61]

Demand and supply side determinants are estimated simultaneously, because the relationship between quantities and prices is, at least in theory, simultaneous. Nonetheless, most empirical studies estimate export demand functions by single equation methods, on the premise that, for an individual country, supply price elasticities for exports are infinite. Similarly, export supply functions are estimated independent of export demand functions, on the assumption that a typical developing country is a small supplier, facing an infinitely elastic foreign demand for the product it produces, and for which changes in foreign demand influence exports only through changes in world prices.

Although export supply is affected by forces that influence both domestic supply of and demand for the exported good, many of the studies naturally focus on domestic supply responses, because there is little or no domestic demand for many export commodities, particularly primary products, or it is assumed that in a perfectly competitive market economy, the diverse factors affecting supply and demand are fully captured in the price (see discussions in Bond (1985) and Riedel and others (1984)). There is, however, theoretical and empirical support for including domestic demand in an export supply equation, in spite of the uncertainty regarding the precise relationship between domestic demand and exports. The traditional argument is that an increase in domestic demand reduces the supply of export goods to the extent that it creates strong competition for resources that would have been devoted to export, while the alternate view posits that domestic demand reduces the average cost per unit and induces technological progress, making it easier for exporters to compete with foreign producers.[62] Empirical studies that explicitly incorporated domestic demand also found it to be a significant explanatory variable of export supply.[63]

Equilibrium Model

In an economy where governmental intervention is pervasive, the diverse factors affecting supply and demand cannot be adequately captured by relative price changes. In Nigeria's circumstances, the predominance of administrative controls in resource allocation and the treatment of exports as a residual activity indicate that the state of domestic demand could exert a negative and far more powerful influence on export performance than marginal fluctuations in relative prices at home and abroad, particularly because export commodities enter directly or indirectly into domestic consumption. Similarly, the shift in the direction of economic policy since 1986 has potential to foster greater export consciousness and thus increase the export growth rate.

The supply of Nigeria's exports is therefore assumed to depend positively on the price of exports, negatively on input prices, and positively on productive capacity. In addition, an increase in domestic demand is posited to curtail exportable surplus, while

---

[59]Surveys of econometric work, on foreign trade price elasticities and their weaknesses, are available in Leamer and Stern (1970), Magee (1975), and Goldstein and Khan (1985).

[60]The prominent controversial issues are outlined in Riveros (1989) and Faini (1988) and include the use of either partial or general equilibrium models, the definition of the prevailing market structure, the assumed degree of substitution between domestically consumed and exported goods, the treatment given to factor costs, and the role taken with regard to relative prices and productive capacity vis-à-vis more "Keynesian" variables such as domestic absorption.

[61]Satisfactory results have been obtained in many studies that applied the model in its basic form, to both developed and developing countries, and for agricultural and manufactured exports. See for instance Goldstein and Khan (1978), Lundborg (1981), Arize (1988), Balassa (1987, 1989), Okonkwo (1989), Lord (1989), and N'geno (1991).

[62]The competing views on the impact of domestic demand on exports are discussed in Artus (1970) and Dunlevy (1980).

[63]See for instance the country study Spain by Donges (1972). The study by Islam and Subramanian (1989) is one of the few studies that estimated an export supply function for agricultural exports and incorporated domestic demand among the explanatory variables. The variable was, however, not found to be statistically significant even though it yielded the expected sign.

APPENDIX III

export promotion policies are expected to cause a shift in the supply function.

The relationship is presented in log-linear form as follows:

$$\log X_t = \beta_0 + \beta_1 \log(P_x/P_d) +$$
$$\beta_2 \log Y^*_t + \beta_3 \log Dd_t + \beta_4 Dum, \quad (1)$$

where
- X_t = quantity of exports supplied
- P_x = price of exports
- P_d = domestic price index
- Y^*_t = an index of domestic capacity
- Dd_t = domestic demand
- Dum = 0 for years prior to policy change, 1 for years after policy change.

The supply function is specified independently of an export demand function, on the premise that Nigeria is a price taker in world markets and that primary commodities, which constitute a large proportion of Nigeria's exports, are generally homogeneous in quality and are sold in perfectly competitive markets.[64]

The relative price variable incorporates the theory that the supply of exports will increase with the profitability of producing and selling exports.[65] The use of the domestic price as divisor to the export price serves a dual role. First, for a given level of export price, the profitability of producing exports falls when factor costs in the export industries increase, and since these factor costs are likely to move with the general level of domestic prices, domestic prices serve as a proxy. Second, to the extent that resources involved in exportable production can be transferred to other uses, the relative profitability of selling exports falls with an increase in domestic prices. Finally, besides capturing production substitution elasticities between exports and nontradables, use of a relative price avoids problems of multicollinearity, because the two prices tend to move together.

The capacity variable embodies the hypothesis that exports will rise, ceteris paribus, where there is an increase in the country's capacity to produce and thus captures shifts in the supply function associated with productivity gains or technological changes. The dummy is designed to capture shifts in the intercept or slope of the function induced by policy changes, which are distinct from movements along the function that are captured by the relative price variable. The domestic demand variable accommodates the "exportable surplus" approach to exports.

Equation (1) is presented in log-linear form because the relationship is assumed to be nonlinear, and, as such, the coefficients deriving thereof represent elasticities. Therefore, β_1 and β_2 are "price" and "capacity" elasticities, respectively, and are expected to be positive. β_3, the elasticity of exports with respect to changes in domestic demand, is posited to assume a negative sign, while β_4 is expected to be positive.

Finally, the relationships specified above reflect a static equilibrium framework, according to which changes in the explanatory variables affect the dependent trade variable within the same period. To incorporate lags in the adjustment of actual to equilibrium values, a short-run model, herein referred to as a disequilibrium model, is formulated below.

Disequilibrium Model

The long gestation period of tree crops suggests that exports may respond to changes in the explanatory variables with a lag.[66] Therefore, in the short-run model, we assume the supply of exports adjusts partially to the difference between desired exports in period t and the actual supply of exports in period $t-1$.[67] Thus

$$\Delta \log X_t = \gamma[\log X^*_t - \log X_{t-1}], \quad (2)$$

where γ, the coefficient of adjustment, is $0 < \gamma \leq 1$ and Δ is a first difference operator. Since, desired supply is not observed, but the determinants of export supply are known, we substitute equation (1) into equation (2), and derive the estimating equation as follows:

$$\log X_t = c_0 + c_1 \log(P_x/P_d) + c_2 \log Y^*_t + c_3 \log Dd_t$$
$$+ c_4 Dum + c_5 \log X_{t-1}, \quad (3)$$

where $c_0 = \gamma\beta_0$, $c_1 = \gamma\beta_1$, $c_2 = \gamma\beta_2$, $c_3 = \gamma\beta_3$, $c_4 = \gamma\beta_4$, and $c_5 = 1 - \gamma$.

The γ denotes the speed of adjustment of actual exports to the desired quantity that occurs in a year. The mean time lag for a complete adjustment is therefore equal to γ^{-1}, and can be calculated from the parameters of equation (3) as $(1 - c_5)^{-1}$.

---

[64]The procedure adopted is fairly standard, see Stern and Zupnick (1962), Basevi (1973), Isard (1977). Besides, attempts to estimate the supply and demand functions simultaneously yielded poor results, particularly for export demand.

[65]A detailed discussion on the rationale for including particular variables in the export supply function is available in Goldstein and Khan (1985).

[66]For a detailed discussion of the sources and types of lags in adjustment see for instance Junz and Rhomberg (1973), Goldstein and Khan (1985), Moran (1988).

[67]The adjustment mechanism adopted has been used in other similar studies, including Goldstein and Khan (1978), Okonkwo (1989), N'geno (1991).

Appendix III

Table 21. Equilibrium Model, Export Supply Elasticities for Selected Export Crops

	Constant	Log $(P_x/P_d)_{t-1}$	LogY^e	LogDd	$Dum1$	R^2	SE	DW
Cocoa	13.75	0.56	−2.02	−0.43	0.27	0.76	0.21	2.1
	(3.87)[1]	(4.51)	(−2.67)	(−4.03)	(3.28)			
Palm kernel	3.37	−0.09	1.21	−0.83	0.14	0.48	0.48	1.66
	(0.39)	(−0.26)	(0.65)	(−2.44)	(0.59)			
Rubber	4.4	1.02	−0.68	−0.28	0.34	0.9	0.26	2.2
	(1.02)	(7.11)	(−0.74)	(−2.22)	(3.75)			
Expected sign		+	+	−	+			

[1] t-values are in parentheses.

Empirical Results

The determinants of Nigeria's export performance were estimated for three commodities only: cocoa, palm kernels, and rubber. This is because aggregate relationships covering all commodities could produce misleading results, in view of the restrictions governing export trade of most commodities during the estimation period.[68] In addition, aggregate relationships conceal intercommodity variations in sensitivity to price and income.

OLS estimation procedures were used to obtain the estimates. Where there was evidence of autocorrelation, the Maximum Likelihood iterative technique and Cochrane Orcutt iterative technique were used to correct for autocorrelation in the equilibrium and disequilibrium models, respectively.

Equilibrium Model

The model generally performs well in explaining the variation in export performance, yielding parameter estimates that are both of the expected sign and statistically significant, particularly for cocoa and rubber. The preferred equation includes a relative price variable lagged by one year (Table 21).[69]

Cocoa and rubber yielded statistically significant price elasticities with the expected positive sign, indicating that the two commodities respond positively, albeit with a lag, to changes in relative prices. The coefficient for palm kernels, on the other hand, appeared insignificant with a wrong sign. The price elasticity marginally exceeds unity for rubber, but yielded coefficients below unity for both cocoa and palm kernels. Such a finding implies a fairly limited response of exports to changes in relative prices. Unfortunately, no estimates of export supply elasticities were found in the literature that could be compared to the estimates obtained here to draw inferences on their precise size.[70]

The dummy yielded statistically significant coefficients with the expected positive sign in the cocoa and rubber equations, denoting a change in intercept and slope since 1986. Estimates of palm kernel exports carried the expected positive sign, but appeared statistically insignificant. These results provide prima facie evidence that the export promotion policies introduced as part of the structural adjustment program increased the export growth rate and support the view that domestic market conditions strongly influence export behavior.

The weak relationship between the tonnage of palm kernel exports and the price incentives, indicated by the low coefficients for both relative prices and the dummy, is not surprising. Palm kernels and palm oil are joint products derived from the same fruit—"palm fruits." The former is primarily produced for export while the latter is wholly consumed domestically. In a subsistence economy based on the

---

[68] The export of groundnuts, cotton, hides and skins, timber, and palm oil has been prohibited for several years and available data do not provide sufficient observations to permit some econometric analysis.

[69] Lagging the relative price variable allows for the possibility of delayed supply adjustment beyond the period of one year. This form of specification was also adopted by Bond (1987) and yielded equally good results.

[70] In Arize's (1989) study, export demand and supply functions were estimated for Nigeria's aggregate exports. However, to the extent that oil exports account for over 90 percent of total exports, the results are technically incomparable and are of limited use for our purposes. Similarly, although N'geno (1991) estimated export supply equations for Kenya's agricultural exports and for the individual commodities, coffee and tea, the results were of equal limited importance for our purposes because of the difference in the composition of the commodities and also because the commodity markets are constrained by the quota system.

APPENDIX III

Table 22. Disequilibrium Model, Export Supply Elasticities for Selected Export Crops

	Constant	Log $(Px/Pd)_{t-1}$	LogY^*	LogDd	LogX_{t-1}	Dum1	R^2	SE	Rho
Cocoa	13.79	0.49	−2.20	−0.41	0.28	0.29	0.7	0.20	−0.57
	(3.77)[1]	(3.69)	(−2.92)	(−3.77)	(1.45)	(3.53)			
Palm kernel	1.00	−0.07	1.01	−0.53	0.38	0.11	0.33	0.50	0.07
	(0.10)	(−0.18)	(0.44)	(−1.05)	(0.66)	(0.47)			
Rubber	5.09	0.97	−0.81	−0.31	0.07	0.36	0.87	0.28	−0.45
	(1.06)	(3.63)	(−0.81)	(−2.07)	(0.30)	(3.48)			
Expected sign		+	+	−	+	+			

[1] t-values are in parentheses.

products of a single species of a tree, which are both consumed locally and also exported, inducement to produce and export may be influenced by factors that bear little relationship to the export price.

The coefficient with respect to productive capacity indicates the degree of export bias associated with agricultural expansion, and our estimates lead to the conclusion that Nigerian agriculture is primarily oriented toward the domestic market. Cocoa yielded statistically significant coefficients carrying a wrong sign, while the capacity elasticity for rubber appeared insignificant with an incorrect sign. Estimates for palm kernels yielded the correct sign but appeared statistically insignificant. These results denote a weak relationship between agricultural output and export trends.

Domestic demand appears as a central explanatory variable, yielding statistically significant coefficients that carry the expected negative sign for all three commodities. This result confirms the earlier assertion that domestic demand posed a major impediment to export during the estimation period and is also consistent with the direction and size of the capacity elasticities obtained in the model, which indicate that Nigerian agriculture is primarily oriented toward domestic consumption. The outcome may be attributed to the Government's interventionist and restrictive policies that accord priority to satisfying domestic consumption and local processing in order to promote the export of value-added items.

Disequilibrium Model

The disequilibrium model captures the short-run response of exports to the explanatory variables. Overall, the results obtained resemble the long-run responses, in terms of direction, but the coefficients are generally lower in magnitude (Table 22).

Cocoa and rubber exhibit a positive response to relative price changes even in the short term, whereas the size of the elasticities were uniformly lower than those obtained in the long-run model. Similarly, the coefficient with respect to the dummy appears with a correct sign in all equations and is statistically significant for cocoa and rubber. The negative effect of domestic demand on exports continues to feature prominently, yielding the expected negative sign for all commodities and appearing statistically significant in the equations for cocoa and rubber.

The equations perform relatively poorly with regard to the estimated elasticity to lagged exports, yielding coefficients with the expected sign, but none of them were statistically significant. The average lag computed from them shows that the adjustment of export supply to changes in the explanatory variables, on average, occurs in less than two years (Table 23).

Implications of Results

The empirical results generally support the view that domestic market conditions strongly influenced export behavior. Nigeria's supply of commodity exports is sensitive to relative price changes, even though the magnitude of response is fairly low, while export promotion measures generally accelerate the export growth rate. Commodity exports show greater sensitivity to prices in the long run than in the short run. These results provide evidence of, and support for, the usefulness of pricing policy in eliciting export supply, particularly for cocoa and rubber.

The restrictive policies of the Government adversely affected the export performance of agricultural products. The Government's unrelenting dedication to self-sufficiency amplifies the restrictive

Table 23. Average Time Lags
(In years)

Commodity	Time Lag
Cocoa	1.38
Palm kernels	1.61
Rubber	1.07

effect of domestic demand, while the requirement to export only processed or manufactured products, for which a comparative advantage may not have been established, negates the translation of output increases into corresponding export growth and limits the positive effect of growth promoting policies on export performance.

The lag in the response of exports to changes in relative prices, estimated to average one year, is relatively short considering the long gestation period of the export crops in our sample. The short-term response indicated by these results may therefore be attributed to improvements in yield, or the redirection of unrecorded exports into official channels, rather than an expansion of capacity arising from new plantings.

To a lesser extent, the results also reflect basic data inadequacies, such as large unrecorded exports. There is considerable disagreement among the different data sources about the actual amounts and growth rates of agricultural crops produced in Nigeria. Data problems in Nigeria's agricultural sector can be explained by the nature of the sector, which is dominated by smallholders, shifting cultivation, fragmented farm holdings, and an enormous variety of intercropping systems, all of which combine to make record keeping difficult. The problems are compounded by severe weaknesses in the capacity of institutions charged with monitoring performance of the sector.

Annex I Data Definitions and Sources

The Sample

Data for the study consist of 21 observations pertaining to the years 1970–90. Annual observations are used because of the lack of monthly or quarterly series.

The Dependent Variable (X_s)

The dependent variable is represented by actual export volumes of the respective commodity exports, obtained from various editions of the Central Bank of Nigeria's *Annual Report*.

Relative Prices (P_x/P_d)

The choice of an export price is complicated in Nigeria's case, because until 1986 producers of export crops received the administratively determined "producer price," which diverged from the export price. Arguably, however, to the extent that producer prices accrue to agricultural producers, while the export price accrues to the exporters, the two prices constitute incentives to produce and export, respectively, and therefore export prices are the appropriate prices in modeling export supply.

In this study, like in previous studies, the numerator (P_x) represents world export prices of the respective commodities converted into domestic prices by the average exchange rate. Domestic costs are proxied by the CPI. Data on export prices were obtained from the Commodity Division of the International Monetary Fund, while the average exchange rate and the CPI were extracted from the *International Financial Statistics*.

Productive Capacity (Y^*)

The ideal construct, for our purposes, would be the index of agricultural production. This series was, however, only available commencing in 1975 and therefore provided insufficient observation for regression analysis. As an alternative, domestic capacity is proxied by the value of agriculture in real GDP, at constant prices. Data were obtained from the World Bank's World Tables.

Domestic Demand Pressure (D_d)

The index of manufacturing has been used as a proxy for domestic demand on the grounds that Nigeria's export commodities are not consumed directly but are intermediate inputs in the manufacture of consumption goods. Data for this series were obtained from the *Annual Report and Statement of Accounts* of the Central Bank of Nigeria.

References

Anwar, S., 1985, "Export Functions for Pakistan: A Simultaneous Equations Approach," *Pakistan Journal of Applied Economics,* Vol. 4, No. 1, pp. 29–34.

Arize, A., 1988, "Modelling Export Prices and Quantities in Selected Developing Economies," *Atlantic Economic Journal,* Vol. 16, No. 1 (March), pp. 19–34.

———, 1989, "The Demand and Supply for Exports in Nigeria in a Simultaneous Model," *The Indian*

Economic Journal, Vol. 35, No. 4 (April–June), pp. 33–43.

Artus, J.R., 1970, "The Short-Run Effects of Domestic Demand Pressure on British Export Performance," *Staff Papers,* International Monetary Fund, Vol. 17, pp. 247–75.

Balassa, B., 1989, Economic Incentives and Agricultural Exports in Developing Countries," in *The Balance between Industry and Agriculture in Economic Development,* ed. by N. Islam, Proceedings of the Eighth World Congress of the International Economic Association, Delhi, India (London: Macmillan).

———, 1987, "Effects of Exchange Rate Changes in Developing Countries," *Indian Journal of Economics,* Vol. 68, No. 269, pp. 203–22.

Basevi, G., 1973, "Commodity Trade Equations in Project Link," *The International Linkage of National Economic Models,* ed. by R. Ball (Amsterdam: North-Holland).

Bienen, H., 1983, "Oil Revenues and Policy Choice in Nigeria," World Bank Working Paper No. 592 (Washington: World Bank).

Bond, M., 1987, "An Econometric Study of Primary Commodity Exports from Developing Country Regions to the World," *Staff Papers,* International Monetary Fund, Vol. 34, No. 2 (June), pp. 191–227.

———, 1985, "Export Demand and Supply for Groups of Non-Oil Developing Countries." *Staff Papers,* International Monetary Fund, Vol. 32, No. 1 (March), pp. 56–77.

Donges, J.B., 1972, "Spain's Industrial Exports: An Analysis of Supply and Demand," *Weltwirtschaftliches Archiv,* Band 108, Heft 2, pp. 190–233.

——— and J. Riedel, 1977, "The Expansion of Manufactured Exports in Developing Countries: An Empirical Assessment of Supply and Demand Issues," *Weltwirtschaftliches Archiv,* Band 113, Heft 1, pp. 59–87.

Dunlevy, J.A., 1980, "A Test of the Capacity Pressure Hypothesis Within a Simultaneous Equations Model of Export Performance," *The Review of Economics and Statistics,* Vol. 62, No.1, pp. 130–135.

Eicher, C.K., and D.C. Baker, 1982, "Research on Agricultural Development in Sub-Saharan Africa—A Critical Survey," International Development Paper No.1.

Faini, R., 1988, "Export Supply, Capacity, and Relative Prices," World Bank Working Paper No. 123 (Washington: World Bank).

Goldstein, M., and M. Khan, 1978, "The Supply and Demand for Exports: A Simultaneous Approach," *Review of Economics and Statistics,* Vol. 60, No. 2), pp. 275–85.

———, 1985, "Income and Price Effects in Foreign Trade," in *Handbook of International Economics,* ed. by R.W. Jones and P.B. Kenen (Amsterdam: North-Holland).

Haynes, S., and J. Stone, 1983, "Specification of Supply Behavior in International Trade," *Review of Economics and Statistics,* Vol. 65, No. 4, pp. 626–31.

Houthakker, H.S., and D.L. Taylor, 1970, *Consumer Demand in the United States* (Cambridge, Massachusetts: Harvard University Press).

Isard, P., 1977, "How Far Can We Push the Law of One Price?" *American Economic Review,* Vol. 67, No. 5, pp. 942–48.

Islam, N., and A. Subramanian, 1989, "Agricultural Exports of Developing Countries: Estimates of Income and Price Elasticities of Demand and Supply," *Journal of Agricultural Economics,* Vol. 40, No. 2 (May), pp. 221–31.

Junz, H.B., and R. Rhomberg, 1973, "Price Competitiveness in Export Trade and Industrial Countries," *American Economic Review,* Vol. 63, pp. 412–18.

Khan, M.S., and K.Z. Ross, 1977, "The Functional Form of the Aggregate Import Equation," *Journal of International Economics,* Vol. 7, No. 2, pp.149–60.

Leamer, E.E., and R.M. Stern, 1970, *Quantitative International Economics* (Boston: Allyn and Bacon).

Lord, M.J., 1989, "Primary Commodities as an Engine for Export Growth of Latin America," in *The Balance Between Industry and Agriculture in Economic Development,* ed. by N. Islam, Proceedings of the Eighth World Congress of the International Economic Association, Delhi, India (London: Macmillan).

Lundborg, P., 1981, "The Elasticities of Supply and Demand for Swedish Exports in a Simultaneous Model," *Scandinavian Journal of Economics,* Vol. 83, No. 3, pp. 444–48.

Magee, S.P., 1975, "Prices, Income and Foreign Trade: A Survey of Recent Economic Studies," in *International Trade and Finance,* ed. by P. B. Kenen, (Cambridge: Cambridge University Press).

Moran, C., 1988, "A Structural Model for Developing Countries Manufactured Exports," *The World Bank Economic Review,* No. 3, pp. 321–40.

Nigeria, Federal Ministry of Agriculture, 1988, "Agriculture Policy for Nigeria," (February).

N'geno, K.N., 1991, "Kenya's Export Performance," in *Trade and Development in Sub-Saharan Africa,* ed. by Frimpong-Ansa, Kanbur, and Svedberg, Center for Economic Policy Research (Manchester: Manchester University Press).

Ojo, F., 1977, "Nigeria's Export Performance: Trends, Problems and Prospects," *Pakistan Economic and Social Review,* Vol. 15, No. 3–4 (Autumn–Winter), pp. 174–88.

Okonkwo, I.C., 1989, "The Erosion of Agricultural Exports in an Oil Economy: The Case of Nigeria," *Journal of Agricultural Economics,* Vol. 40, No. 3, pp. 375–84.

Olayide, S.O., and N. Olatunbosun, 1970, "An Econometric Analysis of Nigeria's Export Demand," *Indian Journal of Agricultural Economics,* Vol. 40, No. 3 (January-March), pp. 59–73.

Oyejide, A., 1986, "The Effects of Trade and Exchange Rate Policies on Agricultural in Nigeria," *International Food Policy Research Institute.*

Riedel, J., C. Hall, and R. Grawe, 1984, "Determinants of Indian Export Performance in the 1970s," *Weltwirtschaftliches Archiv,* Band 120, Heft 1, pp. 41–63.

Riveros., L.A., 1988, "The Impact of Labour Costs on Manufactured Exports in Developing Countries: An Econometric Analysis." World Bank Working Paper No. 123 (Washington: World Bank).

Scherr, S.J., 1989, "Agriculture in an Export Boom Economy: A Comparative Analysis of Policy and Performance in Indonesia, Mexico and Nigeria," *World Development,* Vol. 17, No. 4, pp. 543–60.

Stern, R.M., and E. Zupnick, 1962, "The Theory and Measurement of Elasticity of Substitution in International Trade," *Kyklos,* Vol. 15, No. 3, pp. 580–93.

Teal, F., 1983, "The Supply of Agricultural Output in Nigeria, 1950–74," *Journal of Development Studies,* Vol. 19, No. 2, pp. 191–206.

World Bank, 1981, "Oil Palm—Subsector Review," World Bank, Washington, D.C. (July).

_____, 1982, "Nigeria: Non-Oil Export Prospects." Report No. 3771-UNI (June).

_____, 1985, "Nigeria: Agricultural Pricing Policy." Report No. 4945-UNI (June).

Yang, Y. Y., 1978, "Estimation of the Manufacture Export Supply Function From Developing Countries," *Weltwirtschaftliches Archiv,* Band 114, Heft 3, pp. 515–25.

Appendix IV Oil Smuggling, Fiscal Policy, and Macroeconomic Imbalances

Scott Rogers

The subsidization of gasoline for domestic use in Nigeria has a direct impact on the Nigerian fiscal balance and on the smuggling of gasoline from Nigeria to other countries in the region. In addition, Nigeria's fiscal policy may itself affect the smuggling of gasoline through its impact on the parallel exchange rate. As many countries in the region depend on domestic gasoline taxes as a source of revenue, the smuggling of gasoline erodes their tax base and consequently worsens their fiscal balances. Thus, Nigeria's fiscal policies have a regional impact.

This appendix analyzes the connections between Nigeria's fiscal and domestic gasoline pricing policies and gasoline smuggling. It demonstrates that an increase in Nigeria's fiscal deficit boosts the incentives for smuggling by causing the parallel exchange rate to depreciate and that an increase in the domestic retail price of gasoline would simultaneously improve the fiscal balance and reduce the incentives for smuggling. The domestic gasoline pricing policy directly affects smuggling by altering the differential between retail gasoline prices in the rest of the region and at home. It also indirectly affects smuggling through its impact on the fiscal deficit. By administratively setting the domestic price of gasoline well below import parity, revenues are forgone that could reduce the fiscal deficit significantly. A reduction in the fiscal deficit would reduce the Government's recourse to domestic bank financing, which has been the principal cause of accelerating inflation and the depreciation of the parallel exchange rate.

Subsidization and Taxation in the Region

The domestic retail price of gasoline in Nigeria is set well below import parity, generating a large implicit subsidy.[71] In contrast, retail gasoline prices in the neighboring CFA franc countries are set well above import parity, resulting in a substantial implicit tax (Figure 24). Retail gasoline prices in Nigeria and the CFA franc countries have changed infrequently; most changes in implicit subsidization and taxation arise from changes in the world price of gasoline and exchange rates (Table 24). Given domestic transportation and distribution costs (Table 25), the difference between the domestic and world price overstates the extent of taxation in the CFA franc countries and understates the extent of subsidization in Nigeria; it is, however, indicative of relative magnitudes and general trends. One trend seems clear: the implicit subsidy in Nigeria, as indicated by the decline in the ratio of the domestic price to the world price of gasoline, increased steadily between 1986 and 1993. The recent upward adjustment in domestic petroleum prices in late 1993 resulted in a sharp decline in the implicit subsidy.

The extent of the subsidy and tax depends on the domestic retail price, the world price of gasoline, and the exchange rate. Changes in world prices affect the implicit tax in the CFA franc countries and the implicit subsidy in Nigeria in opposite directions; an increase in the world price reduces the implicit tax and raises the implicit subsidy. Changes in the CFA franc/U.S. dollar exchange rate reflect the movement in the French franc/U.S. dollar exchange rate. Given the relative stability of the French franc/U.S. dollar exchange rate since 1990, the decline in world petroleum prices between 1990 and 1993 resulted in a general upward trend in the implicit tax in the CFA countries. In Nigeria, the depreciation of the naira in the parallel market has overwhelmed the impact of the decline in world gasoline prices, causing the implicit subsidy to rise substantially.

Incentives for Smuggling

The incentives for smuggling gasoline from Nigeria remain enormous despite the recent CFA franc devaluation and the increase in domestic

---
[71]Import parity is defined as the world price of gasoline valued at the parallel exchange rate. The analysis is limited to the gasoline market for ease of exposition and because most smuggling involves gasoline. The analysis applies to other petroleum products as well.

Appendix IV

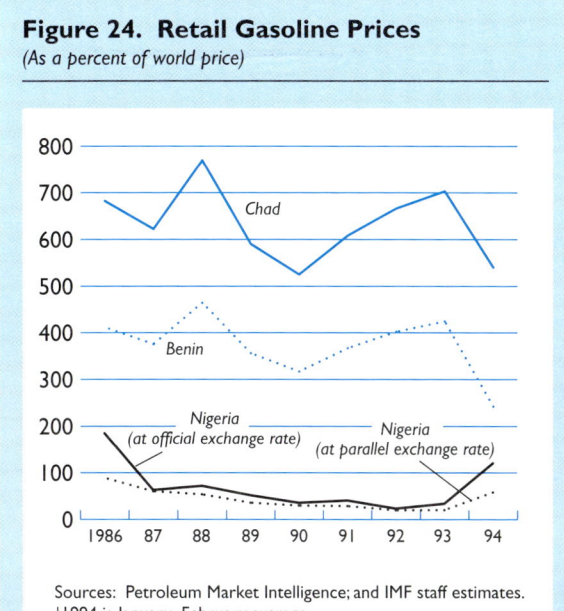

Figure 24. Retail Gasoline Prices
(As a percent of world price)

Sources: Petroleum Market Intelligence; and IMF staff estimates.
[1]1994 is January–February average.

product prices in Nigeria.[72] The current spread between retail prices of premium gasoline in neighboring countries and in Nigeria ranges from a low of ₦10.1 per liter for Benin to a high of ₦26.4 per liter for Chad.

The actual volume of smuggling in the region is not known, although some partial estimates and anecdotal evidence exist. In the case of Benin, it is estimated that unrecorded imports have been rising rapidly since 1986, reaching 133,000 tons in 1991, nearly 70 percent of total consumption. While this represented a substantial share of the gasoline market in Benin, it constituted only 3 percent of the total stock of gasoline allocated to Nigeria's domestic market in that year. Clearly, what may appear as a relatively small amount of smuggling from the point of view of the Nigerian market can constitute a substantial share of certain foreign markets.

The allocation of gasoline for domestic consumption in Nigeria has increased on average by 11.2 percent a year since 1988, reaching 5.3 million tons in 1993. Nonetheless, shortages of gasoline have regularly been reported in the border towns of Nigeria, where the incentives for smuggling are the greatest. More recently, shortages have appeared in Abuja and Lagos as well. The implicit gasoline subsidy amounted to an estimated ₦30 billion in 1993, equivalent to 3.8 percent of GDP. It is estimated that as much as 20 percent of the gasoline allocated to Nigeria's domestic market is smuggled abroad, implying that income derived from gasoline smuggling was equivalent to roughly 0.8 percent of Nigeria's GDP in 1993.

Nigeria's Fiscal Policy and the Incentive to Smuggle

The incentive to smuggle gasoline abroad is a function of the difference between the foreign retail price and the Nigerian retail price, measured at the parallel exchange rate. The quantity of gasoline smuggled (X in equation (1)) is a function of the retail price in CFA franc countries (Pc), converted at the parallel ₦/CFAF exchange rate (En/Ec, where En and Ec are the naira and CFA franc bilateral exchange rates vis-à-vis the U.S. dollar, respectively) relative to the retail price of gasoline in Nigeria (Pn). The quantity of gasoline smuggled is constrained to be less than the total amount officially allocated for domestic consumption (DA).[73] Domestic consumption in Nigeria is determined residually as the difference between the domestic allocation (DA) and the amount smuggled (X). The following equations describe these relationships:

$$
\begin{aligned}
X &= b[(En/Ec)Pc - Pn],^{74} \quad b>0,\ 0<X<DA & (1)\\
En &= P/Pf, & (2)\\
P &= vM/Y, & (3)\\
dM &= -FB, & (4)\\
FB &= R + Pn{*}DA - EXP, & (5)\\
DC &= DA - X. & (6)
\end{aligned}
$$

The naira/U.S. dollar exchange rate in equation (2) is assumed to be determined by purchasing power parity (PPP), where P is the aggregate price level in Nigeria, and Pf is the aggregate price level of its trading partners. The Nigerian price level in equation (3) is equal to money velocity (v) times the stock of money (M) divided by real GDP (Y). The change in the stock of money (dM) in equation (4) is presumed to derive solely from the fiscal balance (FB). For the sake of simplicity, it is assumed that the entire deficit is financed by the domestic banking system. The fiscal balance (in equation (5)) is equal

---

[72]The impact of these two actions, both of which reduced the profitability of smuggling, was partially offset by increases in retail gasoline prices in most CFA franc countries.

[73]It is generally assumed that the gasoline smuggled into the neighboring countries originates from the allocation from domestic consumption.

[74]The smuggling function is derived from the following maximization problem: max Π = $(En/Ec)PcX - C(X)$ where Π represents profits arising from smuggling and $C(X) = PnX + zX^2$ defines the cost of smuggling. Equation (1) follows where $b = 1/zt$.

APPENDIX IV

Table 24. Retail Prices of Premium Gasoline in Nigeria and Neighboring Countries

	1986	1987	1988	1989	1990	1991	1992	1993	Jan.–Feb. 1994
(In local currency per liter)									
Nigeria	0.40	0.40	0.42	0.60	0.60	0.70	0.70	1.13	3.25
Benin	175	175	175	175	175	175	175	175	175
Cameroon	155	190	220	280	280	190	195	195	251
Chad	290	290	290	290	290	290	290	290	390
Niger	280	280	254	263	263	263	263	263	385
(In U.S. cents per liter)									
Nigeria									
At official exchange rate	22.9	10.0	9.3	8.2	7.5	7.1	4.0	5.1	14.8
At parallel exchange rate	11.1	9.5	7.0	5.7	6.3	5.0	3.4	3.1	7.2
Benin	50.5	58.2	58.8	54.9	64.3	62.0	66.1	61.8	29.6
Cameroon	53.4	63.2	73.9	87.8	102.8	67.3	73.7	68.9	42.5
Chad	83.7	96.5	97.4	90.9	106.5	103	109.6	102.4	66.0
Niger	80.9	93.2	853.0	82.4	96.6	93.2	99.4	92.9	65.1
(In percent of world price)									
Nigeria									
At official exchange rate	186.2	64.2	73.1	52.9	36.8	41.8	24.6	35.0	121.5
At parallel exchange rate	90.5	61.6	54.9	37.0	30.8	29.9	20.9	21.4	59.1
Benin	411.7	375.5	464.3	356.1	316.9	367.0	402.0	424.3	242.4
Cameroon	435.2	407.7	583.7	569.8	507.0	398.5	447.9	472.8	347.6
Chad	682.2	6,223	769.4	590.2	525.1	608.2	666.2	703.1	540.2
Niger	658.7	600.8	673.9	535.2	476.2	551.6	604.1	637.7	533.2
Memorandum items:									
(In units indicated)									
World price of gasoline (U.S. cents/liter)[1]	12.3	15.5	127	15.4	20.3	16.9	16.4	14.6	12.2
World price of crude oil (U.S. dollars/bbl)[2]	14.50	18.34	14.97	18.22	23.99	19.99	19.34	17.04	...
Exchange rates									
Official									
Naira/U.S. dollar	1.75	4.02	4.54	7.36	8.04	9.91	17.30	22.05	21.89
CFAF/U.S. dollar	346	301	298	319	272	282	265	283	591
Naira/CFAF	0.0051	0.0134	0.0152	0.0231	0.0295	0.0351	0.0654	0.0779	0.0370
Parallel									
Naira/U.S. dollar	3.60	4.19	6.04	10.52	9.60	13.87	20.38	36.16	45.00
Naira/CFAF	0.0104	0.0139	0.0203	0.0330	—	0.0492	0.0770	0.1277	0.0761

Sources: *Petroleum Market Intelligence*; and IMF staff estimates.
[1]For 1992–94, wholesale price of premium gasoline in U.S. Gulf Coast as reported in *Petroleum Market Intelligence*. Prior years are estimated, using ratio of Gulf Coast price to the price of U.K. Brent crude oil.
[2]Price of U.K. Brent.

to revenues other than those derived from the sale of gasoline for domestic consumption (R) plus the value of domestic gasoline sales valued at the official retail price ($Pn*DA$), less expenditure (EXP). Equation (6) shows that domestic consumption (DC) equals the difference between domestic allocation (DA) and the amount smuggled (X).

Substituting equations (2) through (5) into (1) yields equation (7), which describes smuggling in terms of exogenous variables and parameters only:

$$X = b\left[\frac{n(M_{t-1} - R - Pn*DA + EXP)}{Y*P_f*E_c} * P_c - P_n\right]. \quad (7)$$

Taking the total differential of (7) and dividing through by X yields an expression that describes the percentage change in the quantity of gasoline smuggled as a function of percentage changes in exogenous variables.

Appendix IV

Table 25. Composition of Retail Prices of Premium Gasoline in Selected CFAF Countries, 1991
(In CFA francs per liter)

Country	Import or Ex-Refinery Price	Distribution Cost	Taxes	Retail Price	Taxes as Percent of Retail Price
Benin	61.1	23.6	90.3	175.0	51.6
Cameroon	32.9	37.5	120.2	190.0	63.3
Chad	95.0	37.0	140.0	290.0	48.3
Niger	62.4	93.7	106.9	263.0	40.6

Source: World Bank (1991), *A Tax Reform Strategy for Cameroon.*

$$\hat{X} = S_1[-S_2\hat{R} + S_4 E\hat{X}P] + S_1[\hat{P}_c - \hat{E}_c - \hat{Y} - \hat{P}_f]$$
$$-[(S_1 - 1) + S_1 S_3]\hat{R} \quad , \quad (8)$$

where $S_1 = [(En/Ec)P_c]/[(En/Ec)P_c - P_n]$
$S_2 = R/FB$
$S_3 = Pn*DA/FB$
$S_4 = EXP/FB.$

The first term in brackets in equation (8) represents the impact of changes in non-gasoline related fiscal revenue and expenditure on smuggling. A decline in revenue or an increase in expenditure causes the deficit to rise. The stock of money rises, causing the aggregate price level to rise and the parallel exchange rate to depreciate. Smuggling increases because the depreciation increases the naira value of the retail price of gasoline in the neighboring countries. Since the cost of smuggling (Pn) is constant, the profitability of smuggling rises. This result clearly implies that the incentive for smuggling is affected not just by Nigeria's domestic gasoline pricing policy, but by its overall fiscal policy as well. It also implies that smuggling could be curtailed by reducing the Nigerian fiscal deficit, even if the domestic price of gasoline in Nigeria remains unchanged.

The second term in brackets captures the impact of changes in the retail price of gasoline in neighboring countries, the CFAF/U.S. dollar exchange rate, real income in Nigeria, and the price level of Nigeria's trading partners. An increase in the price of gasoline in neighboring countries increases smuggling for the obvious reason; it increases the price differential. An increase in any of the last three variables causes smuggling to decline. A devaluation of the CFA franc vis-à-vis the U.S. dollar reduces the ₦/CFAF cross rate, reducing the profitability of smuggling. An increase in either real GDP in Nigeria or the foreign price level causes smuggling to fall because both cause the ₦/US$ exchange rate to appreciate.

The last term in equation (8) defines the impact of a change in the domestic price of gasoline in Nigeria, and two separate effects can be identified. The first term in parentheses defines the direct impact; an increase in the Nigerian price reduces the price differential. The second term in parentheses defines the indirect impact; an increase in the retail price of gasoline reduces the fiscal deficit and hence indirectly induces an appreciation of the ₦/CFAF exchange rate, which reduces the profitability of smuggling.

Equation (8) indicates that the increase in the domestic price of gasoline in Nigeria in November 1993 and the devaluation of the CFA franc in January should both serve to reduce the amount of smuggling in the region. However, it also indicates that the impact of these policy actions could be overwhelmed by Nigerian fiscal policies if the deficit continues to expand.

Conclusion

It is well known that Nigeria's policy of maintaining a highly subsidized domestic price of gasoline generates an incentive to smuggle gasoline to neighboring countries, where the retail prices of gasoline are substantially higher. However, Nigeria's expansionary fiscal policy of the past few years has also indirectly increased the incentive to smuggle gasoline by contributing to the rapid growth in broad money and the resulting acceleration of inflation and the depreciation of the naira in the parallel foreign exchange market. To the extent that this smuggling erodes the tax base of neighboring countries, Nigeria's expansionary fiscal policy has had a regional impact. Raising the domestic retail price of gasoline in Nigeria would reduce the size of the fiscal deficit, thereby reducing the rate of growth of money, inflation, and depreciation, while simultaneously contributing to fiscal adjustment in the region as a whole.

Appendix V   Statistical Appendix

The tables on the following pages provide a statistical overview of the Nigerian economy. Starting with selected economic and financial indicators, the tables move on to fiscal and monetary statistics, as well as statistics on the balance of payments, public and publicly guaranteed debt, the gross domestic product at current and constant prices, and gross national expenditure. Other tables provide statistics on the evolution of petroleum prices, the index of agricultural production, the index of manufacturing production, and the structure of Nigeria's exports. The final table provides figures on selected financial institutions—banks, foreign exchange bureaus, stockbrokers, and discount houses—in the Nigerian economy.

APPENDIX V

Table 26. Selected Economic and Financial Indicators

	1980	1981	1982	1983	1984	1985	1986	1987	1988	1989	1990	1991	1992	1993	1994 Est.
(Annual percentage changes, unless otherwise indicated)															
National income and prices															
Real GDP (at market prices)[1]	2.9	−2.9	−0.6	−4.9	−4.8	9.7	2.5	−0.7	9.9	7.2	8.2	4.8	2.9	2.3	1.3
Oil GDP (at 1984 factor cost)	−11.6	−31.6	−11.4	−3.2	13.0	8.5	−5.2	−9.8	8.1	15.0	5.5	9.2	2.7	−2.6	−6.0
Non-oil GDP (at 1984 factor cost)	7.8	5.7	1.5	−5.7	−7.7	9.5	4.6	1.0	10.2	6.3	8.6	4.1	3.0	3.0	2.4
Of which: agriculture	(...)	(...)	(2.3)	(−2.9)	(−4.5)	(24.0)	(11.3)	(−4.0)	(−10.8)	(−5.0)	(−4.4)	(−4.5)	(−3.0)	(−2.9)	(3.0)
GDP deflator	12.1	7.7	2.5	16.3	17.0	3.7	−1.5	50.1	21.4	44.4	7.2	18.7	64.9	23.9	27.1
Consumer prices (annual average)	10.0	20.8	7.7	23.2	39.6	5.5	5.4	10.2	34.5	50.5	7.4	13.0	44.6	57.2	57.0
Consumer prices (end of period)	16.0	17.3	7.1	38.7	22.6	1.1	13.6	9.7	39.0	44.7	3.5	23.0	48.8	61.3	76.8
Nominal GDP (in billions of naira)	49.8	50.7	51.7	57.1	63.6	72.4	73.1	108.9	145.2	224.8	260.6	324.0	549.8	697.1	897.5
Oil production volume (in m/b per day)	2.1	1.4	1.3	1.2	1.4	1.5	1.5	1.4	1.4	1.7	1.8	2.0	2.0	2.0	2.0
Population (millions)	61.4	63.5	65.7	67.9	70.2	72.6	75.1	77.6	80.2	82.9	85.7	88.5	91.4	94.3	97.1
Nominal per capita GDP (in U.S. dollars)	1,482	1,294	1,170	1,169	1,177	1,120	556	349	399	368	378	369	348	335	420
External sector															
Exports f.o.b. (in billions of U.S. dollars)	26.0	17.7	12.2	10.4	11.9	12.6	6.8	7.5	7.1	9.8	13.9	12.1	12.3	11.3	9.5
Of which: oil (in billions of U.S. dollars)	(24.9)	(17.2)	(11.9)	(10.0)	(11.6)	(12.2)	(6.4)	(7.0)	(6.5)	(9.4)	(13.5)	(11.7)	(12.0)	(11.0)	(9.3)
Imports f.o.b. (in billions of U.S. dollars)	−14.7	−18.4	−14.9	−11.5	−8.9	−8.3	−6.7	−5.8	−5.8	−5.9	−7.1	−7.9	−8.7	−8.1	−6.7
Oil export volume	−12.9	−36.0	−18.3	−6.7	17.3	13.6	−0.4	−9.0	6.2	9.7	9.7	3.3	6.7	3.1	−6.9
Non-oil export volume	5.2	−33.9	−23.1	59.3	−38.6	10.3	10.8	16.0	14.0	17.5	3.0	19.0	−39.8	−5.5	−26.9
Import volume	11.0	31.2	−15.4	−20.1	−19.8	−7.1	−27.9	−23.7	−6.4	−28.7	9.2	11.5	7.3	−3.4	−20.1
Average oil export price (in U.S. dollars per barrel, f.o.b.)	35.4	38.3	32.4	29.2	28.9	26.9	14.3	17.2	14.9	18.5	24.3	20.2	19.6	17.4	15.8
Nominal effective exchange rate[2]	11.1	3.4	4.6	3.9	7.2	−8.3	−44.2	−69.9	−18.0	−33.0	1.6	−17.5	−35.4	−22.3	33.0
Real effective exchange rate[2]	6.5	10.8	2.7	18.1	37.7	−10.3	−45.4	−68.1	0.2	−10.7	−7.4	−15.7	−17.2	9.1	83.3
Average official exchange rate (naira/U.S. dollar)	0.55	0.62	0.67	0.72	0.77	0.89	1.75	4.02	4.54	7.36	8.04	9.91	17.30	22.05	22.00
Terms of trade	52.0	12.2	−12.1	−7.4	3.9	−7.3	−52.2	4.1	−16.1	22.6	18.5	−16.4	−5.5	−7.3	−11.2
Money and credit															
Net foreign assets	73.7	−54.5	−61.7	−61.8	172.9	78.8	1.0	−38.6	805.3	126.2	93.7	31.2	−33.9	47.4	0.1
Net domestic assets	33.5	72.5	26.1	18.9	7.9	−34.1	76.3	26.2	20.3	−33.1	−2.5	35.0	339.5	3.3	54.4
Net credit to the Federal Government	−6.5	116.8	58.1	48.9	15.0	12.1	−4.1	12.4	28.6	−33.7	15.1	61.0	138.3	121.6	27.8
Credit to the rest of the economy	61.9	46.5	24.1	9.8	3.1	12.2	34.0	15.7	37.2	4.4	20.6	23.4	36.8	50.3	32.7
Broad money	48.9	15.6	10.6	14.0	11.3	16.7	2.7	22.7	43.3	7.2	42.3	32.3	51.3	48.0	38.4
Velocity (GDP/average broad money)	...	3.7	3.4	3.3	3.3	3.3	3.0	4.0	4.0	4.9	4.9	4.3	5.1	4.3	4.4
Savings deposit rate (end of period)	6.0	6.0	8.5	7.5	9.5	9.5	9.5	11.0	12.4	16.5	17.8	14.0	16.1	16.7	12.3
Treasury bill rate (end of period)	...	5.0	7.0	7.0	8.5	8.5	8.5	11.8	11.8	17.5	17.5	14.5	21.0	28.0	12.5
(In percent of GDP)															
Federal Government budget															
Federally collected revenue	30.5	25.7	25.2	20.1	19.3	20.9	21.7	21.4	20.3	24.6	35.9	31.2	31.1	27.6	18.3
Of which: oil revenues	(24.8)	(19.7)	(16.5)	(12.3)	(14.4)	(15.1)	(17.4)	(17.0)	(16.3)	(20.8)	(30.6)	(25.9)	(26.1)	(22.8)	(13.7)
Federally retained revenue	24.2	15.9	16.0	13.1	11.5	12.4	13.9	11.6	11.1	13.8	21.5	17.9	17.8	15.3	10.9

Appendix V

Expenditure and net lending	24.5	25.2	25.0	23.8	16.1	15.2	19.1	23.3	24.7	20.7	24.5	24.7	25.6	33.3	19.6
Current expenditure	10.5	9.7	8.2	11.9	10.1	8.3	10.5	16.5	15.5	14.3	15.9	14.5	14.7	17.7	13.5
Capital expenditure	14.0	15.5	16.8	11.9	6.1	7.0	8.8	6.2	7.5	4.9	4.9	5.2	3.8	4.4	5.8
Supplementary/extrabudgetary outlays	—	—	—	—	—	—	—	0.7	1.7	1.8	4.1	5.3	8.2	11.5	0.6
Federal Government budget deficit	-0.3	-9.3	-9.0	-10.8	-4.6	-2.8	-5.2	-11.7	-13.6	-7.0	-2.9	-6.8	-7.9	-18.1	-8.8
External sector															
Current account balance	4.7	-7.4	-9.4	-6.3	-1.3	-0.3	-9.1	-4.6	-6.0	1.3	7.8	0.1	-1.9	-2.9	-2.4
Overall balance of payments	5.0	-7.5	-6.9	-7.3	-0.5	-0.1	-20.1	-15.8	-15.3	-5.1	-1.8	-7.0	-24.2	-10.6	-6.1
External debt	4.5	7.4	16.1	22.4	21.0	23.3	58.9	104.5	94.1	102.9	104.0	103.2	90.7	94.2	76.4

(In billions of U.S. dollars, unless otherwise indicated)

Current account balance	4.3	-6.0	-7.2	-5.0	-1.1	-0.2	-3.8	-1.2	-1.9	0.4	2.5	0.0	-0.6	-0.9	-1.0
Overall balance of payments	4.5	-6.2	-5.3	-5.8	-0.4	-0.1	-8.4	-4.3	-4.9	-1.5	-0.6	-2.3	-7.7	-3.3	-2.5
External public and publicly guaranteed debt	4.1	6.1	12.4	17.8	17.3	18.9	24.6	28.3	30.1	31.4	33.7	33.7	28.8	29.8	31.2
Gross international reserves (end of period)	10.4	4.5	2.0	1.2	1.5	1.7	0.9	0.8	0.3	1.6	4.1	4.2	0.8	0.7	0.9
(in months of imports of goods and nonfactor services)	5.9	2.3	1.3	1.1	1.7	1.9	1.3	1.4	0.5	2.5	5.3	4.8	0.9	0.8	1.3

Sources: Data provided by the Nigerian authorities; and IMF staff estimates.
[1] Figures prior to 1982 are based on constant 1977/78 prices.
[2] Based on the weighted average of the official and foreign exchange bureau exchange rates.

APPENDIX V

Table 27. Federal Government Fiscal Operations

	1981	1982	1983	1984	1985	1986	1987	1988	1989	1990	1991	1992	1993	1994 Est.
	(In billions of naira)													
Federally collected revenue	13.0	13.0	11.5	12.3	15.1	15.9	23.3	29.5	55.4	93.7	101.2	171.2	192.3	164.0
Petroleum revenue	10.0	8.5	7.0	9.1	10.9	12.7	18.5	23.6	46.7	79.8	83.9	143.5	159.0	122.7
Of which: FGN dedicated	...	...	...	...	...	(3.3)	(0.5)	(0.8)	(4.5)	(19.9)	(18.0)	(29.8)	(34.7)	(37.6)
NNPC dedicated	...	...	...	...	...	(0.4)	(1.1)	(1.5)	(3.5)	(4.6)	(5.6)	(10.0)	(18.3)	...
Non-petroleum revenue	3.0	4.5	4.4	3.1	4.2	3.2	4.8	5.8	8.7	13.8	17.4	27.7	33.3	41.3
Inland revenue	0.6	0.7	1.1	1.1	1.1	1.0	1.3	1.5	1.9	2.8	3.8	5.4	9.4	12.3
Customs, excise, and fees	2.3	2.3	2.0	1.6	2.2	1.7	3.1	3.8	5.8	8.6	11.5	16.1	15.7	18.3
Independent revenue	0.1	1.5	1.3	0.4	0.9	0.4	0.4	0.5	0.9	2.3	2.1	6.2	8.1	10.7
Federally retained revenue	8.1	8.3	7.5	7.3	9.0	10.2	12.6	16.1	31.0	56.2	57.9	97.6	106.4	97.5
Total expenditure and net lending	12.8	12.9	13.6	10.3	11.0	14.0	25.4	35.8	46.6	63.8	80.0	141.0	232.5	176.3
Of which: non-debt	(12.2)	(11.6)	(11.6)	(7.7)	(8.1)	(10.5)	(11.7)	(20.2)	(22.3)	(32.9)	(45.3)	(76.0)	(150.5)	(106.8)
Recurrent expenditure	4.9	4.2	6.8	6.4	6.0	7.7	18.0	22.5	32.1	41.4	47.1	80.6	123.2	120.9
Personnel costs	1.3	1.1	1.2	1.1	1.5	1.6	2.4	2.8	3.4	5.1	5.7	7.1	18.2	22.2
Overhead costs	2.1	1.7	3.0	2.6	1.6	2.6	1.9	4.1	4.4	5.3	6.7	8.6	20.5	25.5
Foreign interest due	0.3	0.3	0.6	0.8	0.8	1.0	8.4	10.4	16.4	21.0	22.6	36.0	41.5	41.1
Domestic interest due	0.2	1.0	1.4	1.8	2.1	2.5	3.8	4.2	6.0	8.5	10.5	26.3	38.7	28.5
Pre-SFEM payments	—	—	—	—	—	—	1.5	1.0	1.9	1.5	1.7	2.7	1.7	—
Capital expenditure	7.9	8.7	6.8	3.9	5.0	6.4	6.8	10.9	11.0	12.9	16.8	21.1	30.5	52.3
Of which: domestically financed	...	...	...	...	...	(6.7)	(3.8)	(8.6)	(5.6)	(7.4)	(9.7)	(12.0)	(18.6)	(39.0)
Net lending to state governments	...	...	...	...	...	-0.1	-0.2	-0.1	-0.5	-1.2	-1.1	-5.9	-1.4	-2.6
Supplementary/extrabudgetary outlays	...	...	...	...	...	—	0.8	2.5	4.0	10.8	17.3	45.2	80.1	5.7
Overall balance	-4.7	-4.7	-6.1	-2.9	-2.0	-3.8	-12.8	-19.7	-15.6	-7.7	-22.1	-43.4	-126.0	-78.8
Primary fiscal balance	-4.2	-3.3	-4.1	-0.3	0.9	-0.4	1.0	-4.2	8.7	23.3	12.7	21.6	-44.1	-9.2
Financing	4.7	4.7	6.1	2.9	2.0	3.8	12.8	19.7	15.6	7.7	22.1	43.4	126.0	78.8
Foreign (net)	0.5	0.3	0.2	-0.1	-0.4	-0.3	3.5	5.4	8.2	-0.3	-0.5	-9.0	19.2	16.1
Borrowing	...	...	...	...	...	...	3.0	2.9	9.4	7.8	7.4	9.1	12.0	13.3
Amortization due	...	...	...	...	...	...	-16.4	-18.0	-25.5	-33.0	-31.1	-83.7	-58.4	-58.8
Changes in arrears	...	...	...	...	...	...	-0.5	20.5	0.9	12.5	-1.2	38.9	65.6	61.6
Debt relief	...	...	...	...	...	...	17.5	—	23.4	12.4	24.4	26.6	—	—
Domestic (net)	4.2	4.4	6.0	3.0	2.4	4.1	9.3	14.3	7.4	7.9	22.6	52.4	106.8	62.7
Banking system	3.5	3.8	5.1	2.3	1.6	-0.8	2.4	6.1	-9.3	2.8	12.8	46.8	98.1	49.8
Non-bank	0.7	0.6	0.9	0.7	0.8	4.9	6.9	8.2	16.7	5.1	9.7	5.6	8.7	12.9
	(In percent of GDP)													
Federally collected revenue	25.7	25.2	20.1	19.3	20.9	21.7	21.4	20.3	24.6	35.9	31.2	31.1	27.6	18.3
Oil revenue	19.7	16.5	12.3	14.4	15.1	17.4	17.0	16.3	20.8	30.6	25.9	26.1	22.8	13.7
Non-oil revenue	6.0	8.7	7.8	4.9	5.8	4.3	4.4	4.0	3.9	5.3	5.4	5.0	4.8	4.6
(percent of non-oil GDP)	7.5	10.5	9.1	5.9	7.1	5.1	5.9	5.2	6.0	8.1	8.7	9.6	7.5	6.3

Appendix V

Federally retained revenue	15.9	16.0	13.1	11.5	12.4	13.9	11.6	11.1	13.8	21.5	17.9	17.8	15.3	10.9
Total expenditure and net lending	25.2	25.0	23.8	16.1	15.2	19.1	23.3	24.7	20.7	24.5	24.7	25.6	33.3	19.6
Of which: nondebt expenditure	(24.1)	(22.3)	(20.3)	(12.0)	(11.2)	(14.4)	(10.7)	(13.9)	(9.9)	(12.6)	(14.0)	(13.8)	(21.6)	(11.9)
Recurrent expenditure	9.7	8.2	11.9	10.1	8.3	10.5	16.5	15.5	14.3	15.9	14.5	14.7	17.7	13.5
Personnel costs	2.5	2.2	2.1	1.8	2.1	2.1	2.2	1.9	1.5	2.0	1.7	1.3	2.6	2.5
Overhead costs	4.2	3.4	5.3	4.0	2.2	3.6	1.7	2.8	2.0	2.0	2.1	1.6	2.9	2.8
Interest due	1.1	2.6	3.6	4.1	4.0	4.7	11.2	10.0	10.0	11.3	10.2	11.3	11.5	7.8
Of which: foreign interest	(0.7)	(0.7)	(1.1)	(1.2)	(1.1)	(1.4)	(7.7)	(7.1)	(7.3)	(8.1)	(7.0)	(6.6)	(6.0)	(4.6)
Capital expenditure	15.5	16.8	11.9	6.1	7.0	8.8	6.2	7.5	4.9	4.9	5.2	3.8	4.4	5.8
Supplementary/extrabudgetary outlays	—	—	—	—	—	—	0.7	1.7	1.8	4.1	5.3	8.2	11.5	0.6
Overall fiscal balance	-9.3	-9.0	-10.8	-4.6	-2.8	-5.2	-11.7	-13.6	-7.0	-2.9	-6.8	-7.9	-18.1	-8.8
Primary fiscal balance	-8.2	-6.4	-7.2	-0.5	1.2	-0.5	0.9	-2.9	3.9	8.9	3.9	3.9	-6.3	-1.0
Domestic financing	8.3	8.5	10.4	4.7	3.3	5.6	8.5	9.8	3.3	3.0	7.0	9.5	15.3	7.0
Of which: bank financing	(6.9)	(7.4)	(8.9)	(3.6)	(2.2)	(-1.1)	(2.2)	(4.2)	(-4.1)	(1.1)	(4.0)	(8.5)	(14.1)	(5.5)

Sources: Data provided by the Nigerian authorities; and IMF staff estimates.

APPENDIX V

Table 28. Summary of Budgetary Operations of State and Local Governments and Special Funds[1]

	1981	1982	1983	1984	1985	1986	1987	1988	1989	1990	1991	1992	1993	1994 Est.
(In billions of naira)														
Revenue	6.02	6.11	5.37	6.31	6.55	7.18	11.59	14.10	22.52	35.63	40.90	68.90	75.19	76.49
Statutory share of Federation Account (gross)	4.98	4.79	4.00	4.93	4.97	5.32	9.64	11.92	14.69	22.94	26.93	39.56	55.00	56.98
Statutory share of Federation Stabilization Account (gross)	—	—	—	—	—	—	—	—	6.23	9.96	10.82	24.13	12.56	2.60
Independent revenue[2]	1.05	1.32	1.37	1.38	1.58	1.86	1.95	2.18	1.60	2.73	3.15	5.21	7.63	16.90
Expenditure and net lending	6.50	6.54	5.48	6.19	5.53	7.51	10.97	16.32	22.81	34.09	32.15	63.95	70.44	73.89
Recurrent	2.71	2.90	2.60	5.35	4.55	5.92	7.49	10.85	14.01	23.18	18.96	33.74	45.49	47.22
Capital	3.79	3.64	2.88	0.84	0.98	1.51	3.33	5.41	8.32	9.74	12.07	24.28	23.55	24.10
Net lending	—	—	—	—	—	0.08	0.15	0.06	0.48	1.17	1.11	5.93	1.40	2.57
Balance (deficit −)	−0.48	−0.43	−0.11	0.12	1.02	−0.33	0.62	−2.22	−0.28	1.54	8.75	4.95	4.76	2.60
Financing	0.48	0.43	0.11	−0.12	−1.02	0.33	−0.62	2.22	0.28	−1.54	−8.75	−4.95	−4.76	−2.60
Foreign (net)	—	—	—	—	—	—	—	—	—	—	—	—	—	—
Domestic (net)	0.48	0.43	0.11	−0.12	−1.02	0.33	−0.62	2.22	0.28	−1.54	−8.75	−4.95	−4.76	−2.60
Banking system	0.48	0.43	0.11	−0.12	−1.02	0.33	−0.62	2.22	0.28	0.24	−0.03	0.35	0.28	0.42
Non-bank[3]	—	—	—	—	—	—	—	—	—	−1.78	−8.72	−5.30	−5.04	−3.02
(In percent of GDP)														
Revenue	11.9	11.8	9.4	9.9	9.1	9.8	10.6	9.7	10.0	13.7	12.6	12.5	10.8	8.5
Statutory share of Federation Account (gross)	9.8	9.3	7.0	7.8	6.9	7.3	8.8	8.2	6.5	8.8	8.3	7.2	7.9	6.3
Statutory share of Federation Stabilization Account (gross)	0.0	0.0	0.0	0.0	0.0	0.0	0.0	0.0	2.8	3.8	3.3	4.4	1.8	0.3
Independent revenue[2]	2.1	2.5	2.4	2.2	2.2	2.5	1.8	1.5	0.7	1.0	1.0	0.9	1.1	1.9
Expenditure and net lending	12.8	12.6	9.6	9.7	7.6	10.3	10.1	11.2	10.1	13.1	9.9	11.6	10.1	8.2
Recurrent	5.3	5.6	4.6	8.4	6.3	8.1	6.9	7.5	6.2	8.9	5.9	6.1	6.5	5.3
Capital	7.5	7.0	5.0	1.3	1.3	2.1	3.1	3.7	3.7	3.7	3.7	4.4	3.4	2.7
Net lending	—	—	—	—	—	—	—	—	—	—	—	—	—	—
Balance (deficit −)	−0.9	−0.8	−0.2	0.2	1.4	−0.4	0.6	−1.5	−0.1	0.6	2.7	0.9	0.7	0.3
Financing														
Foreign (net)	…	…	…	…	…	…	…	…	…	…	…	…	…	…
Domestic (net)	0.9	0.8	0.2	−0.2	−1.4	0.4	−0.6	1.5	0.1	−0.6	−2.7	−0.9	−0.7	−0.3
Banking system	0.9	0.8	0.2	−0.2	−1.4	0.4	−0.6	1.5	0.1	0.1	—	0.1	—	—
Non-bank[3]	—	—	—	—	—	—	—	—	—	−0.7	−2.7	−1.0	−0.7	−0.3

Sources: Data provided by the Nigerian authorities; and IMF staff estimates.

[1] These data, which are based on limited budgetary data and staff estimates, should be viewed only as illustrative of general budgetary trends.
[2] State government only.
[3] Lending to the Federal Government via the Federation Stabilization Account.

Appendix V

Table 29. Consolidated General Government Fiscal Operations[1]

	1981	1982	1983	1984	1985	1986	1987	1988	1989	1990	1991	1992	1993	1994 Est.
	(In billions of naira)													
Revenue	14.1	14.4	12.9	13.7	16.7	17.3	24.2	30.1	53.5	91.8	98.8	166.5	181.6	180.9
Federally collected revenue[2]	13.0	13.0	11.5	12.3	15.1	15.5	22.2	28.0	51.9	89.1	95.6	161.2	174.0	164.0
State and local government independent revenue	1.0	1.3	1.4	1.4	1.6	1.9	2.0	2.2	1.6	2.7	3.1	5.2	7.6	16.9
Expenditure	19.3	19.5	19.1	16.5	16.5	21.5	36.4	52.1	69.4	97.9	112.2	204.9	302.9	250.2
Recurrent[3]	7.6	7.1	9.4	11.8	10.5	13.6	25.9	34.6	48.1	69.9	74.7	137.0	208.8	171.0
Capital[3]	11.7	12.3	9.7	4.7	6.0	7.9	10.5	17.6	21.3	28.0	37.5	68.0	94.1	79.2
Overall balance (deficit −)	−5.2	−5.1	−6.3	−2.8	0.2	−4.2	−12.2	−22.0	−15.9	−6.1	−13.4	−38.5	−121.3	−69.3
Financing	5.2	5.1	6.3	2.8	−0.2	4.2	12.2	22.0	15.9	6.1	13.4	38.5	121.3	69.3
Foreign	0.5	0.3	0.2	−0.1	−0.4	−0.3	3.5	5.4	8.2	−0.3	−0.5	−9.0	19.2	16.1
Domestic	4.7	4.8	6.1	2.9	0.2	4.4	8.7	16.6	7.7	6.4	13.8	47.5	102.1	53.2
Banking system	4.0	4.2	5.2	2.2	1.1	−0.5	1.7	8.4	−9.0	3.0	12.8	47.2	98.4	50.3
Non-bank	0.7	0.6	0.9	0.7	−0.9	4.9	6.9	8.2	16.7	3.4	1.0	0.3	3.7	3.0
	(In percent of GDP)													
Revenue	27.7	27.8	22.5	21.5	23.1	23.7	22.2	20.7	23.8	35.2	30.5	30.3	26.1	20.2
Federally collected revenue[2]	25.7	25.2	20.1	19.3	20.9	21.2	20.4	19.2	23.1	34.2	29.5	29.3	25.0	18.3
State and local government independent revenue	2.1	2.5	2.4	2.2	2.2	2.5	1.8	1.5	0.7	1.0	1.0	0.9	1.1	1.9
Expenditure	38.0	37.6	33.4	25.9	22.9	29.4	33.4	35.9	30.9	37.6	34.6	37.3	43.5	27.9
Recurrent[3]	15.0	13.8	16.5	18.5	14.5	18.6	23.7	23.8	21.4	26.8	23.0	24.9	29.9	19.0
Capital[3]	23.0	23.8	17.0	7.4	8.3	10.8	9.6	12.1	9.5	10.7	11.6	12.4	13.5	8.8
Overall balance (deficit −)	−10.3	−9.8	−10.9	−4.4	0.2	−5.7	−11.2	−15.1	−7.1	−2.4	−4.1	−7.0	−17.4	−7.7
Financing	10.3	9.8	10.9	4.4	−0.2	5.7	11.2	15.1	7.1	2.4	4.1	7.0	17.4	7.7
Foreign	1.0	0.5	0.3	−0.1	−0.5	−0.3	3.2	3.7	3.7	−0.1	−0.1	−1.6	2.8	1.8
Domestic	9.3	9.3	10.6	4.5	0.3	6.0	8.0	11.4	3.4	2.4	4.3	8.6	14.6	5.9
Banking system	7.9	8.2	9.1	3.5	1.5	−0.7	1.6	5.8	−4.0	1.2	4.0	8.6	14.1	5.6
Non-bank	1.4	1.2	1.6	1.1	−1.2	6.7	6.4	5.7	7.4	1.3	0.3	0.1	0.5	0.3

Sources: Data provided by the Nigerian authorities; and IMF staff estimates.
[1] These data, which are based on limited budgetary data and staff estimates, should be viewed only as illustrative of general budgetary trends.
[2] Excludes dedicated oil revenue earmarked for NNPC.
[3] Includes 50 percent of estimated extrabudgetary expenditure by the Federal Government.

APPENDIX V

Table 30. Monetary Survey

	1981	1982	1983	1984	1985	1986	1987	1988	1989	1990	1991	1992	1993	1994 Est.
	(In billions of naira, unless otherwise indicated)													
Net foreign assets	2.6	1.0	0.4	1.0	1.8	1.8	1.1	10.2	23.1	44.8	58.8	38.8	57.2	57.3
Central Bank of Nigeria (net)	2.4	1.0	0.3	0.7	1.5	−0.3	(2.2)	3.2	13.4	34.9	44.2	13.2	27.6	34.7
Foreign assets	2.8	1.3	0.9	1.2	1.7	3.0	3.1	3.3	13.5	35.0	44.3	14.0	29.1	36.3
Foreign liabilities	−0.4	−0.4	−0.6	−0.5	−0.1	−3.2	5.3	—	—	—	—	−0.8	−1.5	−1.6
Commercial and merchant banks (net)	0.1	0.0	0.1	0.3	0.3	2.1	3.3	7.0	9.7	9.9	14.5	25.6	29.6	22.6
Foreign assets	0.3	0.3	0.3	0.4	0.6	2.9	4.3	7.6	11.1	10.4	15.6	28.0	31.4	25.4
Foreign liabilities	−0.1	−0.2	−0.3	−0.1	−0.3	−0.8	−1.0	−0.6	−1.4	−0.5	−1.1	−2.4	−1.8	−2.9
Net domestic assets	11.9	15.0	17.9	19.3	12.7	22.4	28.3	34.1	22.8	22.2	30.0	131.9	136.3	210.5
Net domestic credit	14.9	20.8	26.8	29.5	33.1	36.8	41.9	55.7	47.6	56.4	77.5	140.4	268.6	347.7
Federal Government (net)	6.6	10.4	15.4	17.7	19.9	19.1	21.4	27.6	18.3	21.0	33.9	80.7	178.9	228.6
Rest of the economy	8.4	10.4	11.4	11.7	13.2	17.7	20.5	28.1	29.4	35.4	43.7	59.8	89.8	119.2
State government	−0.6	−0.2	−0.1	−0.2	−1.1	−0.8	1.3	0.5	0.8	1.0	0.9	1.2	1.4	1.9
Local government	−0.2	−0.1	−0.1	−0.1	−0.3	−0.2	0.3	0.1	0.1	0.1	0.2	0.3	0.3	0.3
Private sector	9.1	10.7	11.6	12.1	14.5	18.7	22.1	27.5	28.5	34.3	42.6	58.3	88.1	117.0
Other items (net)[1]	−3.0	−5.7	−9.0	−10.2	−20.4	−14.3	−13.6	−21.6	−24.9	−34.2	−47.5	−8.5	−132.3	−137.3
Broad money	14.5	16.0	18.3	20.3	23.7	24.4	29.9	42.8	45.9	65.3	86.4	130.7	193.5	267.8
Valuation account[1]	…	…	…	…	9.2	−0.1	−0.5	−0.3	—	1.7	2.4	40.0	—	—
	(Annual percentage change)													
Net domestic assets	72.5	26.1	18.9	7.9	−34.1	76.3	26.2	20.3	−33.1	−2.5	35.0	339.5	3.3	54.4
Net domestic credit	70.7	39.0	29.3	9.9	12.1	11.1	13.9	33.0	−14.4	18.5	37.3	81.2	91.3	29.4
Federal Government	116.8	58.1	48.9	15.0	12.1	−4.1	12.4	28.6	−33.7	15.1	61.0	138.3	121.6	27.8
Rest of economy	46.5	24.1	9.8	3.1	12.2	34.0	15.7	37.2	4.4	20.6	23.4	36.8	50.3	32.7
Of which: private sector	(31.6)	(17.5)	(8.5)	(4.0)	(20.3)	(28.7)	(18.2)	(24.4)	(3.6)	(20.4)	(24.2)	(36.9)	(51.1)	(32.8)
Broad money	15.6	10.6	14.0	11.3	16.7	2.7	22.7	43.3	7.2	42.3	32.3	51.3	48.0	38.4
Velocity (GDP/average broad money)	3.7	3.4	3.3	3.3	3.3	3.0	4.0	4.0	4.9	4.9	4.3	5.1	4.3	4.4
Contribution to the growth of broad money														
Net foreign assets	−24.4	−10.9	−3.8	3.5	4.0	0.1	−2.9	30.4	30.1	47.2	21.4	−23.1	14.1	—
Net domestic assets	40.0	21.5	17.7	7.7	−32.4	41.0	24.1	19.3	−26.3	−1.2	11.9	118.0	3.4	38.3
Net domestic credit	49.4	40.2	38.0	14.6	17.6	15.6	20.9	46.2	−18.8	19.2	32.3	72.9	98.1	40.9
Of which:														
Federal Government	28.2	26.3	31.6	12.7	10.5	−3.4	9.7	20.5	−21.7	6.0	19.6	54.2	75.1	25.7
Rest of economy	21.2	14.0	6.4	1.9	7.1	19.0	11.4	25.5	2.9	13.2	12.7	18.6	23.0	15.2
Of which: private sector	(17.4)	(11.0)	(5.7)	(2.6)	(12.1)	(17.6)	(14.0)	(18.1)	(2.3)	(12.6)	(12.7)	(18.2)	(22.8)	(14.9)
Other items (net)	−9.4	−18.7	−20.2	−6.9	−50.0	25.4	3.2	−27.0	−7.5	−20.4	−20.3	45.1	−94.7	−2.5
Valuation account	—	—	—	—	45.1	−38.3	1.5	−0.6	−0.7	−3.7	−1.0	−43.5	30.6	—
Savings deposit rate (end of period)	6.0	8.5	7.5	9.5	9.5	9.5	11.0	12.4	16.5	17.8	14.0	16.1	16.7	12.3
Treasury bill rate (end of period)	5.0	7.0	7.0	8.5	8.5	8.5	11.8	11.8	17.5	17.5	14.5	21.0	28.0	12.5

Source: Data provided by the Nigerian authorities; and IMF staff estimates.
[1]Valuation account included in other items net prior to 1985.

Appendix V

Table 31. Balance of Payments

	1981	1982	1983	1984	1985	1986	1987	1988	1989	1990	1991	1992	1993	1994 Est.
	(In billions of U.S. dollars, unless otherwise indicated)													
Trade balance	−0.67	−2.73	−1.08	3.01	4.29	0.04	1.76	1.29	3.90	6.84	4.23	3.57	3.17	2.86
Exports	17.72	12.15	10.37	11.89	12.57	6.78	7.53	7.07	9.81	13.91	12.13	12.31	11.30	9.54
Petroleum	17.16	11.89	9.95	11.57	12.20	6.39	6.99	6.46	9.41	13.51	11.65	12.03	11.02	9.30
Other	0.56	0.27	0.42	0.32	0.36	0.40	0.54	0.61	0.40	0.41	0.47	0.28	0.28	0.23
Imports	−18.39	−14.88	−11.45	−8.88	−8.28	−6.74	−5.77	−5.78	−5.91	−7.07	−7.89	−8.74	−8.13	−6.68
Services (net)	−4.80	−4.06	−3.54	−3.74	−4.24	−4.39	−3.46	−3.85	−4.27	−5.39	−5.26	−4.89	−4.70	−4.36
Investment income (net)	−0.65	−1.10	−1.53	−2.21	−2.37	−2.93	−2.77	−2.90	−2.67	−3.29	−2.97	−2.80	−2.63	−2.46
Of which: interest due	(−0.50)	(−0.93)	(−1.24)	(−2.11)	(−2.14)	(−2.09)	(−2.11)	(−2.37)	(−2.36)	(−2.74)	(−2.42)	(−2.15)	(−1.91)	(−1.91)
Nonfactor services (net)	−4.15	−2.96	−2.01	−1.54	−1.87	−1.46	−0.69	−0.94	−1.60	−2.10	−2.29	−2.09	−2.07	−1.89
Credits	0.93	0.51	0.37	0.43	0.29	0.34	0.23	0.33	0.17	0.17	0.20	0.12	0.11	0.10
Debits	−5.08	−3.47	−2.38	−1.97	−2.15	−1.79	−0.92	−1.28	−1.77	−2.27	−2.48	−2.21	−2.19	−1.99
Transfers (net)	−0.57	−0.43	−0.40	−0.33	−0.26	0.57	0.46	0.63	0.78	1.08	1.05	0.73	0.61	0.50
Current account balance	−6.04	−7.21	−5.01	−1.07	−0.21	−3.78	−1.24	−1.92	0.41	2.53	0.03	−0.59	−0.93	−1.00
Official capital (net)	0.81	2.98	1.40	−0.18	−1.08	−2.21	−3.23	−3.43	−2.48	−3.09	−2.57	−6.07	−2.48	−2.09
Disbursements	1.39	3.60	2.35	1.85	1.56	0.85	0.74	0.62	1.22	0.93	0.72	0.53	0.54	0.61
Amortization due	−0.58	−0.63	−0.95	−2.03	−2.64	−3.06	−3.97	−4.05	−3.70	−4.02	−3.28	−6.60	−3.02	−2.70
Private capital (net)	0.17	0.43	0.37	0.19	0.33	0.42	0.57	0.33	2.43	0.58	0.61	0.90	0.64	0.58
Direct investment	0.17	0.43	0.37	0.19	0.35	0.42	0.61	0.36	2.44	0.60	0.59	0.84	0.61	0.58
Other					−0.02		−0.05	−0.03	−0.02	−0.02	0.03	0.06	0.03	−0.01
Short-term capital (net)	0.41	−1.14	−2.10	0.02	0.54	−0.10	−0.53	−0.43	−2.42	−1.11	−0.12	−1.82	−0.35	−0.16
Capital account balance	1.39	2.26	−0.33	0.03	−0.21	−1.89	−3.20	−3.53	−2.48	−3.62	−2.07	−6.99	−2.19	−1.67
Errors and omissions	−1.54	−0.35	−0.42	0.66	0.35	−0.28	0.15	0.55	0.52	0.50	−0.25	−0.12	−0.22	0.17
Overall balance	−6.20	−5.30	−5.76	−0.38	−0.07	−8.41	−4.29	−4.90	−1.54	−0.59	−2.29	−7.69	−3.34	−2.50
Financing	6.20	5.30	5.76	0.38	0.07	8.41	4.29	4.90	1.54	0.59	2.29	7.69	3.34	2.50
Net reserves (increase −)	6.20	2.37	1.05	−0.48	−0.70	0.85	0.08	0.33	−1.27	−2.51	−0.05	3.02	0.06	0.20
Net accumulation of arrears (decrease −)		2.93	4.72	0.86	0.77	2.00	−0.13	4.57	−0.36	1.56	−0.12	2.06	3.28	2.70
Rescheduling of arrears			−1.94	−0.26	−1.05	−2.79	−3.24		−4.55	−0.72	−0.83	−0.21		
Exceptional financing			1.94	0.26	1.05	8.35	7.59		7.73	2.27	3.30	2.83		
Debt relief			1.94	0.26	1.05	8.35	7.59		7.73	2.27	3.30	2.83		
Memorandum items:														
	(In units indicated)													
Current account/GDP (in percent)	−7.4	−9.4	−6.3	−1.3	−0.3	−9.1	−4.6	−6.0	1.3	7.8	0.1	−1.9	−2.9	−2.4
Gross official reserves (in billions of US dollars)	4.45	1.96	1.23	1.50	1.69	0.89	0.76	0.32	1.59	4.10	4.15	0.83	0.72	0.92
(In months of imports of goods and nonfactor services)	2.3	1.3	1.1	1.7	1.9	1.3	1.4	0.5	2.5	5.3	4.8	0.9	0.8	1.3
Debt-service ratio (before rescheduling)	5.8	12.3	20.3	33.6	37.2	72.2	78.4	86.2	59.1	47.2	45.8	69.9	43.3	47.7
Debt-service ratio (after rescheduling)	5.8	12.3	20.3	33.6	37.2	25.8	22.3	86.2	27.3	36.3	25.8	48.8	43.3	47.7
	(Index number, 1988=100)													
Export volume	99.7	81.1	77.7	88.6	100.6	100.5	95.8	100.0	113.5	124.1	129.2	134.3	138.2	127.9
Of which: non-oil exports	(82.3)	(63.2)	(100.7)	(61.9)	(68.2)	(75.6)	(87.7)	(100.0)	(71.3)	(73.4)	(87.3)	(52.6)	(49.7)	(36.3)
Import volume	385.7	326.3	260.8	209.1	194.2	140.0	106.8	100.0	102.5	112.0	124.9	134.0	129.5	103.5
Export price index	252.4	212.1	189.2	190.1	177.0	95.6	111.5	100.0	122.3	158.7	132.8	129.6	115.7	105.5
Oil	244	206	185	184	180	95.6	115.1	100.0	124.1	162.4	135.6	131.1	116.5	105.6
Non-oil	114	71	70	88	89.7	143.1	72.4	100.0	91.8	90.2	88.2	87.2	90.3	104.5
Import price index	82.6	79.0	76.1	73.6	73.9	83.5	93.6	100.0	99.8	109.3	109.4	112.9	108.7	111.5
Terms of trade (1988=100)	305.6	268.5	248.7	258.4	239.6	114.5	119.2	100.0	122.6	145.2	121.4	114.8	106.4	94.5
Nominal effective exchange rate (INS)	679.4	710.9	738.4	791.3	725.4	404.7	122.0	100.0	67.0	68.1	56.1	36.2	28.1	37.5
Real effective exchange rate (INS)	382.3	392.4	463.5	638.5	572.5	312.8	99.8	100.0	89.3	82.7	69.7	57.7	63.0	115.4

Sources: Data provided by the Nigerian authorities; and IMF staff estimates.

APPENDIX V

Table 32. Stock of Public and Publicly Guaranteed Debt

	1980	1981	1982	1983	1984	1985	1986	1987	1988	1989	1990	1991	1992	1993	1994 Est.
									(In billions of U.S. dollars)						
Paris Club	...	...	3.34	5.39	5.81	7.85	10.23	12.59	13.77	15.80	17.71	17.79	17.81	18.71	19.93
Medium- and long-term debt[1]	...	...	2.99	3.52	3.72	5.59	7.32	9.64	10.57	12.74	14.71	15.35	16.06	17.56	19.39
Other[2]	...	...	0.35	1.87	2.10	2.27	2.91	2.95	3.20	3.06	3.00	2.43	1.75	1.16	0.54
Multilateral debt	...	...	0.74	0.88	1.10	1.32	1.89	2.99	2.84	3.17	3.85	4.01	4.09	4.22	4.38
Other official debt[1]	...	...	1.11	1.09	1.03	1.64	1.68	2.03	1.36	1.33	1.37	1.45	1.51	1.65	1.74
London Club	...	...	5.73	6.26	5.00	3.56	6.09	5.86	6.13	5.85	5.88	5.96	2.12	2.06	2.05
Medium- and long-term	...	...	4.28	4.33	3.81	3.12	3.25	2.81	3.00	2.87	2.88	2.90	2.12	2.06	2.05
Other[2]	...	...	1.45	1.94	1.19	0.44	2.83	3.05	3.14	2.98	3.00	3.06	—	—	—
Promissory notes	...	...	0.93	3.70	4.13	4.26	4.50	4.85	4.81	4.56	4.51	4.32	3.22	3.16	3.05
Suppliers' credits	...	...	0.52	0.44	0.29	0.28	1.19	—	0.48	0.42	0.06	0.02			
Subtotal	...	...	12.37	17.77	17.35	18.90	24.57	28.32	29.39	31.13	33.39	33.55	28.74	29.79	31.15
Other non-debt arrears[3]	...	...	...	...	...	...	...	...	0.71	0.29	0.33	0.19	0.10	—	—
Total	4.09	6.08	12.37	17.77	17.35	18.90	24.57	28.32	30.09	31.43	33.72	33.74	28.84	29.79	31.15
									(In percent)						
Memorandum items:															
Share in total debt															
Paris Club creditors	...	...	26.97	30.34	33.50	41.54	41.62	44.46	45.75	50.28	52.53	52.71	61.74	62.82	63.98
London Club banks	...	...	46.30	35.25	28.80	18.83	24.77	20.70	20.39	18.61	17.43	17.67	7.34	6.90	6.58
Multilateral organizations	...	...	6.00	4.98	6.32	6.97	7.68	10.54	9.43	10.09	11.43	11.88	14.18	14.15	14.06
Other creditors	...	...	20.72	29.43	31.38	32.66	25.93	24.30	24.43	21.02	18.62	17.74	16.73	16.14	15.38
Debt/GDP	4.5	7.4	16.1	22.4	21.0	23.3	58.9	104.5	94.1	102.9	104.0	103.2	90.7	94.2	76.4

Sources: Central Bank of Nigeria; and IMF staff estimates.
[1] Includes arrears as well as rescheduled medium- and long-term debt. Also includes new disbursements.
[2] Includes short-term arrears, rescheduled short-term claims, and payable debt.
[3] Includes pre-SFEM and dedication account arrears.

Appendix V

Table 33. Domestic Petroleum Prices

	1985	1986[1]	1987	1988[2]	1989	1990[3]	1991[4]	1992	1993[5]	1994[6]
				(In naira per liter, unless otherwise indicated)						
Crude oil transfer price (naira/barrel)	...	8.83	11.75	11.75	11.75	14.80	20.00	20.00	20.00	183.00
Premium motor spirits [7]	0.2	0.39	0.39	0.42	0.60	0.60	0.70	0.70	3.25	11.00
Household kerosene	0.1	0.10	0.10	0.15	0.15	0.40	0.50	0.50	2.75	6.00
Gas oil/diesel	0.1	0.29	0.29	0.35	0.35	0.50	0.55	0.55	3.00	9.00
Fuel oil [3]	0.1	0.19	0.19	0.30	0.30	0.40	0.50	0.50	2.50	7.00
Liquified petroleum gas (naira/kg)	0.2	0.40	0.40	0.40	0.40	0.80	2.00	2.00	2.00	2.00
Aviation kerosene	0.2	0.30	0.30	1.00	1.00	1.00	1.05	1.05	5.50	8.00
Memorandum items:					*(In units indicated)*					
Crude oil transfer price (percent of export price)	...	35.3	17.0	17.3	8.6	7.6	10.0	5.9	5.2	52.6
Premium motor spirits (percent of world price at average official exchange rate)[8]	...	183.9	63.4	73.1	52.9	36.8	41.8	24.6	101.2	371.1

[1] Prices became effective on January 1.
[2] Prices became effective on April 10.
[3] Prices became effective on January 1.
[4] Prices became effective on March 5.
[5] Prices became effective on November 18.
[6] Prices became effective on October 5.
[7] A two-tier pricing system in which private vehicle owners paid ₦0.60 per liter and commercial vehicle owners paid ₦0.42 per liter was implemented in January 1989. The prices were unified toward the end of the year.
[8] For 1992–94, average annual wholesale price of premium unleaded gasoline in U.S. Gulf Coast as reported in *Petroleum Market Intelligence*. Prior years are estimated using ratio of Gulf Coast price to the price of U.K. Brent crude oil.

APPENDIX V

Table 34. Gross Domestic Product by Sector of Origin at Current Prices

	1982	1983	1984	1985	1986	1987	1988	1989	1990	1991	1992	1993	1994 Est.
	(In billions of naira)												
Primary sector	25.20	27.29	33.95	39.16	37.96	64.91	88.17	149.09	171.20	218.31	401.01	478.62	585.49
Agriculture	15.91	18.84	23.80	26.63	27.89	39.20	57.92	69.71	84.34	97.46	145.23	231.83	345.01
Agriculture	11.27	12.87	16.92	19.73	20.44	31.21	48.68	56.58	68.42	80.00	120.72	196.13	293.33
Livestock	2.68	3.51	4.47	4.84	4.99	5.66	6.01	7.97	9.56	10.53	15.57	24.72	36.26
Forestry	1.07	1.16	1.26	1.34	1.44	1.46	1.70	1.99	2.15	2.23	2.74	3.63	5.47
Fishing	0.89	1.30	1.14	0.71	1.01	0.87	1.53	3.17	4.22	4.70	6.20	7.34	9.95
Mining and quarrying	9.29	8.45	10.16	12.54	10.07	25.71	30.24	79.38	86.85	120.85	255.78	246.79	240.48
Of which: crude petrol and gas	(8.43)	(7.79)	(9.57)	(12.11)	(9.83)	(25.42)	(29.92)	(78.79)	(86.19)	(120.10)	(254.85)	(245.58)	(238.99)
Secondary sector	7.90	8.41	7.35	8.29	8.68	9.90	13.74	16.70	19.83	25.09	33.86	48.05	68.86
Manufacturing	4.93	5.61	4.93	6.24	6.30	7.22	10.73	11.77	14.30	18.89	26.35	38.43	57.20
Utilities	0.48	0.54	0.51	0.52	0.47	0.50	0.55	1.07	1.18	1.30	1.41	1.60	1.76
Building and construction	2.49	2.26	1.91	1.53	1.92	2.18	2.47	3.85	4.35	4.90	6.11	8.02	9.91
Tertiary sector	18.47	21.01	21.70	23.91	25.49	32.07	40.77	56.67	66.85	76.84	109.47	164.93	237.43
Transport	2.49	2.46	2.64	3.61	3.76	4.00	4.31	4.57	5.25	5.94	8.75	14.57	27.64
Communication	0.28	0.25	0.26	0.29	0.30	0.32	0.34	0.36	0.41	0.45	0.55	0.72	0.74
Wholesale and retail trade	6.62	8.31	8.60	9.19	9.49	14.82	20.75	32.37	35.84	41.79	62.30	100.85	144.02
Hotel and restaurants	0.40	0.41	0.49	0.47	0.49	0.49	0.49	0.52	0.55	0.59	0.76	1.22	1.99
Finance and insurance	1.93	1.94	2.39	2.70	3.31	3.89	5.00	7.32	11.64	12.98	15.12	16.28	20.55
Real estate	0.23	0.22	0.21	0.23	0.25	0.28	0.31	0.35	0.40	0.47	0.58	0.70	0.92
Housing	1.67	1.98	1.87	2.00	2.21	2.25	2.37	3.37	3.87	4.75	5.92	9.28	16.05
Community and other services	0.49	0.55	0.64	0.59	0.65	0.72	0.77	0.83	0.93	1.07	1.31	2.19	3.48
Government services	4.37	4.88	4.61	4.84	5.03	5.31	6.41	6.99	7.95	8.80	14.17	19.13	22.05
Total GDP at factor cost	51.57	56.71	63.01	71.37	72.13	106.88	142.68	222.46	257.87	320.25	544.33	691.61	891.79
Oil	8.43	7.79	9.57	12.11	9.83	25.42	29.92	78.79	86.19	120.10	254.85	245.58	238.99
Non-oil	43.14	48.92	53.44	59.26	62.30	81.46	112.76	143.67	171.69	200.14	289.48	446.03	652.80
Total indirect taxes (net)	0.81	0.92	1.05	1.33	1.38	2.33	3.15	2.77	3.22	4.27	5.76	5.69	5.90
Subsidies	0.67	0.49	0.45	0.34	0.45	0.33	0.58	0.43	0.46	0.51	0.28	0.20	0.19
GDP at market prices	51.71	57.14	63.61	72.36	73.06	108.89	145.24	224.80	260.64	324.01	549.81	697.10	897.50
Memorandum items:													
	(In percent of GDP at factor cost)												
Oil sector	16.3	13.7	15.2	17.0	13.6	23.8	21.0	35.4	33.4	37.5	46.8	35.5	26.8
Non-oil sector	83.7	86.3	84.8	83.0	86.4	76.2	79.0	64.6	66.6	62.5	53.2	64.5	73.2
Of which: Agriculture	(21.9)	(22.7)	(26.9)	(27.6)	(28.3)	(29.2)	(34.1)	(25.4)	(26.5)	(25.0)	(22.2)	(28.4)	(32.9)
Manufacturing	(9.6)	(9.9)	(7.8)	(8.7)	(8.7)	(6.8)	(7.5)	(5.3)	(5.5)	(5.9)	(4.8)	(5.6)	(6.4)

Sources: Nigerian Federal Office of Statistics and National Planning Commission.

Appendix V

Table 35. Gross Domestic Product by Sector of Origin at Constant 1984 Prices

	1982	1983	1984	1985	1986	1987	1988	1989	1990	1991	1992	1993	1994 Est.
	(In billions of 1984 naira)												
Primary Sector	34.72	34.16	33.95	38.54	40.39	38.48	42.10	45.13	47.19	49.52	50.62	50.80	50.95
Agriculture	25.08	25.01	23.80	27.79	30.36	29.39	32.27	33.85	35.28	36.52	37.27	37.78	38.69
Agriculture	18.25	17.72	16.92	20.98	23.35	22.41	24.83	26.07	27.21	28.43	29.28	30.13	31.04
Livestock	4.04	4.40	4.47	4.79	4.72	4.85	4.97	5.07	5.17	5.09	5.14	5.17	5.22
Forestry	1.22	1.24	1.26	1.29	1.43	1.44	1.47	1.11	1.20	1.23	1.26	1.29	1.32
Fishing	1.57	1.64	1.14	0.74	0.86	0.68	1.00	1.59	1.70	1.77	1.59	1.19	1.12
Mining and quarrying	9.63	9.15	10.16	10.74	10.03	9.09	9.83	11.29	11.91	12.99	13.34	13.02	12.26
Of which: crude petrol and gas	(8.74)	(8.47)	(9.57)	(10.38)	(9.83)	(8.87)	(9.59)	(11.03)	(11.65)	(12.72)	(13.06)	(12.72)	(11.96)
Secondary sector	10.99	8.44	7.35	7.69	7.35	7.79	8.72	8.94	9.59	10.35	10.08	9.88	9.61
Manufacturing	7.86	5.55	4.93	5.90	5.67	5.96	6.73	6.84	7.36	8.05	7.66	7.34	6.97
Utilities	0.48	0.56	0.51	0.47	0.37	0.39	0.42	0.45	0.50	0.51	0.56	0.58	0.61
Building and construction	2.65	2.34	1.91	1.31	1.31	1.43	1.58	1.64	1.73	1.80	1.87	1.96	2.02
Tertiary sector	24.45	23.79	21.70	22.69	23.34	24.48	26.93	29.43	33.56	34.75	36.74	38.97	40.42
Transport	3.30	2.85	2.64	3.16	2.77	2.77	2.79	2.80	2.85	2.95	3.08	3.22	3.24
Communication	0.27	0.24	0.26	0.24	0.24	0.24	0.25	0.25	0.26	0.24	0.27	0.28	0.28
Wholesale and retail trade	9.55	9.32	8.60	8.94	9.25	9.83	10.73	11.15	11.49	11.86	12.22	12.59	12.59
Hotel and restaurants	0.70	0.58	0.49	0.45	0.46	0.47	0.47	0.47	0.48	0.48	0.49	0.50	0.50
Finance and insurance	3.04	3.00	2.39	2.32	2.81	3.04	3.72	5.19	7.88	8.20	8.52	8.85	9.11
Real estate	0.20	0.22	0.21	0.23	0.25	0.25	0.25	0.25	0.26	0.26	0.27	0.28	0.29
Housing	1.83	1.85	1.87	1.89	1.91	1.93	1.95	1.98	2.08	2.16	2.25	2.34	2.41
Community and other services	0.82	0.77	0.64	0.61	0.63	0.64	0.64	0.65	0.67	0.68	0.72	0.80	0.87
Government services	4.74	4.95	4.61	4.84	5.02	5.31	6.13	6.67	7.60	7.91	8.90	10.12	11.12
Total GDP at factor cost	70.16	66.39	63.01	68.92	71.08	70.74	77.75	83.50	90.34	94.61	97.43	99.65	100.98
Oil	8.74	8.47	9.57	10.38	9.83	8.87	9.59	11.03	11.65	12.72	13.06	12.72	11.96
Non-oil	61.42	57.92	53.44	58.54	61.24	61.87	68.16	72.46	78.70	81.90	84.37	86.93	89.02
Total indirect taxes (net)	0.86	0.94	1.05	1.17	0.68	0.34	0.38	0.23	0.24	0.27	0.20	0.24	0.24
Subsidies	0.71	0.50	0.45	0.30	0.22	0.05	0.07	0.04	0.03	0.03	0.01	0.01	—
GDP at market prices	70.30	66.83	63.61	69.78	71.54	71.03	78.07	83.69	90.55	94.85	97.62	99.89	101.22
Memorandum items:													
	(In percent of GDP at constant factor cost)												
Oil sector	12.5	12.8	15.2	15.1	13.8	12.5	12.3	13.2	12.9	13.4	13.4	12.8	11.8
Non-oil sector	87.5	87.2	84.8	84.9	86.2	87.5	87.7	86.8	87.1	86.6	86.6	87.2	88.2
Of which:													
Agriculture	(26.0)	(26.7)	(26.9)	(30.4)	(32.8)	(31.7)	(31.9)	(31.2)	(30.1)	(30.0)	(30.1)	(30.2)	(30.7)
Manufacturing	(11.2)	(8.4)	(7.8)	(8.6)	(8.0)	(8.4)	(8.7)	(8.2)	(8.1)	(8.5)	(7.9)	(7.4)	(6.9)

Sources: Nigerian Federal Office of Statistics and National Planning Commission.

APPENDIX V

Table 36. Gross National Expenditure

	1981	1982	1983	1984	1985	1986	1987	1988	1989	1990	1991	1992	1993	1994 Est.
	(In billions of current naira)													
GDP at market prices	50.75	51.71	57.14	63.61	72.36	73.06	108.89	145.24	224.80	260.64	324.01	549.81	697.10	897.50
External balance	–2.98	–3.83	–2.22	1.13	2.15	–2.48	4.29	1.59	16.95	38.11	19.30	25.56	24.14	21.16
Exports of goods and nonfactor services	11.52	8.53	7.73	9.49	11.44	12.46	31.15	33.58	73.50	113.20	122.11	214.91	251.60	210.79
Imports of goods and nonfactor services	14.50	12.35	9.96	8.35	9.28	14.94	26.86	31.99	56.55	75.09	102.82	189.35	227.46	189.64
Gross domestic demand	53.73	55.54	59.37	62.47	70.20	75.54	104.60	143.65	207.85	222.53	304.71	524.25	672.96	876.34
Consumption	40.80	41.41	48.29	55.05	59.01	59.65	87.20	117.50	168.00	184.12	228.87	389.63	555.58	717.74
Public	6.11	5.76	6.83	9.06	7.64	10.12	12.12	18.99	23.46	39.35	39.92	71.95	124.33	101.39
Federal	3.40	2.86	4.23	3.71	3.09	4.20	4.65	8.14	9.76	15.81	20.96	38.21	81.35	54.25
Other government	2.71	2.90	2.60	5.35	4.55	5.92	7.47	10.85	13.70	23.53	18.96	33.74	42.98	47.14
Private	34.69	35.65	41.46	45.98	51.38	49.53	75.07	98.51	144.54	144.78	188.95	317.68	431.25	616.35
Gross investment	12.93	14.13	11.07	7.42	11.19	15.89	17.40	26.16	39.85	38.40	75.84	134.62	117.38	158.60
Stock exchanges	–0.62	–1.19	–0.66	–1.16	–0.45	0.41	–1.06	–1.90	0.01	0.50	0.20	0.30	0.45	0.32
Fixed investment	13.55	15.32	11.73	8.58	11.64	15.48	18.46	28.06	39.84	37.90	75.64	134.32	116.93	158.29
Public	11.67	12.33	9.71	4.70	6.01	7.91	10.50	17.56	21.14	28.12	37.48	67.98	94.94	79.27
Federal	7.88	8.69	6.83	3.86	5.04	6.40	7.18	12.15	13.00	18.23	25.40	43.70	70.58	55.15
Other government	3.79	3.64	2.88	0.84	0.98	1.51	3.32	5.40	8.13	9.89	12.07	24.28	24.36	24.12
Private	1.88	2.98	2.02	3.88	5.63	7.57	7.96	10.50	18.70	9.79	38.16	66.34	22.00	79.02
	(In percent of GDP)													
Memorandum items:														
Gross domestic savings	19.6	19.9	15.5	13.5	18.4	18.4	19.9	19.1	25.3	29.4	29.4	29.1	20.3	20.0
General government	12.7	14.0	6.0	3.0	7.0	5.2	–1.5	–3.0	2.4	8.4	7.4	5.4	–3.9	0.3
Federal	6.2	7.8	1.2	1.5	4.2	3.4	–5.3	–5.3	–1.4	3.6	0.7	–1.0	–8.2	–2.9
Other	6.5	6.2	4.8	1.5	2.8	1.7	3.8	2.2	3.8	4.8	6.8	6.4	4.3	3.3
Private sector	6.9	5.9	9.4	10.5	11.5	13.2	21.4	22.1	22.9	21.0	21.9	23.8	24.2	19.7
Gross national savings	18.1	17.9	13.1	10.4	15.2	12.7	11.4	12.0	19.1	22.5	23.5	22.6	13.9	15.2
General government	12.7	14.0	6.0	3.0	7.0	5.2	–1.5	–3.0	2.4	8.4	7.4	5.4	–3.9	0.3
Federal	6.2	7.8	1.2	1.5	4.2	3.4	–5.3	–5.3	–1.4	3.6	0.7	–1.0	–8.2	–2.9
Other	6.5	6.2	4.8	1.5	2.8	1.7	3.8	2.2	3.8	4.8	6.8	6.4	4.3	3.3
Private sector	5.4	3.9	7.0	7.4	8.2	7.5	12.9	15.0	16.7	14.2	16.0	17.3	17.8	14.9
Foreign savings	7.4	9.4	6.3	1.3	0.3	9.1	4.6	6.0	–1.3	–7.8	–0.1	1.9	2.9	2.4
Gross investment	25.5	27.3	19.4	11.7	15.5	21.8	16.0	18.0	17.7	14.7	23.4	24.5	16.8	17.7
General government	23.0	23.8	17.0	7.4	8.3	10.8	9.6	12.1	9.4	10.8	11.6	12.4	13.6	8.8
Federal	15.5	16.8	11.9	6.1	7.0	8.8	6.6	8.4	5.8	7.0	7.8	7.9	10.1	6.1
Other	7.5	7.0	5.0	1.3	1.3	2.1	3.0	3.7	3.6	3.8	3.7	4.4	3.5	2.7
Private sector	2.5	3.5	2.4	4.3	7.2	10.9	6.3	5.9	8.3	3.9	11.8	12.1	3.2	8.8
Savings–investment balance	–7.4	–9.4	–6.3	–1.3	–0.3	–9.1	–4.6	–6.0	1.4	7.8	0.1	–1.9	–2.9	–2.4
General government	–10.3	–9.8	–10.9	–4.4	–1.4	–5.7	–11.1	–15.1	–7.0	–2.4	–4.1	–7.0	–17.5	–8.5
Federal	–9.3	–9.0	–10.8	–4.6	–2.8	–5.3	–11.9	–13.6	–7.2	–3.4	–7.2	–9.0	–18.3	–9.1
Other	–0.9	–0.8	–0.2	0.2	1.4	–0.3	0.7	–1.5	0.2	1.0	3.0	2.0	0.8	0.6
Private sector	2.9	0.5	4.6	3.1	1.1	–3.4	6.5	9.1	8.4	10.2	4.2	5.1	14.6	6.0

Sources: Data provided by the Nigerian authorities; and IMF staff estimates.

Appendix V

Table 37. Index of Agricultural Production
(1985=100)

	1980	1981	1982	1983	1984	1985	1986	1987	1988	1989	1990	1991	1992	1993	1994 Est.
Total	88.4	91.0	94.0	89.8	95.6	100.0	103.5	111.0	132.4	146.3	153.6	163.8	173.6	183.6	191.0
Crops	88.9	90.4	92.5	87.4	96.6	100.0	107.4	119.2	146.6	163.9	173.9	187.9	201.5	218.0	227.4
Staples	83.2	84.6	88.5	86.2	96.8	100.0	106.5	121.6	154.0	172.9	183.3	199.3	215.8	235.3	246.0
Other crops	102.3	103.8	101.6	90.5	96.3	100.0	111.5	110.9	119.2	132.1	139.6	146.1	149.0	153.7	156.5
Livestock	72.0	84.8	92.1	88.1	95.9	100.0	103.6	99.6	105.8	112.9	116.3	115.2	116.3	117.0	122.6
Fish	246.2	213.0	219.6	235.8	160.5	100.0	111.6	107.2	137.6	143.2	124.2	135.3	135.3	69.8	65.3
Forestry	88.4	91.0	94.0	89.8	95.6	100.0	103.5	111.0	104.3	107.7	112.0	114.2	116.8	119.2	122.4

Source: *Statistical Bulletin*, Vol. 4, December 1993, Central Bank of Nigeria, and *Annual Report and Statement of Accounts*, various issues, Central Bank of Nigeria.

APPENDIX V

Table 38. Index of Manufacturing Production
(1985=100)

	1981	1982	1983	1984	1985	1986	1987	1988	1989	1990	1991	1992	1993	1994 Est.
Total manufacturing	117.4	132.8	94.8	83.4	100.0	96.1	130.8	135.2	154.3	162.9	178.1	169.5	145.5	132.8
Sugar confections	219.2	186.0	131.0	111.8	100.0	71.8	136.0	190.1	97.4	93.7	129.1	176.7	134.4	104.8
Soft drinks	104.2	128.1	111.2	117.3	100.0	71.2	128.1	185.5	222.5	364.4	243.5	186.5	159.7	147.8
Beer	101.6	104.1	62.6	85.7	100.0	125.5	83.4	76.0	101.6	97.8	100.7	104.5	99.0	95.0
Cotton textiles	193.5	235.0	131.6	94.5	100.0	37.9	120.6	123.6	104.1	118.0	147.5	151.1	106.4	92.1
Synthetic fabrics	303.1	3,45.4	3,71.2	1,87.9	100.0	196.1	1,125.7	1,318.6	1,309.3	1,501.6	1,921.1	1,891.6	1,229.0	1,023.0
Footwear	377.5	76.6	128.7	122.7	100.0	75.4	93.9	73.8	41.5	45.8	85.9	92.0	88.0	59.0
Paints and allied products	266.3	267.7	119.1	137.2	100.0	79.1	89.1	98.7	82.7	62.7	98.0	99.7	110.6	94.4
Refined petroleum	93.6	98.5	71.3	70.2	100.0	50.3	74.0	84.6	110.1	108.8	116.0	113.7	112.0	109.7
Cement	76.6	89.8	31.8	20.0	100.0	108.1	92.0	119.9	126.2	88.7	98.7	100.5	104.1	95.0
Roofing sheet	52.1	85.3	37.5	39.7	100.0	184.5	54.7	50.6	149.0	79.6	57.9	41.2	39.3	30.8
Vehicle assembly	128.5	406.5	153.9	51.3	100.0	46.8	27.0	4.4	15.7	24.1	17.1	18.3	18.9	17.4
Soap and detergent	263.9	261.9	313.3	95.9	100.0	49.3	135.5	104.6	157.8	153.1	153.9	154.1	164.0	153.0
Radio and TV	95.7	112.3	104.4	90.9	100.0	154.8	45.8	14.7	12.5	12.2	11.8	11.6	10.1	8.9
Memorandum items:														
Manufacturing capacity utilization rate	73.3	63.6	49.7	43.0	38.3	38.8	40.4	42.4	43.8	40.3	42.0	38.1	37.2	30.4
Textiles	76.9	73.6	57.4	46.7	44.6	41.3	48.0	54.8	59.7	52.2	54.9	44.3	61.0	46.6
Motor vehicle assembly	79.1	61.4	38.1	24.9	26.1	24.9	30.6	22.2	18.9	27.9	19.6	12.7	12.5	15.0

Source: *Statistical Bulletin*, Vol. 4, December 1993, Central Bank of Nigeria, and *Annual Report and Statement of Accounts*, various issues, Central Bank of Nigeria.

Table 39. Non-Oil Exports, 1970–80[1]

(In millions of U.S. dollars)

	1970	1971	1972	1973	1974	1975	1976	1977	1978	1979	1980
Major agricultural products	371.4	343.3	261.4	380.1	438.1	374.4	437.2	582.8	649.3	766.6	622.5
Cocoa	186.3	200.8	153.6	170.8	252.4	293.8	349.1	482.6	595.1	715.6	568.7
Palm kernels	30.5	36.2	23.9	28.7	69.4	30.0	43.1	50.5	20.0	19.5	25.8
Rubber	24.4	17.4	11.2	29.5	52.7	24.7	23.0	17.2	19.8	21.5	25.8
Groundnuts	61.1	34.2	29.0	69.1	10.8	—	0.3	—	—	—	—
Pineapples	—	—	—	—	—	—	—	—	—	—	—
Coffee	—	2.8	3.2	2.0	0.2	1.8	8.6	7.1	—	1.0	—
Fish and shrimp	—	—	—	—	—	—	—	—	—	—	—
Cashew nuts	—	—	—	—	—	—	—	—	—	—	—
Spices	—	—	—	—	—	—	—	—	—	—	2.2
Cotton and yarn	18.5	15.4	0.9	7.1	—	—	—	15.7	6.6	4.6	—
Hides and skins	7.8	6.7	10.3	19.0	16.8	14.3	10.8	8.8	6.0	4.3	—
Timber (log and sawn)	8.7	7.3	12.3	17.9	17.8	7.5	1.4	0.8	0.2	—	—
Palm oil	1.7	4.8	0.3	—	—	1.9	0.8	—	1.6	—	—
Groundnut oil	32.5	17.7	16.6	35.9	18.1	0.3	—	—	—	—	—
Other agricultural products											
Mineral products	2.8	1.4	1.7	2.1	6.5	3.6	4.8	9.9	1.1	1.7	—
Columbite	2.8	1.4	1.7	2.1	2.2	2.4	4.0	9.8	0.9	1.5	—
Other	—	—	—	—	4.3	1.1	0.8	0.2	0.2	0.2	—
Manufactures and semi-manufactures of											
Agricultural products	37.3	25.8	27.5	58.7	50.3	41.4	36.4	96.1	49.4	45.7	51.9
Cocoa butter	18.5	11.5	15.3	22.8	33.3	33.1	23.1	59.7	27.7	34.4	36.6
Cocoa powder	0.3	2.0	—	0.3	1.3	0.5	2.9	6.4	7.1	9.1	7.9
Cocoa cake	3.1	2.8	3.2	8.2	8.1	6.8	4.9	28.5	14.6	2.2	7.5
Cocoa paste	—	—	—	—	—	—	—	—	—	—	—
Groundnut cake	15.4	9.5	9.0	27.4	7.6	1.0	5.4	1.6	—	—	—
Wood products	—	—	—	—	—	—	—	—	—	—	—
Other	—	—	—	—	—	—	—	—	—	—	—
Manufactured exports	47.3	33.9	29.0	23.6	41.9	33.1	24.7	20.6	14.8	17.9	26.0
Textiles	—	—	—	—	—	—	—	—	—	—	—
Tin metal	47.3	33.9	29.0	23.6	41.9	33.1	24.7	20.6	14.8	17.9	26.0
Chemicals	—	—	—	—	—	—	—	—	—	—	—
Other exports	56.3	55.3	53.6	106.8	127.0	126.8	170.0	141.9	298.7	250.7	259.2
Total non-oil exports	515.1	459.7	373.3	571.3	663.8	579.2	673.0	851.3	1,013.4	1,082.5	959.6

Source: Central Bank of Nigeria, *Annual Report and Statement of Accounts*, various editions.
[1]Figures were converted from naira into U.S. dollars using average exchange rates.

APPENDIX V

Table 40. Non-Oil Exports, 1981–90[1]

(In millions of U.S. dollars)

	1981	1982	1983	1984	1985	1986	1987	1988	1989	1990
Major agricultural products	288.7	295.1	357.7	271.2	214.9	232.1	395.5	394.5	248.9	283.8
Cocoa	230.9	223.5	312.4	238.3	203.7	211.2	373.0	325.3	141.7	130.3
Palm kernels	29.0	16.6	22.9	11.0	6.9	4.3	7.5	15.0	15.7	11.8
Rubber	28.8	23.8	20.6	21.6	4.3	16.6	15.1	44.8	69.0	95.7
Groundnuts	—	—	1.8	0.3	—	—	—	0.3	0.2	0.4
Pineapples	—	—	—	—	—	—	—	0.4	0.4	4.7
Coffee	—	2.8	—	—	—	—	—	0.1	0.2	12.1
Fish and shrimp	—	—	—	—	—	—	—	—	—	—
Cashew nuts	—	—	—	—	—	—	—	6.9	0.6	1.1
Spices	—	0.4	—	—	—	—	—	1.0	0.4	0.5
Cotton and yarn	—	—	—	—	—	—	—	—	1.2	12.0
Hides and skins	—	—	—	—	—	—	—	—	—	—
Timber (log and sawn)	—	—	—	—	—	—	—	—	—	—
Palm oil	—	—	—	—	—	—	—	—	—	—
Groundnut oil	—	—	—	—	—	—	—	—	—	—
Other agricultural products	—	27.9	—	—	—	—	—	0.7	19.5	15.2
Mineral products	—	—	—	—	—	—	—	—	0.7	3.3
Columbite	—	—	—	—	—	—	—	—	—	—
Other	—	—	—	—	—	—	—	—	0.7	3.3
Manufactures and semi-manufactures of										
Agricultural products	138.5	6.8	58.4	51.4	63.9	30.9	15.3	18.1	15.5	16.7
Cocoa butter	121.2	—	39.8	30.8	52.3	25.5	13.4	16.4	13.8	13.4
Cocoa powder	14.2	—	—	—	4.3	1.1	1.3	0.3	—	—
Cocoa cake	3.1	—	—	—	7.3	4.3	0.6	1.1	—	—
Cocoa paste	—	—	—	—	—	—	—	0.2	—	—
Groundnut cake	—	—	—	—	—	—	—	—	—	—
Wood products	—	—	—	—	—	—	—	—	1.7	3.3
Other	—	6.8	18.6	20.6	—	—	—	—	—	—
Manufactured exports	43.4	—	—	—	4.6	0.7	7.5	1.9	18.2	31.8
Textiles	—	—	—	—	—	—	—	—	17.4	12.8
Tin metal	43.4	—	—	—	4.6	0.7	7.5	1.9	0.8	0.6
Chemicals	—	—	—	—	—	—	—	—	—	18.3
Other exports	165.0	—	—	—	272.7	50.8	117.5	195.3	117.9	69.9
Total non-oil exports	635.6	301.9	416.2	322.6	556.0	314.6	535.9	609.9	401.1	405.5

Source: Central Bank of Nigeria, *Annual Report and Statement of Accounts*, various editions.
[1] Figures were converted from naira into U.S. dollars using average exchange rates.

Appendix V

Table 41. Structure of Exports, 1970–80

	1970	1971	1972	1973	1974	1975	1976	1977	1978	1979	1980
	(Share in total exports; in percent)										
Major agricultural products	28.3	18.3	11.4	10.1	4.6	4.7	4.1	4.9	6.8	4.3	2.4
Cocoa	15.6	11.3	7.2	5.0	2.8	3.7	3.2	4.1	6.3	4.0	2.2
Palm kernels	2.6	2.0	1.1	0.8	0.8	0.4	0.4	0.4	0.2	0.1	0.1
Rubber	2.0	1.0	0.5	0.9	0.6	0.3	0.2	0.1	0.2	0.1	0.1
Groundnuts	5.1	1.9	1.4	2.0	0.1	—	—	—	—	—	—
Pineapples	—	—	—	—	—	—	—	—	—	—	—
Coffee	—	0.2	0.1	0.1	—	—	0.1	0.1	—	—	—
Fish and shrimp	—	—	—	—	—	—	—	—	—	—	—
Cashew nuts	—	—	—	—	—	—	—	—	—	—	—
Spices	1.5	0.9	—	0.2	—	—	—	—	0.1	—	—
Cotton and yarn	0.7	0.4	0.5	0.6	0.2	0.2	0.1	0.1	0.1	—	—
Hides and skins	0.7	0.4	0.6	0.5	0.2	0.1	—	0.1	—	—	—
Timber (log and sawn)	0.1	0.3	—	—	—	—	—	—	—	—	—
Palm oil	2.7	1.0	0.8	1.1	0.2	—	—	—	—	—	—
Groundnut oil	—	—	—	—	—	—	—	—	—	—	—
Other agricultural products	0.2	0.1	0.1	0.1	0.1	—	—	0.1	—	—	—
Mineral Products	0.2	0.1	0.1	0.1	—	—	—	0.1	—	—	—
Columbite	—	—	—	—	—	—	—	—	—	—	—
Other											
Manufactures and semi manufactures of											
Agricultural products	3.1	1.5	1.3	1.7	0.5	0.5	0.3	0.8	0.5	0.3	0.2
Cocoa butter	1.5	0.6	0.7	0.7	0.4	0.4	0.2	0.5	0.3	0.2	0.1
Cocoa powder	—	0.1	—	—	—	—	—	0.1	0.1	0.1	—
Cocoa cake	0.3	0.2	0.1	0.2	0.1	0.1	—	0.2	0.2	—	—
Cocoa paste	—	—	—	—	—	—	—	—	—	—	—
Groundnut cake	1.3	0.5	0.4	0.8	0.1	—	0.1	—	—	—	—
Wood products	—	—	—	—	—	—	—	—	—	—	—
Other	—	—	—	—	—	—	—	—	—	—	—
Manufactured exports	4.0	1.9	1.4	0.7	0.5	0.4	0.2	0.2	0.2	0.1	0.1
Textiles	—	—	—	—	—	—	—	—	—	—	—
Tin metal	4.0	1.9	1.4	0.7	0.5	0.4	0.2	0.2	0.2	0.1	0.1
Chemicals	—	—	—	—	—	—	—	—	—	—	—
Other exports	4.7	3.1	2.5	3.1	1.4	1.6	1.6	1.2	3.1	1.4	1.0
Total non-oil exports	40.3	24.9	16.6	15.7	7.0	7.2	6.3	7.2	10.6	6.0	3.7
Oil exports	59.7	75.1	83.4	84.3	93.0	92.8	93.7	92.8	89.4	94.0	96.3
Total exports	100.0	100.0	100.0	100.0	100.0	100.0	100.0	100.0	100.0	100.0	100.0

Source: Central Bank of Nigeria, *Annual Report and Statement of Accounts*, various editions.

APPENDIX V

Table 42. Structure of Exports, 1981–90

	1981	1982	1983	1984	1985	1986	1987	1988	1989	1990
	(Share in total exports; in percent)									
Major agricultural products										
Cocoa	1.6	2.4	3.5	2.3	1.6	4.6	5.2	5.7	3.2	2.1
Palm kernels	1.3	1.8	3.0	2.0	1.6	4.2	4.9	4.7	1.8	1.0
Rubber	0.2	0.1	0.2	0.1	0.1	0.1	0.1	0.2	0.2	0.1
Groundnuts	0.2	0.2	0.2	0.2	—	0.3	0.2	0.7	0.9	0.7
Pineapples	—	—	—	—	—	—	—	—	—	—
Coffee	—	—	—	—	—	—	—	—	—	—
Fish and shrimp	—	—	—	—	—	—	—	—	—	0.1
Cashew nuts	—	—	—	—	—	—	—	0.1	—	—
Spices	—	—	—	—	—	—	—	—	—	—
Cotton and yarn	—	—	—	—	—	—	—	—	—	0.1
Hides and skins	—	—	—	—	—	—	—	—	—	—
Timber (log and sawn)	—	—	—	—	—	—	—	—	—	—
Palm oil	—	—	—	—	—	—	—	—	—	—
Groundnut oil	—	—	—	—	—	—	—	—	—	—
Other agricultural products	—	0.2	—	—	—	—	—	—	0.2	0.1
Mineral products										
Columbite	—	—	—	—	—	—	—	—	—	—
Other	—	—	—	—	—	—	—	—	—	—
Manufactures and semi-manufactures of										
Agricultural products	0.8	0.1	0.6	0.4	0.5	0.6	0.2	0.3	0.2	0.1
Cocoa butter	0.7	—	0.4	0.3	0.4	0.5	0.2	0.2	0.2	0.1
Cocoa powder	0.1	—	—	—	—	—	—	—	—	—
Cocoa cake	—	—	—	—	0.1	0.1	—	—	—	—
Cocoa paste	—	—	—	—	—	—	—	—	—	—
Groundnut cake	—	—	—	—	—	—	—	—	—	—
Wood products	—	—	—	—	—	—	—	—	—	—
Other	—	0.1	0.2	0.2	—	—	—	—	—	—
Manufactured exports	0.2	—	—	—	—	—	0.1	—	0.2	0.2
Textiles	—	—	—	—	—	—	—	—	0.2	0.1
Tin metal	0.2	—	—	—	—	—	0.1	—	—	—
Chemicals	—	—	—	—	—	—	—	—	—	0.1
Other exports	0.9	—	—	—	2.1	1.0	1.6	2.8	1.5	0.5
Total non-oil exports	3.5	2.5	4.0	2.7	4.2	6.2	7.1	8.9	5.1	3.0
Oil exports	96.5	97.5	96.0	97.3	95.8	93.8	92.9	91.1	94.9	97.0
Total exports	100.0	100.0	100.0	100.0	100.0	100.0	100.0	100.0	100.0	100.0

Source: Central Bank of Nigeria, *Annual Report and Statement of Accounts*, various editions.

Appendix V

Table 43. Structure of Non-Oil Exports, 1970–80

	1970	1971	1972	1973	1974	1975	1976	1977	1978	1979	1980
	\multicolumn{11}{c}{(Share in total non-oil exports; in percent)}										
Major agricultural products	70.2	73.7	68.6	64.3	65.0	64.6	65.0	68.5	64.1	70.8	64.9
Cocoa	38.6	45.4	43.1	31.9	39.1	50.8	51.9	56.7	58.7	66.1	59.3
Palm kernels	6.3	8.2	6.7	5.4	10.7	5.2	6.4	5.9	2.0	1.8	2.7
Rubber	5.0	3.9	3.2	5.5	8.2	4.3	3.4	2.0	2.0	2.0	2.7
Groundnuts	12.7	7.7	8.1	12.9	1.7	—	—	—	—	—	—
Pineapples	—	—	—	—	—	—	—	—	—	—	—
Coffee	—	0.6	0.9	0.4	—	0.3	1.3	0.8	—	0.1	—
Fish and shrimp	—	—	—	—	—	—	—	—	—	—	—
Cashew nuts	—	—	—	—	—	—	—	—	—	—	—
Spices	3.8	3.5	0.3	1.3	—	—	—	1.8	0.7	0.4	0.2
Cotton and yarn	1.6	1.5	2.9	3.5	2.6	2.5	1.6	1.0	0.6	0.4	—
Hides and skins	1.8	1.6	3.5	3.3	2.8	1.3	0.2	0.1	—	—	—
Timber (log and sawn)	0.3	1.1	0.1	—	—	0.3	0.1	—	0.2	—	—
Palm oil	6.7	4.0	4.6	6.7	2.8	0.1	—	—	—	—	—
Groundnut oil	—	—	—	—	—	—	—	—	—	—	—
Other agricultural products	—	—	—	—	—	—	—	—	—	—	—
Mineral products	0.6	0.3	0.5	0.4	1.0	0.6	0.7	1.2	0.1	0.2	—
Columbite	0.6	0.3	0.5	0.4	0.3	0.4	0.6	1.1	0.0	0.1	—
Other	—	—	—	—	0.7	0.2	0.1	—	—	—	—
Manufactures and semi-manufactures of											
Agricultural products	7.7	5.8	7.7	11.0	7.8	7.2	5.4	11.3	4.9	4.2	5.4
Cocoa butter	3.8	2.6	4.3	4.3	5.2	5.7	3.4	7.0	2.7	3.2	3.8
Cocoa powder	0.1	0.4	—	0.1	0.2	0.1	0.4	0.7	0.7	0.8	0.8
Cocoa cake	0.6	0.6	0.9	1.5	1.3	1.2	0.7	3.4	1.4	0.2	0.8
Cocoa paste	—	—	—	—	—	—	—	—	—	—	—
Groundnut cake	3.2	2.2	2.5	5.1	1.2	0.2	0.8	0.2	—	—	—
Wood products	—	—	—	—	—	—	—	—	—	—	—
Other	—	—	—	—	—	—	—	—	—	—	—
Manufactured exports	9.8	7.7	8.1	4.4	6.5	5.7	3.7	2.4	1.5	1.7	2.7
Textiles	—	—	—	—	—	—	—	—	—	—	—
Tin metal	9.8	7.7	8.1	4.4	6.5	5.7	3.7	2.4	1.5	1.7	2.7
Chemicals	—	—	—	—	—	—	—	—	—	—	—
Other exports	11.7	12.5	15.0	20.0	19.7	21.9	25.3	16.7	29.5	23.2	27.0
Total non-oil exports	100.0	100.0	100.0	100.0	100.0	100.0	100.0	100.0	100.0	100.0	100.0

Source: Central Bank of Nigeria, *Annual Report and Statement of Accounts*, various editions.

APPENDIX V

Table 44. Structure of Non-Oil Exports, 1981–90

	1981	1982	1983	1984	1985	1986	1987	1988	1989	1990
	(Share in total non-oil exports; in percent)									
Major agricultural products	45.4	97.7	86.0	84.1	38.6	73.8	73.8	64.7	62.0	70.0
Cocoa	36.3	74.0	75.1	73.9	36.6	67.1	69.6	53.3	35.3	32.1
Palm kernels	4.6	5.5	5.5	3.4	1.2	1.4	1.4	2.5	3.9	2.9
Rubber	4.5	7.9	4.9	6.7	0.8	5.3	2.8	7.3	17.2	23.6
Groundnuts	—	—	0.4	0.1	—	—	—	0.1	0.1	0.1
Pineapples	—	—	—	—	—	—	—	0.1	0.1	1.2
Coffee	—	0.9	—	—	—	—	—	—	—	3.0
Fish and shrimp	—	—	—	—	—	—	—	1.1	0.1	0.3
Cashew nuts	—	—	—	—	—	—	—	0.2	0.1	0.1
Spices	—	0.1	—	—	—	—	—	—	0.3	3.0
Cotton and yarn	—	—	—	—	—	—	—	—	—	—
Hides and skins	—	—	—	—	—	—	—	—	—	—
Timber (log and sawn)	—	—	—	—	—	—	—	—	—	—
Palm oil	—	—	—	—	—	—	—	—	—	—
Groundnut oil	—	—	—	—	—	—	—	—	—	—
Other agricultural products	—	9.3	—	6.4	—	—	—	0.1	4.9	3.7
Mineral products	—	—	—	—	—	—	—	—	0.2	0.8
Columbite	—	—	—	—	—	—	—	—	—	—
Other	—	—	—	—	—	—	—	—	0.2	0.8
Manufactures and semi-manufactures of										
Agricultural products	21.8	2.3	14.0	15.9	11.5	9.8	2.9	3.0	3.9	4.1
Cocoa butter	19.1	—	9.6	9.5	9.4	8.1	2.5	2.7	3.4	3.3
Cocoa powder	2.2	—	—	—	0.8	0.3	0.3	0.1	—	—
Cocoa cake	0.5	—	—	—	1.3	1.4	0.1	0.2	—	—
Cocoa paste	—	—	—	—	—	—	—	—	—	—
Groundnut cake	—	—	—	—	—	—	—	—	—	—
Wood products	—	—	—	—	—	—	—	—	0.4	0.8
Other	—	2.3	4.5	6.4	—	—	—	—	—	—
Manufactured exports	6.8	—	—	—	0.8	0.2	1.4	0.3	4.5	7.8
Textiles	—	—	—	—	—	—	—	—	4.3	3.2
Tin metal	6.8	—	—	—	0.8	0.2	1.4	0.3	0.2	0.2
Chemicals	—	—	—	—	—	—	—	—	—	4.5
Other exports	26.0	—	—	—	49.0	16.2	21.9	32.0	29.4	17.2
Total non-oil exports	100.0	100.0	100.0	100.0	100.0	100.0	100.0	100.0	100.0	100.0

Source: Central Bank of Nigeria, *Annual Report and Statement of Account*, various editions.

Appendix V

Table 45. Agricultural Exports—Selected Indicators, 1970–80

	1970	1971	1972	1973	1974	1975	1976	1977	1978	1979	1980
Incentive indicators[1]											
Real effective exchange rate											
Index (1985=100)	36.5	39.14	38.81	34.99	36.69	43.78	52.91	52.33	54.22	55.8	59.6
Annual change (in percent)	...	7.2	–0.8	–9.8	4.9	19.3	20.9	–1.1	3.6	2.9	6.8
Consumer price index (1985=100)	10.3	12	12.4	13	14.7	19.7	24.4	27.8	33.9	37.8	41.6
Ratio of producer price[2] to international price											
Cocoa	61.7	75.7	57.7	50.5	62.5	72.2	66.0	45.2	49.2	60.6	91.3
Palm Kernels	45.8	61.0	72.7	108.3	51.6	150.0	130.4	64.7	68.7	63.3	95.4
Rubber	...	...	...	...	...	...	...	...	...	75.9	68.7
Groundnuts	62.1	45.6	43.3	34.9	49.8	83.3	108.7	71.1	81.0	108.6	168.2
Coffee	...	...	...	...	...	...	...	...	...	...	...
Cotton	...	...	49.2	42.5	22.3	38.9	31.2	74.3	31.5	30.2	30.6
Performance indicators											
Export volume index (1970=100)[3]											
Total non-oil exports	100.0	130.8	110.1	104.9	94.7	84.2	104.8	79.6	85.3	96.4	70.3
Cocoa	100.0	138.8	116.2	109.3	99.1	89.3	111.9	85.6	98.0	111.3	80.3
Palm kernels	100.0	130.1	114.5	74.2	100.2	92.5	146.8	100.4	30.7	27.5	26.8
Rubber	100.0	83.1	66.8	80.1	99.4	98.7	55.1	44.9	50.1	55.4	50.2
Groundnuts	100.0	47.0	36.3	68.0	10.4	—	0.5	0.3	—	—	—
Coffee	...	...	...	...	...	...	...	...	...	...	...
Cotton	100.0	79.1	3.5	29.1	—	—	—	32.6	11.3	9.2	8.5
Palm oil	100.0	265.8	25.0	—	—	140.8	43.4	—	42.1	9.2	—
Groundnut oil	100.0	45.9	44.1	123.1	26.1	—	—	—	—	—	—
Share in world trade[4]											
Cocoa	...	22.8	18.2	19.3	16.5	16.8	19.3	17.3	17.7	12.4	12.6
Palm kernels	...	49.0	52.7	44.9	51.7	55.3	69.2	66.2	63.4	40.1	47.9
Rubber	...	1.7	1.4	1.5	1.9	1.6	0.8	0.8	0.9	0.8	0.4
Groundnuts	...	15.6	11.5	20.7	3.5	0.2	0.2	0.1	0.3	0.3	—
Coffee	...	0.1	0.1	0.1	...	—	0.2	0.1	—	—	0.1
Cotton	...	0.6	—	0.2	...	—	0.2	0.2	0.2	0.5	—
Palm oil	...	13.6	15.5	19.0	12.5	8.5	5.0	5.3	14.0	15.1	12.8
Groundnut oil	...	11.9	7.5	21.9	6.0	—	—	—	—	—	—
Export/output[5]											
Cocoa	64.2	105.7	94.4	99.5	90.7	80.9	120.9	86.0	122.1	144.2	102.7
Palm kernels	62.0	78.5	78.6	59.5	59.9	58.1	92.2	65.5	20.2	18.2	17.8
Rubber	94.9	82.7	72.3	74.8	78.6	89.6	64.2	46.9	53.3	61.1	68.9
Groundnuts	18.5	10.0	7.9	22.6	1.6	0.3	0.1	—	—	—	—
Coffee	...	...	...	...	...	...	...	...	...	...	...
Cotton	7.9	5.2	1.0	9.6	—	—	—	3.4	1.5	2.1	3.1
Palm oil	1.6	4.0	0.4	—	—	2.1	0.6	—	0.6	0.1	—
Share of agricultural exports in GDP	4.7	3.4	2.2	2.2	1.5	1.1	1.0	1.1	1.1	1.1	0.7
Share of non-oil exports in GDP	6.5	4.6	3.2	3.4	2.2	1.6	1.5	1.7	1.8	1.5	1.0
Share of agricultural exports in total exports	31.0	19.3	12.2	11.1	4.8	4.7	4.1	4.9	6.8	4.3	2.4
Share of non-oil exports in total exports	43.0	25.8	17.4	16.7	7.2	7.3	6.3	7.2	10.6	6.0	3.7

[1] International Monetary Fund, *International Financial Statistics Yearbook* 1992.
[2] Producer prices were obtained from Central Bank of Nigeria, *Annual Report and Statement of Accounts*, various editions; international prices were obtained from IMF, Commodities Special Division.
[3] Central Bank of Nigeria, *Annual Report and Statement of Accounts*, various editions.
[4] Nigeria's exports were obtained from Central Bank of Nigeria, *Annual Report and Statement of Accounts*, various editions; world exports were extracted from UNCTAD, *Commodity Year Book*, various issues.
[5] Export volumes were obtained from Central Bank of Nigeria, *Annual Report and Statement of Accounts*, various editions; output figures were extracted from Central Bank of Nigeria, *Statistical Bulletin*, Vol. 4, No. 1, 1993.

APPENDIX V

Table 46. Agricultural Exports—Selected Indicators, 1981–90

	1981	1982	1983	1984	1985	1986	1987	1988	1989	1990
Incentive indicators[1]										
Real effective exchange rate Index (1985=100)	66.0	67.7	80.1	110.1	100.0	42.7	17.8	22.4	20.9	18.0
Annual change (in percent)	10.7	2.6	18.3	37.5	–9.1	–57.3	–58.3	26.0	–6.9	–14.0
Consumer price index (1985=100)	50.3	54.1	66.7	93.1	100.0	105.7	117.7	181.8	273.5	293.7
Ratio of producer price[2] to international price										
Cocoa	101.3	110.9	91.3	81.6	79.4	96.4	93.6	152.6	110.1	83.2
Palm kernels	102.0	129.0	86.9	98.6	153.6	161.0	116.7	83.6	96.5	132.1
Rubber	77.2	82.9	91.7	104.4	111.1	85.7	25.1	28.5	28.6	20.1
Groundnuts	123.1	168.1	...	...	...	...	...	...	...	...
Coffee	...	...	...	...	...	...	...	...	...	...
Cotton	40.2	48.6	...	...	...	...	...	...	...	...
Palm oil	128.7	151.8	91.2	75.4	121.8	197.7	70.1	61.4	37.7	43.2
Performance indicators										
Export volume index (1970=100)[3]										
Total non-oil exports	66.6	56.7	78.5	46.5	41.5	67.3	91.2	136.6	64.9	66.3
Cocoa	99.4	64.0	88.8	52.8	47.5	75.8	103.0	155.3	67.1	70.8
Palm kernels	49.8	34.3	47.7	14.5	17.5	33.1	49.9	59.6	62.1	33.5
Rubber	39.5	43.3	31.3	44.7	9.7	53.5	62.6	109.2	166.9	171.5
Groundnuts	—	—	1.7	0.3	—	—	—	0.1	—	—
Coffee	...	...	...	...	...	...	...	—	...	...
Cotton	—	—	—	—	—	—	—	—	—	—
Palm oil	—	—	513.2	—	—	—	—	—	—	—
Groundnut oil	—	—	—	—	—	—	—	—	—	—
Share in world trade[4]										
Cocoa	14.5	10.9	17.1	9.7	6.7	9.5	6.3	12.3	6.1	7.0
Palm kernels	32.8	40.4	45.2	31.7	32.6	64.6	76.8	76.6	65.9	51.3
Rubber	0.7	0.9	0.8	0.8	0.8	0.9	0.9	1.1	1.4	2.1
Groundnuts	—	0.4	—	—	—	—	—	—	—	—
Coffee	—	—	0.1	—	—	—	—	—	0.1	0.1
Cotton	—	—	—	—	—	—	—	—	—	—
Palm oil	11.6	8.4	7.2	2.4	1.0	1.1	0.2	1.1	0.2	—
Groundnut oil	0	—	—	—	—	—	—	—	—	—
Export/Output[5]										
Cocoa	105.5	80.3	124.1	68.9	84.5	148.4	191.9	132.1	51.3	62.7
Palm kernels	47.6	20.5	31.7	7.9	9.0	17.5	26.2	20.3	19.2	10.0
Rubber	124.4	53.4	42.9	47.6	10.3	55.0	68.9	99.1	128.8	120.2
Groundnuts	...	...	1.3	0.2	—	...	...	...	...	...
Coffee	...	...	...	...	...	...	...	...	...	...
Cotton	...	...	—	—	...	...	...	—	—	—
Palm oil	...	...	—	—	...	...	...	—	—	—
Groundnut oil	...	...	7.8	—	...	...	...	—	—	—
Share of agricultural exports in GDP	0.4	0.4	0.5	0.3	0.3	0.6	1.5	1.2	0.8	0.9
Share of non-oil exports in GDP	0.8	0.4	0.5	0.4	0.7	0.8	2.0	1.9	1.3	1.3
Share of agricultural exports in total exports	1.6	2.4	3.5	2.3	1.6	4.6	5.2	5.7	3.2	2.1
Share of non-oil exports in total exports	3.5	2.5	4.0	2.7	4.2	6.2	7.1	8.9	5.1	3.0

[1] International Monetary Fund, *International Financial Statistics Yearbook* 1992.
[2] Producer prices were obtained from Central Bank of Nigeria, *Annual Report and Statement of Accounts*; international prices were obtained from IMF, Commodities Special Division.
[3] Central Bank of Nigeria, *Annual Report and Statement of Accounts*, various editions.
[4] Nigeria's exports were obtained from Central Bank of Nigeria, *Annual Report and Statement of Accounts*; World exports were extracted from UNCTAD, *Commodity Year Book*, various editions.
[5] Export volumes were obtained from Central Bank of Nigeria, *Annual Report and Statement of Accounts*, various editions; output was extracted from Central Bank of Nigeria, *Statistical Bulletin*, Vol. 4, No. 1, 1993.

Appendix V

Table 47. Export Volumes, Export Prices, Consumer Price Index, GDP at Factor Cost, and Index of Manufacturing

Period	Export Volumes [1]			Export Prices of Nigeria's Commodities [2]			Nigeria, CPI [3]	Agriculture at Factor Cost [4]	Index of Manufacturing [1]
	Cocoa	Palm kernels	Rubber	Cocoa	Palm kernels	Rubber			
	(In thousands of metric tons)			(U.S. dollars per metric ton)			(1985=100)	(In millions of 1987 naira)	(1972=100)
1970	195.7	185.3	61.7	673.9	167.6	407.2	10.3	38,023	81
1971	271.7	241.1	51.3	538.5	144.9	332.5	12.0	40,004	82
1972	227.5	212.2	41.2	642.6	116.1	331.8	12.4	37,092	100
1973	213.9	137.5	49.4	1,130.8	258.6	678.0	13.0	40,401	123
1974	194.0	185.6	61.3	1,560.2	464.3	751.6	14.7	44,589	120
1975	174.7	171.4	60.9	1,245.9	206.8	560.9	19.7	39,958	148
1976	218.9	272.0	34.0	2,045.8	229.9	773.7	24.4	39,332	182
1977	167.5	186.0	27.7	3,791.1	326.3	814.7	27.8	42,017	194
1978	191.7	56.8	30.9	3,404.6	363.7	985.6	33.9	38,385	221
1979	217.8	50.9	34.2	3,292.8	499.5	1,262.1	37.8	37,223	328
1980	157.1	49.6	31.0	2,603.4	344.5	1,424.6	41.6	39,061	345
1981	194.6	92.2	24.4	2,076.6	317.3	1,122.8	50.3	32,630	395
1982	125.2	63.5	26.7	1,741.8	264.8	857.7	54.1	33,459	447
1983	173.8	88.4	19.3	2,118.7	365.3	1,064.2	66.7	33,361	319
1984	103.4	26.8	27.6	2,395.7	524.8	957.7	93.1	31,747	281
1985	92.9	32.4	6.0	2,254.6	284.7	758.7	100.0	37,076	337
1986	148.4	61.3	33.0	2,068.3	141.4	806.5	105.7	40,495	324
1987	201.5	92.4	38.6	1,997.8	181.4	984.7	117.7	39,204	432
1988	303.9	110.4	67.4	1,583.8	264.0	1,185.0	181.8	43,051	505
1989	131.3	115.1	103.0	1,242.2	268.0	969.9	273.5	45,088	538
1990	138.5	62.0	105.8	1,268.0	188.4	864.7	293.7	46,922	545

[1] Central Bank of Nigeria, Annual Report and Statement of Accounts, various editions.
[2] International Monetary Fund, Commodities Special Division.
[3] International Monetary Fund, International Financial Statistics Yearbook, 1992.
[4] World Bank, World Tables, 1992.

APPENDIX V

Table 48. Selected Financial Institutions

	1980	1981	1982	1983	1984	1985	1986	1987	1988	1989	1990	1991	1992	1993	1994 Est.
Total deposit banks	26	26	30	35	38	40	41	50	66	81	109	186	521	999	1,087
Commercial deposit banks	20	20	22	25	27	28	29	34	42	47	58	65	65	65	65
Merchant banks	6	6	8	10	11	12	12	16	24	34	49	54	54	54	51
Community banks	—	—	—	—	—	—	—	—	—	—	—	66	401	879	970
People's Bank of Nigeria	—	—	—	—	—	—	—	—	—	—	1	1	1	1	1
Foreign exchange bureaus	—	—	—	—	—	—	—	—	—	52	88	102	132	144	183
Finance companies	...	...	...	...	...	...	...	...	...	...	...	48	666	310	292
Deposit insurance corporation	—	—	—	—	—	—	—	—	—	1	1	1	1	1	1
Unit trusts	—	—	—	—	—	—	—	—	—	—	—	11	11	11	11
Stockbrokers	...	...	...	...	16	19	23	33	43	61	80	110	140	140	140
Federal mortgage bank	—	—	—	—	—	—	—	—	—	—	—	1	1	1	1
Secondary mortgage banks	—	—	—	—	—	—	—	—	—	—	—	—	—	—	—
Discount houses	—	—	—	—	—	—	—	—	—	—	—	—	3	3	3
Memorandum items:															
Total number of deposit bank branches[1]	692	884	1,010	1,132	1,274	1,323	1,394	1,516	1,711	1,911	2,182	2,307	2,619	2,794	2,816
Commercial bank branches	680	869	991	1,108	1,249	1,297	1,367	1,483	1,665	1,855	1,939	2,023	2,275	2,397	2,397
Rural branches	168	240	308	407	432	451	481	529	602	756	765	765	774	763	763
Urban branches	512	629	683	701	817	846	886	954	1,063	1,099	1,174	1,258	1,501	1,634	1,634
Merchant bank branches	12	15	19	24	25	26	27	33	46	56	74	84	116	126	144
People's Bank of Nigeria	...	...	...	...	...	...	...	...	...	...	169	200	228	271	275
Insurance companies	70	66	79	85	88	87	88	91	92	98	103	107	132	132	187

Source: Central Bank of Nigeria.
[1] Excluding community banks.

Recent Occasional Papers of the International Monetary Fund

148. Nigeria: Experience with Structural Adjustment, by Gary Moser, Scott Rogers, and Reinold van Til, with Robin Kibuka and Inutu Lukonga. 1997.

147. Aging Populations and Public Pension Schemes, by Sheetal K. Chand and Albert Jaeger, 1996

146. Thailand: The Road to Sustained Growth, by Kalpana Kochhar, Louis Dicks-Mireaux, Balazs Horvath, Mauro Mecagni, Erik Offerdal, and Jianping Zhou. 1996.

145. Exchange Rate Movements and Their Impact on Trade and Investment in the APEC Region, by Takatoshi Ito, Peter Isard, Steven Symansky, and Tamim Bayoumi. 1996.

144. National Bank of Poland: The Road to Indirect Instruments, by Piero Ugolini. 1996.

143. Adjustment for Growth: The African Experience, by Michael T. Hadjimichael, Michael Nowak, Robert Sharer, and Amor Tahari. 1996.

142. Quasi-Fiscal Operations of Public Financial Institutions, by G.A. Mackenzie and Peter Stella. 1996.

141. Monetary and Exchange System Reforms in China: An Experiment in Gradualism, by Hassanali Mehran, Marc Quintyn, Tom Nordman, and Bernard Laurens. 1996.

140. Government Reform in New Zealand, by Graham C. Scott. 1996.

139. Reinvigorating Growth in Developing Countries: Lessons from Adjustment Policies in Eight Economies, by David Goldsbrough, Sharmini Coorey, Louis Dicks-Mireaux, Balazs Horvath, Kalpana Kochhar, Mauro Mecagni, Erik Offerdal, and Jianping Zhou. 1996.

138. Aftermath of the CFA Franc Devaluation, by Jean A.P. Clément, with Johannes Mueller, Stéphane Cossé, and Jean Le Dem. 1996.

137. The Lao People's Democratic Republic: Systemic Transformation and Adjustment, edited by Ichiro Otani and Chi Do Pham. 1996.

136. Jordan: Strategy for Adjustment and Growth, edited by Edouard Maciejewski and Ahsan Mansur. 1996.

135. Vietnam: Transition to a Market Economy, by John R. Dodsworth, Erich Spitäller, Michael Braulke, Keon Hyok Lee, Kenneth Miranda, Christian Mulder, Hisanobu Shishido, and Krishna Srinivasan. 1996.

134. India: Economic Reform and Growth, by Ajai Chopra, Charles Collyns, Richard Hemming, and Karen Parker with Woosik Chu and Oliver Fratzscher. 1995.

133. Policy Experiences and Issues in the Baltics, Russia, and Other Countries of the Former Soviet Union, edited by Daniel A. Citrin and Ashok K. Lahiri. 1995.

132. Financial Fragilities in Latin America: The 1980s and 1990s, by Liliana Rojas-Suárez and Steven R. Weisbrod. 1995.

131. Capital Account Convertibility: Review of Experience and Implications for IMF Policies, by staff teams headed by Peter J. Quirk and Owen Evans. 1995.

130. Challenges to the Swedish Welfare State, by Desmond Lachman, Adam Bennett, John H. Green, Robert Hagemann, and Ramana Ramaswamy. 1995.

129. IMF Conditionality: Experience Under Stand-By and Extended Arrangements. Part II: Background Papers. Susan Schadler, Editor, with Adam Bennett, Maria Carkovic, Louis Dicks-Mireaux, Mauro Mecagni, James H.J. Morsink, and Miguel A. Savastano. 1995.

128. IMF Conditionality: Experience Under Stand-By and Extended Arrangements. Part I: Key Issues and Findings, by Susan Schadler, Adam Bennett, Maria Carkovic, Louis Dicks-Mireaux, Mauro Mecagni, James H.J. Morsink, and Miguel A. Savastano. 1995.

127. Road Maps of the Transition: The Baltics, the Czech Republic, Hungary, and Russia, by Biswajit Banerjee, Vincent Koen, Thomas Krueger, Mark S. Lutz, Michael Marrese, and Tapio O. Saavalainen. 1995.

126. The Adoption of Indirect Instruments of Monetary Policy, by a staff team headed by William E. Alexander, Tomás J.T. Baliño, and Charles Enoch. 1995.

OCCASIONAL PAPERS

125. United Germany: The First Five Years—Performance and Policy Issues, by Robert Corker, Robert A. Feldman, Karl Habermeier, Hari Vittas, and Tessa van der Willigen. 1995.

124. Saving Behavior and the Asset Price "Bubble" in Japan: Analytical Studies, edited by Ulrich Baumgartner and Guy Meredith. 1995.

123. Comprehensive Tax Reform: The Colombian Experience, edited by Parthasarathi Shome. 1995.

122. Capital Flows in the APEC Region, edited by Mohsin S. Khan and Carmen M. Reinhart. 1995.

121. Uganda: Adjustment with Growth, 1987–94, by Robert L. Sharer, Hema R. De Zoysa, and Calvin A. McDonald. 1995.

120. Economic Dislocation and Recovery in Lebanon, by Sena Eken, Paul Cashin, S. Nuri Erbas, Jose Martelino, and Adnan Mazarei. 1995.

119. Singapore: A Case Study in Rapid Development, edited by Kenneth Bercuson with a staff team comprising Robert G. Carling, Aasim M. Husain, Thomas Rumbaugh, and Rachel van Elkan. 1995.

118. Sub-Saharan Africa: Growth, Savings, and Investment, by Michael T. Hadjimichael, Dhaneshwar Ghura, Martin Mühleisen, Roger Nord, and E. Murat Uçer. 1995.

117. Resilience and Growth Through Sustained Adjustment: The Moroccan Experience, by Saleh M. Nsouli, Sena Eken, Klaus Enders, Van-Can Thai, Jörg Decressin, and Filippo Cartiglia, with Janet Bungay. 1995.

116. Improving the International Monetary System: Constraints and Possibilities, by Michael Mussa, Morris Goldstein, Peter B. Clark, Donald J. Mathieson, and Tamim Bayoumi. 1994.

115. Exchange Rates and Economic Fundamentals: A Framework for Analysis, by Peter B. Clark, Leonardo Bartolini, Tamim Bayoumi, and Steven Symansky. 1994.

114. Economic Reform in China: A New Phase, by Wanda Tseng, Hoe Ee Khor, Kalpana Kochhar, Dubravko Mihaljek, and David Burton. 1994.

113. Poland: The Path to a Market Economy, by Liam P. Ebrill, Ajai Chopra, Charalambos Christofides, Paul Mylonas, Inci Otker, and Gerd Schwartz. 1994.

112. The Behavior of Non-Oil Commodity Prices, by Eduardo Borensztein, Mohsin S. Khan, Carmen M. Reinhart, and Peter Wickham. 1994.

111. The Russian Federation in Transition: External Developments, by Benedicte Vibe Christensen. 1994.

110. Limiting Central Bank Credit to the Government: Theory and Practice, by Carlo Cottarelli. 1993.

109. The Path to Convertibility and Growth: The Tunisian Experience, by Saleh M. Nsouli, Sena Eken, Paul Duran, Gerwin Bell, and Zühtü Yücelik. 1993.

108. Recent Experiences with Surges in Capital Inflows, by Susan Schadler, Maria Carkovic, Adam Bennett, and Robert Kahn. 1993.

107. China at the Threshold of a Market Economy, by Michael W. Bell, Hoe Ee Khor, and Kalpana Kochhar with Jun Ma, Simon N'guiamba, and Rajiv Lall. 1993.

106. Economic Adjustment in Low-Income Countries: Experience Under the Enhanced Structural Adjustment Facility, by Susan Schadler, Franek Rozwadowski, Siddharth Tiwari, and David O. Robinson. 1993.

105. The Structure and Operation of the World Gold Market, by Gary O'Callaghan. 1993.

104. Price Liberalization in Russia: Behavior of Prices, Household Incomes, and Consumption During the First Year, by Vincent Koen and Steven Phillips. 1993.

103. Liberalization of the Capital Account: Experiences and Issues, by Donald J. Mathieson and Liliana Rojas-Suárez. 1993.

102. Financial Sector Reforms and Exchange Arrangements in Eastern Europe. Part I: Financial Markets and Intermediation, by Guillermo A. Calvo and Manmohan S. Kumar. Part II: Exchange Arrangements of Previously Centrally Planned Economies, by Eduardo Borensztein and Paul R. Masson. 1993.

Note: For information on the title and availability of Occasional Papers not listed, please consult the IMF Publications Catalog or contact IMF Publication Services.